VBA Programming for
Microsoft Office Project
Versions 98 Through 2007

Rod Gill
Microsoft Project MVP

VBA Programming for Microsoft Office Project
Versions 98 Through 2007

Copyright © 2006 Rod Gill
Portions Copyright © 2006 Soho Corp. dba msProjectExperts

Publisher: Soho Corp. dba msProjectExperts
Author: Rod Gill
Editors: Gary L. Chefetz, Dale A. Howard
Technical Editor: Ed Morrison
Copy Editor: Rodney Walker

ISBN: 0-9759828-7-7

Library of Congress Control Number: 2006931790

Official book website: http://www.projectvbabook.com

Published and distributed by Soho Corp. dba msProjectExperts, 90 John Street, Suite 404, New York, NY 10038 (646) 736-1688 http://www.msprojectexperts.com

EPM Learning

EPM Learning is a complete series of role-based training manuals for professional trainers and corporate training programs. To learn more about the EPM Learning courseware series for Technical Administrators, PMO Administrators, Project Managers, Resource Managers, Executives and Team Members, or to obtain instructor companion products and materials, contact Soho Corp. by phone (646) 736-1688 or by email info@msprojectexperts.com.

Contents

About the Author xi

About the Editors.. xii

Introduction xiii

SECTION 1: INTRODUCTION TO VBA 1

Downloading the Sample Files 3

Introducing VBA 3

VBA Programming Skills Needed.. 4

Support for Your VBA Macros.. 5

Module 01: Creating and Editing VBA Code............................ 7

Understanding the Visual Basic Editor 9

Using the Project Explorer 12

Entering and Editing Code.. 13

What is IntelliSense? 15

Understanding Modules 17

Using Sub Procedures 17

Using Functions 18

Using GoSub Subroutines 18

Using Class Modules.. 18

Using UserForms.. 19

Module 02: Common VBA Code for All Office Programs 21

Using Office VBA Code 23

Adding Comments to Your Code...................................... 23

Understanding Objects, Methods, Properties, and Parameters ... 24

Using the With Statement 27

Using the MsgBox Function 29

Prompting the User for Inputs 30

Understanding Functions and Procedures............................ 31

Using Help to Learn More about VBA................................ 33

Contents

Module 03: Using Variables and Constants 35

Using Variables to Store Data 37
Declaring Variables..37
Using a Naming Convention for Variables..................................39

Using Constants to Store Fixed Values............................ 39

Controlling Variable Scope 41
Forcing Declared Variables...41
Protecting Variables from Unwanted Change 42
Sharing Variables with Another File..42

Storing Data in the Registry.. 42

Working with Data Types.. 43
Handling Dates 43
Handling Text 45
Using Numbers 48
Using Variant Variables 49
Converting Between Variable Types 49

Compiling Your Code... 50

Module 04: Using Conditional Statements and Loops 53

Structuring Your VBA Code 55

Using the Conditional IF Statement 56

Working with Loops 58
Using the Do Loop 58
Using the For Next Loop 60
Using the For Each Next Loop 60

Module 05: Using Classes 63

Creating a Simple Class.. 65

Module 06: Working with Other Applications.................... 71

Understanding VBA Automation.................................... 73

Adding References to Other Applications 73

Managing VBA Security 75
Creating a Digital Certificate 76

Module 07: Writing and Debugging Your Code 81

Using a Simple Approach to Create a VBA Macro................ 83

Estimating Development Time **84**

Running and Debugging Your VBA Code **85**

Using VBA's Debugging Features *86*

Making Your Code Easier to Maintain **88**

Making Your Code Easier to Debug **90**

SECTION 2: MICROSOFT PROJECT VBA ESSENTIALS **93**

Introducing Project VBA **95**

Downloading the Sample Files **95**

Module 08: Defining and Using Custom Fields **97**

Overview of Custom Fields **99**

Using Formulas to Support Project VBA **102**

Defining Custom Fields **103**

Using a Value List in a Custom Field *105*

Using a Formula in a Custom Field *109*

Testing for an NA Date Value *113*

Using Graphical Indicators in a Custom Field *113*

Defining Custom Outline Codes **119**

Deleting a Custom Field or Outline Code **124**

Module 09: Using Objects, Methods, and Properties **127**

Understanding the Project Object Model **129**

Using Application-Related Objects, Methods, and Properties **131**

Using Project-Related Objects, Methods, and Properties **133**

Using Project Objects *133*

Using Project Methods *134*

Using Project Properties *134*

Using Task-Related Objects, Methods, and Properties **135**

Using Resource-Related Objects, Methods, and Properties **137**

Using Assignment-Related Objects, Methods, and Properties ... **138**

Using the Object Browser **138**

Module 10: Recording Macros **145**

Understanding When to Record a Macro **147**

Recording a Macro **147**

Modifying a Recorded Macro **151**

Storing Your VBA Code... **153**

Controlling the Size of Project .MPP Files................................. **155**

Repairing Corrupted Files **156**

Module 11: Looping Through Your Schedule......................... 157

Looping Through All Tasks in a Project **159**

Clearing a Custom Field for Non-Summary Tasks...................... **160**

Using Loops to Set Custom Field Values.................................... **161**

Module 12: Creating New Objects in Microsoft Project 163

Safely Creating New Objects.. **165**

Creating New Views, Tables, and Filters **165**

Creating a New Toolbar.. **166**

Creating a New Menu **167**

Module 13: Managing Run-Time Errors................................ 171

Managing Errors... **173**

Using Resume Next Error Handling *175*
Using Goto Error Handling *175*
Selecting an Error Handling Method *176*
Using the Err Object *176*

Module 14: Creating and Running UserForms....................... 179

Understanding UserForms.. **181**

Creating a UserForm **182**

Adding Code to a UserForm... **184**

Module 15: Using Events 187

What Are Events?... **189**

Using Project Events **189**

Using Task Events **190**

Module 16: Creating the Project Control Center Macro 195

Structuring Your Macros **197**

Project Control Center Macro Overview **198**

Designing the Project Control Center.. *198*

Deliverables for Project Control Center *199*

Understanding the Project Control Center Code *200*

Module 17: Displaying Driving Tasks 209

Designing the Driving Task Macro 211

Designing the Main Procedure *212*

Understanding Task Dependencies *213*

Understanding the Task Driver Code *213*

Adding a UserForm to Display the Results 222

Running the Macro from a Toolbar 228

Module 18: Distributing Your Macros 231

Making Your Procedures Private 233

Calling a Procedure from Another File 233

Using the Global.mpt File 234

Moving Macros into the Global.mpt File 234

Copying Modules and Forms to the Global.mpt *235*

Adding the CopyToGlobal Toolbar Button *236*

Creating a Global Macros Toolbar *237*

Module 19: Working with Timephased Data 241

Understanding Timephased Data 243

Reading Timephased Data 244

Exporting Timephased Data to a .csv file 246

Writing Timephased Data 250

Updating the Project Control Center 252

Designing the Get Resource Procedure *253*

Module 20: Controlling Excel with Project VBA 261

Using Excel for Project Reporting 263

Understanding VBA Automation 263

Using Late Binding *264*

Using Early Binding *265*

Connecting to an Already Open Copy of Excel 267

Exporting a List of Resources to Excel 268

Running Excel VBA Code Using Project VBA 270

Controlling Microsoft Project from Excel 271

Creating the S-Curves Macro in Excel..............................**272**

Completing the Who Does What When Macro **278**

Module 21: Create a Cost Margin Report.................... **287**

Understanding the Cost Margin Report **289**

Module 22: Consolidate Multiple Projects........................... **295**

Creating Consolidated Project Reports.....................**297**

Module 23: Changing Working Time **303**

Working with Calendars...**305**

Designing the Update Calendars Macro **305**

Create the Calendar Exceptions UserForm....................*306*

Add the Text Class to Store Calendar Exceptions *319*

Apply Calendar Changes to All Projects.......................*323*

Add the Macro to the Project Control Center Toolbar *326*

Module 24: Display Predecessor and Successor Tasks.......... **329**

Working with Task Dependencies **331**

Designing the LinkedTasks Macro **331**

Understanding the TaskDependency Object.............................**333**

Understanding the TaskLinks Macro Code.............................**334**

Module 25: Miscellaneous Useful Code **343**

Indenting Tasks Using VBA.....................................**345**

Reorganizing Task Sequences.................................**348**

Creating Formulas in Custom Fields..........................**349**

Working with Hyperlinks...**350**

Working with Subprojects.......................................**352**

Making Your Code Run Faster **352**

Timing Code Execution..*354*

Using the Windows API to Open and Save Files **356**

Using File Open...*357*

Using File Save as *359*

Using Get Folder *360*

Applying the clsBrowse Class to a New Project............................*360*

SECTION 3: WORKING WITH DATABASES **363**

Developing Project Database Code **365**

Downloading the Sample Files **366**

Module 26: Importing Data from Other Sources **367**

Importing Data from an Excel Workbook **369**

Importing Data from an Access Database **376**

Importing Data from a SQL Server Database **379**

Module 27: Reading and Writing Data in a Database **385**

Using the PJDB.HTM File **387**

Looping Through all Projects in a Database **389**

Reading Data from a Database **391**

Creating the Database View *391*
Creating the Excel VBA Macro *392*

Writing Data to a Database **395**

Module 28: Using the OLE DB **403**

Understanding OLEDB **405**

Using the OLEDB Driver for Your Project Version *405*
Using the OLEDB driver with Project 2007 .... *406*

Connecting to an .MPP File Using OLEDB **406**

Module 29: Accessing Project Server Data from Excel **415**

Understanding the PJSVRDB.HTM File **417**

Weekly Reporting on Project Server Data **418**

Looping through All Projects *418*
Starting Project Professional and Logging into Project Server *419*
Setting up the Excel Report *421*
Reading a List of All Project Titles *421*
Reading Milestone and Current Task Data *425*
Reading all Issues and Risks for a Project *427*
Writing the Final VBA Code for the Excel Report Macro *431*

Creating a Project Program Report **435**

Module 30: Using Project 2007 VBA **437**

    Introducing Project 2007 VBA **439**

    Using Named Parameters.. **440**

    Undoing a Macro **440**

    Managing Custom Fields **442**

    Controlling Visual Reports **443**

    Managing Calendars.. **443**

    Formatting Cell Background Colors **444**

    Managing Deliverables.. **445**

    Converting SQL Views from 2003 to 2007................................. **446**

Index.. **451**

About the Author

Rod Gill is founder of New Zealand based ACE Project Systems Ltd. He has been involved with project management his entire career and with the advanced use of Microsoft Project since its release. Apart from doing project management training, consulting, and Project Server implementations, Rod has a regular sideline in VBA development, mostly for Microsoft Project.

After 8 years of software engineering to develop control systems and their operator interfaces, Rod was drawn to VBA development and integrating Microsoft Project with other systems. Rod is a long-time Microsoft Project Most Valuable Professional (MVP), first winning this prestigious technical award in 1998 for his contributions to the Microsoft communities. Rod's passion for Microsoft Project and Project VBA and for helping others has kept him in the forefront of using Microsoft Project. Contact Rod online in the microsoft.public.project.developer newsgroup at msnews.microsoft.com, or e-mail him at:

rodg@msproject-systems.com

About the Editors

Gary Chefetz is the founder and President of the Soho Corp. and msProjectExperts, which exist to support businesses and organizations that choose the Microsoft enterprise project management platform. Gary has worked with Microsoft Project since 1995 and has supported Microsoft Project users since the introduction of Project Central in early 2000. Gary continues to receive the prestigious Microsoft Project Most Valuable Professional (MVP) award for his contributions. As a long-time MVP, he works closely with the Microsoft Project product team and support organizations. Gary is dedicated to supporting Microsoft Project Server implementations through his business efforts with clients and through his contributions in the newsgroups. Contact Gary Chefetz online in one of the Microsoft Project newsgroups at msnews.microsoft.com or e-mail him at:

gary_chefetz@msprojectexperts.com

Dale Howard is an enterprise project management trainer/consultant and is Vice President of Educational Services of msProjectExperts. Dale is a Certified Technical Trainer (CTT) who has more than 11 years of experience training and consulting in productivity software. He has worked with Microsoft Project since 1997 and volunteers many hours each week answering user questions in the various Microsoft Project communities. Dale has continued to receive the prestigious Microsoft Project Most Valuable Professional (MVP) award since 2004 for his expertise with the software and for his contributions to the user communities. Dale is married to Mickey and lives in Denver, Colorado. Contact Dale online in one of the Microsoft Project newsgroups at msnews.microsoft.com or e-mail him at:

dale_howard@msprojectexperts.com

Ed Morrison is responsible for technology operations at msProjectExperts. His first forays into project management began with Y2K efforts at a large benefits consulting firm. Before joining our team, Ed ran numerous software development and IT projects in several industries including pharmaceutical, marketing, and IT.

As VP of Technology, Ed wears lots of hats including training, custom development, and implementation consulting. A graduate of Rutgers University in New Jersey, Ed holds a Bachelor of Arts degree. He holds a Microsoft Certified Professional (MCP) certificate in Microsoft Project Server and Microsoft Visual Basic. Contact Ed Morrison via e-mail at:

ed_morrison@msprojectexperts.com

Introduction

Thank you for reading VBA Programming for Microsoft Office Project, Versions 98 Through 2007. This book teaches you to develop VBA macros for Microsoft Project that are productive, quick to develop, and easy to maintain. The learning examples included in this book give you a great jump start for your own Project VBA programming projects. I document an array of useful macros, including routines for viewing all tasks linked to the selected one, automatically creating a consolidated snapshot of multiple project files, a Who Does What When report exported to Excel, and more. In this book, I teach you how to write VBA macros for Microsoft Project by explaining how to design them for easier code maintenance.

For those of you new to VBA programming, Section 1 explains the part of Project VBA that is common to VBA for all Microsoft Office applications. Section 2 is specific to Project VBA and covers the full range of skills you need to automate Microsoft Project. Section 3 documents how to read and write data to Project databases and how to report on projects in a Project Server database.

By reading this book, I believe you will be much more effective as a VBA programmer. If you have specific questions, contact me in the public Microsoft Project newsgroup (server msnews.microsoft.com):

microsoft.public.project.developer

If you are still finding programming Project VBA a hard task, please feel free to e-mail me at rodg@msproject-systems.com to discuss how I can help you.

Rod Gill, Microsoft Project MVP

SECTION 1

INTRODUCTION TO VBA

Learning Objectives

After completing the Modules in this Section, you will be able to:

- Understand and write VBA code common to all Office VBA implementations
- Know how to write code that is easy to maintain and understand
- Perform basic debugging of VBA code in the Visual Basic Editor

Downloading the Sample Files

You can download the Microsoft Project sample files containing all of the sample code in this workbook from the following URL:

http://www.projectvbabook.com/dl

Important Note: Before you begin Module 01, download all these sample files so they are available to you as you work through this book.

Microsoft Project 98 uses a different file format, so if you do have Project 98, make sure you download the Project 98 zip file. The Project 2000-2003 file format is suitable for use with any recent version of Microsoft Project, from 2000 to 2003.

Warning: Microsoft Project 2007 uses a different file format, so if you have Project 2007, you must open and re-save the files in Project 2007 format. When Microsoft releases Project 2007, a Project 2007 zip file will be available with all sample files in Project 2007 format.

 It is possible that a certain version of Project updated to a specific patch level on a particular version and patch level of Windows, might not run the sample macros as expected. If that does happen, I will make sure the sample projects are updated or release a new version that does work. That means that if a sample file has slightly different code than shown in the workbook, then the sample project code is more likely to be correct.

Introducing VBA

First of all, what is VBA? VBA stands for Visual Basic for Applications. Essentially, it is a macro language that can be added to any application (not just Microsoft Office programs, since programs such as AutoCAD have implemented Microsoft's VBA as well). The VBA language is based on early versions of Microsoft's Visual Basic language, but has been modified to handle the host program. Microsoft Project includes a full implementation of VBA so that practically everything you can do manually in Microsoft Project you can do programmatically using its VBA macro language.

I divide this book into three sections:

- Section 1 is a beginner's guide on how to enter, edit, test, and debug VBA code in any implementation of VBA.

- Section 2 teaches you how to write VBA code specifically for Microsoft Project.

- Section 3 is an introduction to VBA reporting from Project Server 2002 and 2003 (with an introduction to programming with the new Project Server Interface (PSI) in Project Server 2007 provided as a download from our web site).

Section 1 is not intended to be a comprehensive guide to the VBA language. My intention is only to provide enough knowledge to let you understand and work with, all the great Project VBA examples that are in Section 2 of the workbook.

If you already know how to write VBA code for another Office product, you can skip Section 1 and proceed directly to Section 2.

VBA Programming Skills Needed

The first skill you need to program in VBA is easy: you need a good working knowledge of Microsoft Project, understanding how it works and what it can and cannot do. Simply stated, if you cannot do something manually in Microsoft Project, then you cannot do it using VBA. It is also pointless to spend days creating a macro to do something for which Project has a built-in function. For example, do not write code to sort your project's tasks when you can use Microsoft Project's built-in Sort function.

The second skill you need is an aptitude for programming. The good news is that if you can create and maintain complex schedules, then you probably have the aptitude to program in VBA as well. If you are a software developer but do not know how to use Microsoft Project, then you should find someone who does know Microsoft Project to help you, or you need to learn to use it yourself!

Using Microsoft Project VBA is a relatively straightforward process. You can create much of your macro code by recording it, and then editing the recorded code to make it more useful, robust, flexible, and easier to maintain.

So, are you ready to start? If you have not previously coded in VBA before, the first step is to understand the Visual Basic Editor, in which you will edit and debug all your code. If you already know VBA for another product (such as Excel, Word, or Access) then proceed directly to Section 2.

Support for Your VBA Macros

The Microsoft Project newsgroups provide great support for Project VBA development. In Outlook Express (or any other newsgroup reader), enter the following server name:

msnews.microsoft.com

From your newsgroup reader, search the list for Project groups. The newsgroup you want for Project VBA is:

microsoft.public.project.developer

In all of the Microsoft newsgroups, Microsoft awards MVP (Most Valuable Professional) status to those who demonstrate expert-level knowledge in their support of the newsgroup communities. The Project MVP's maintain an FAQ list and provide other help at the following URL:

http://www.mvps.org/project

If you have problems using, or getting to work, any of the macros in this book, contact me (Rod Gill) at **vba@msproject-systems.com** and I will be happy to help you via email. If you need more help than this, or need help developing a macro, contact me using the same email address and I will quote you a price for the development.

Module 01

Creating and Editing VBA Code

Learning Objectives

After completing this module, you will be able to:

- Enter and edit VBA code in the Visual Basic Editor
- Navigate in the Visual Basic Editor
- Know the function of each window in the Visual Basic Editor
- Understand the different types of Modules used in the Visual Basic Editor

Understanding the Visual Basic Editor

The Visual Basic Editor (VBE) is where you create, edit, and debug all VBA code. The VBE screen consists of a number of areas, with which you must become familiar and then use. These areas (with keyboard shortcuts, if available) are as follows:

- **Code Window** - Use this window to enter and edit your code. Opening a Module or Class Module from Project Explorer or inserting one from the Insert Menu displays that module in the Code Window.

- **Immediate Window** - This window allows you to enter code for immediate execution. Use this window to test code snippets and to evaluate the state of variables and objects. (Ctrl+G)

- **Locals Window** - This window displays the values of declared variables in the current procedure. You will probably not use this window very frequently.

- **Object Browser Window** - Use this window to search for and learn about all the Objects, Methods, and Properties of the Project Object Library and all other Libraries your macros reference. This window is great for finding objects such as methods and properties. (F2)

- **Project Explorer Window** - This window displays all open projects and all Modules, Forms, and their Classes. It is essential for navigating to the various components and managing them. (Ctrl+R)

- **Properties Window** - Use this window to edit the properties of objects, such as renaming a Module or UserForm. (F4)

- **Toolbox** - While you work with a UserForm, this window displays all the available controls that you can add to the selected UserForm.

- **UserForm Window** - Use this window to create and edit UserForms. The system displays this window in the Code Window when you insert a UserForm from the Insert menu or open one from the Project Explorer.

- **Watch Window** - Use this window for debugging to allow advanced monitoring of your code, including creating a break under conditions you nominate.

To display the VBE, launch Microsoft Project and then click Tools ➤ Macro ➤ Visual Basic Editor. To return to Project from the VBE, press Alt+Tab to return to Project. To close the VBE, click File ➤ Close and Return to Microsoft Project.

Because you will be going in and out of the VBE many times, Rod Gill recommends that you use the Alt+F11 shortcut key for this purpose. Pressing this shortcut key alternately displays the Microsoft Project and VBE windows. Note also that this shortcut key works for all Office programs.

Hands On Exercise

Exercise 1-1

Add a Sub procedure to a project.

1. Create a new project (do not change a live project).
2. Press Alt+F11 to display the VBE.
3. Select Insert ➢ Module.

The system displays a new blank Code Window.

4. In the Code Window, type Sub FirstProcedure and then press the Enter key.

Notice that the system automatically adds the End Sub line for you. You must enter all code for this Sub procedure between the Sub and End Sub lines.

5. Press the F4 function key to display the Properties window.
6. In the Properties window, select the Module1 name and change its name to FirstProcedureCode.

Note: The system does not allow you to use spaces in the name of the Module.

7. Press Alt+F11 to return to Project.
8. Press Alt+F11 to return once more to the VBE.

Using the Project Explorer

The Project Explorer is essential for navigating between different parts of your macro and is visible by default when you first open the VBE. To display the Project Explorer if it is not visible, click View ➤ Project Explorer or press Ctrl+R.

When you have more than one project file open, the Project Explorer shows all of them in a Windows Explorer type display. By navigating down the folders in the relevant project, it is easy to open modules and classes from any open file.

If you right-click any object in the Project Explorer window, the system displays a shortcut menu with options such as exporting or removing the object. You can use the Project Explorer window and the Properties Window together to rename objects. For example, to rename a module, complete the following steps:

1. Open the Project Explorer (Ctrl+R).

2. Open the Properties Window (F4).

3. In the Project Window, select the module you wish to rename.

4. Edit the Name field in the Properties Window and then press the Enter key when finished.

> The Properties Window shows properties relevant to the selected object. For example, if you have a UserForm open with a TextBox control selected, the Properties window shows all properties for the selected TextBox.

Using the Project Explorer window, you can copy a module from one project to another using either of the following techniques:

- Export the module from the first project and Import it into the second project.

- Press and hold the Ctrl key and then drag the module from the first project and drop it into the second project.

If you use either of the preceding techniques, remember that module names only need to be unique within a Project file. If you drag and drop a module without pressing and holding the Ctrl key, the system moves the selected object rather than copying it.

Entering and Editing Code

To enter your VBA code, you need a Module or Class Module in which to add the code. To insert a module, click Insert ➤ Module in the VBE.

You can use all the usual keystroke shortcuts to navigate in your VBA code, such as using Ctrl+Right Arrow (or Left Arrow) to move a word at a time, or using Ctrl+Up Arrow (or Down Arrow) to move a Sub or Function at a time. You can search the VBA Help for other keyboard shortcuts, as they can save you a lot of time.

As you enter your VBA code, you will soon notice that the system "color codes" parts of the code. For example, the system formats comments and reserved words, such as Loop or IF, in different colors. To see the system behavior and to change those colors, complete the following steps:

1. In the VBE, click Tools ➤ Options.

2. Click the *Editor Format* tab.

3. In the *Code Colors* list, select a text type, such as the Comment Text item.

4. Change any of the formatting as desired for the selected text type.

5. Click the *OK* button.

 Rod Gill recommends that you set the Comment text to a more visible color, such as dark green. This makes it easier to read and differentiates Comment text visually from code.

Hands On Exercise

Exercise 1-2

Change the color of all comments in your code:

1. In the VBE, click Tools ➤ Options.
2. Click the *Editor Format* tab.
3. In the *Code Colors* list, select the *Comment Text* item.
4. Click the *Foreground* pick list and select the third color from the list, which is the dark green color.
5. Click the *OK* button.

The system now formats all text following a ' (single quote) character with the dark green format once your cursor leaves the line you edited.

What is IntelliSense?

IntelliSense is a very powerful and useful tool for all VBA programmers. Most code in VBA starts with the name of an object, followed by a period character, and then by a method or property. For example, ActiveProject is an object that represents the currently active project in Microsoft Project itself. To determine the name of the active project, use the following code:

```
ActiveProject.Name
```

To see the name of the active Task, for example, use the following code:

```
ActiveCell.Task.Name
```

When writing your VBA code, IntelliSense shows you the list of available Parameters, and whether each parameter is optional or not. IntelliSense shows optional parameters in square brackets, such as [optional parameter]. IntelliSense also allows you to browse and find the Method or Property you need without looking all the way through the Object Browser or the Help articles.

 Tip: If you cannot find the Method or Property you want with IntelliSense, then you may need to navigate the object hierarchy by going down one or more levels, or you may have the wrong Object selected. For example, the Bold property belongs to the Font Object, so you need to select the Font Object before IntelliSense will show you the Bold property.

Hands On Exercise

Exercise 1-3

Display the values of a property using IntelliSense in the Immediate Window.

1. In the VBE, press Ctrl+G to open the Immediate Window.

2. Type "? ActiveProject" (without the double quotes).

The leading "?" character in step #2 is a shortcut for the word print.

3. Type the period character (.).

Notice that IntelliSense displays a pick list of all Methods and Properties for the ActiveProject object.

4. Type the N character.

Notice that IntelliSense displays the entries starting with N. In this case, the Name property is highlighted.

5. Press the Tab key to select the Name field.

6. Press the Enter key.

The system displays the VBA code, ? ActiveProject.Name, and then shows the value of the Name property, which might be Project1 if you have the default new project selected. The system prints the name because in the Immediate Window, the "?" character is shorthand for the Print command. Therefore, the system evaluates the statement and displays the result on the next line in the immediate window.

 In your code, you can use the Debug.Print statement to display the debug test results in the Immediate Window. For example, you might use something like Debug.Print "Count=0 at start of loop".

Understanding Modules

A Module is the most common place to enter your code. If you are creating a large macro, then you may insert and use several Modules. For example one Module might contain your main code and another might hold all your utility code. By keeping that utility code in a separate Module, you can copy it easily from one project file to another, allowing you to re-use it easily.

Each Module can hold as many procedures as you like, but a good practice is to limit the number of procedures in each module for readability purposes. If you are finding it hard to locate a procedure within a module, insert another Module and then cut and paste logically similar procedures into the new module.

 Tip: A great keyboard shortcut in the Code Window is Ctrl+Up Arrow or Ctrl+Down Arrow to move down or up one procedure at a time.

Using Sub Procedures

A Sub Procedure is a block of code that performs a series of actions. Other code can call a Sub Procedure, and a Sub Procedure can call even more code in turn. A Sub Procedure cannot return a value to the calling code, but it can change shared variables. For example:

```
Sub ShowManagementReport()
   'Code to show the management report
End Sub
```

Values can be passed to the Sub as in:

```
Sub ShowManagementReport(ReportName as String)
   'Code to show the management report
End Sub
```

Note that the names ShowManagementReport and ReportName do not (and are not allowed to) have spaces.

For readability purposes, Rod Gill recommends that you capitalize the first letter of each word in the name of each Module, Procedure, and Variable.

Using Functions

Functions are effectively the same as Sub Procedures, but do return a value and have the same naming restrictions as Sub Procedures (no spaces). Consider the following example:

```
Function GetHoursPerDay()
   GetHoursPerDay=ActiveProject.HoursPerDay
End Function
```

The above code simply returns the Hours Per Day value you set by clicking Tools ➤ Options in the active project. Putting the code in a function allows you to call it when needed. If you ever need to force a value rather than read the current value, you only need to edit the code in one place. This makes for quick, cheap, and accurate changes.

Using GoSub Subroutines

You can use GoSub Subroutines to call small blocks of code within the same procedure. However, these legacy statements are time consuming to debug, difficult to maintain, and cannot have parameters, so I do not recommend their use. If you want to learn more about how to use GoSub Subroutines, type the word GoSub in the Immediate window then press the F1 function key for help on it.

Using Class Modules

When you have numerous things to do, or you want to interact with an object such as Excel, you can use a Class Module as an efficient way to write your code. Do know, however, that you can write all your macros in Modules and never use Class Modules.

Class Modules can make code easier to use and maintain, making them attractive to more advanced developers. Anyone who is familiar with Object Oriented Programming (OOP) knows Class Modules. VBA Class Modules are quite simple; for example, there is no inheritance.

Because Class Modules are a more advanced topic, I give you an example for using them in Module 5.

Using UserForms

UserForms let you create a simple form to display data and to accept user input. In VBA, UserForms are not nearly as sophisticated as they are in Visual Studio or Microsoft Access, but they can be useful in some circumstances. **Note:** UserForms are not the same as the Forms you can show and customize using Tools ➤ Customize ➤ Forms in Microsoft Project.

Module 02

Common VBA Code for All Office Programs

Learning Objectives

After completing this module, you will be able to:

- Understand and use VBA code that is common to all Office applications
- Understand how to use Comments to annotate your code
- Understand Objects, Methods, Properties, and Parameters
- Code some useful functions in VBA common to most Project VBA macros

Using Office VBA Code

You can use VBA macros in all Microsoft Office applications, including Project, Excel, Access, Word, Outlook, FrontPage, and others. Microsoft also licenses VBA to other organizations. For example, AutoCAD uses VBA as its macro language.

Now that you are familiar with the Visual Basic Editor (VBE), I dedicate the remaining Modules in Section 1 to the core parts available to VBA in any application. In this module, I discuss how to use the following elements of VBA code common to all Office programs:

- Comments
- Objects, Methods, Properties, and Parameters
- With statement
- MsgBox function
- InputBox function
- VBA Help

Adding Comments to Your Code

You create a Comment by typing a ' (single quote) character followed by the text of the Comment. Comments are essential to clearly describe what your code does (or should do). A good way of writing VBA code is to first write Comments describing what the code should do, and then write the VBA code according to the comment statement. Some good comments are:

```
'Loop through all tasks counting Assignments
'Open the project referenced in the active task's Hyperlink
```

Some poor comments are:

```
'Add 1 to the loop counter
'Set T to the active task
```

Poor comments simply describe the obvious while the good comments describe what the solution should be. All the comments in the sample code in this workbook describe what the code does rather than explaining the obvious!

By the time a macro is no longer useful to you, you may have spent more time maintaining and modifying it than the time you spent originally writing it. Good comments are essential in reducing maintenance times (and costs) by making it easier to understand the code.

 Tip: When editing code in an existing procedure, start the comment for the change with either the date or the new version number for the code. This makes it easy to track what changes you made and when you made them. For example:

'Nov 11 2006 or
'v2.1

Understanding Objects, Methods, Properties, and Parameters

You used the ActiveProject object in your VBA code in Exercise 1-3. Other examples of Objects are Project, Task, Resource, Assignment, and Calendar.

Not only can you manipulate a single Object, you can work with collections of Objects. The most common collection with which a Project VBA programmer works is the collection of all Tasks in a project. Other collections include Resources, Assignments, and Calendars. In fact, if you see a word and its plural version in the Object browser or in an IntelliSense list (for example Task and Tasks), the plural version is a Collection. A Collection, therefore, is a number of similar Objects grouped together and manageable as a group (collection). I show you how to loop through collections in an upcoming topic.

A Property is a value associated with the Object or a descriptor associated with it. For example, in the ActiveProject.Name code, ActiveProject is the Object and Name is a Property of the Object. ActiveProject.Tasks.Count provides the count of all tasks in the Tasks collection, which is the count of all tasks in the active Project. All collections of Objects have a Count property.

To change an object property, use the following code:

```
Object.Property = NewValue
```

A Method is something you can do with or to an Object. In other words, a Method **does** something. For example, when you apply the Delete method to a Task object, the system deletes the task. When you apply the Add method to the Tasks Collection, the system adds a new Task to the collection and to the project itself.

To set an Object to point to something new you need to use the Set statement as in this example:

```
Set ProjectObject = ActiveProject
```

Objects, Methods, and Properties are essential to your VBA code. You will use them frequently as you write your code.

Parameters are items of information you pass to a Method that communicate options for the Method. For example, consider the following code:

```
Application.Sort "ID", True
```

There are two parameters in the preceding code. The "ID" text string is the parameter representing the name of the Field to sort, while the True parameter says sort in ascending order.

The Application Object refers to Microsoft Project when in Project VBA, but this works unchanged in Excel VBA where Application would refer to Excel (you would need to change the Field name to a cell references). In Help you may also notice that the Application Object qualifier is optional. Sort "ID", True therefore works on its own.

All Parameters have names. In the previous Sort example, the two parameters are the Key1 (set to "ID") and Ascending1 (set to True) parameters. Parameters are either required or optional. With required parameters you must supply a value, and appear as the first parameters in the parameter list. In fact, your code will not run if you leave out a required parameter.

Optional parameters follow required parameters. To find out if a parameter is required or optional, look at Help or the IntelliSense message. The system shows optional parameters in square brackets, like this [optional parameter].

If you only want to supply several of the available parameters, such as only the first and fourth parameters, because the other parameters are optional and not needed, then you have two ways to do this:

- Use placeholders for the missing parameters by adding the commas that separate each parameter, such as in the following example:

```
Object.Method FirstParameter,,, FourthParameter
```

 The preceding code example assumes that there are actually six parameters available for the Method, and assumes that you only want to use the first and fourth parameters, but not the second, third, fifth, and sixth parameters. In this case, you supply commas for the second and third parameters, but you do not supply commas for the fifth and sixth parameters.

- Provide only the parameters you want and declare each of them, such as in the following example:

```
Object.Method ParameterOneName:= ParameterOne, _
    ParameterFourName:= ParameterFour
```

 Notice in the preceding code example the := (colon and equals sign combination) between the parameter name and value are required. Your code will not work without it.

Note that the True parameter in the Application.Sort example is hard to understand unless you have remembered that it refers to the Ascending property. The following code is more readable and useful:

```
Sort Key1:="ID", Ascending1:=True
```

 Of the two preceding methods, Rod Gill recommends that you supply Parameter names because it provides code that is both easier to understand and to modify.

Using the With Statement

Sometimes you may want to perform several actions on the same Object or read or write a number of Properties for the same Object. To simplify this code and to make it run faster, use the With statement.

For example, to print a number of properties in the Immediate Window for the ActiveProject object, use a procedure such as the following:

```
With ActiveProject.ProjectSummaryTask
    Debug.Print "Name:", .Name
    Debug.Print "Duration:", .Duration
    Debug.Print "% Complete:", .PercentComplete
End With
```

If I did not use the With statement, I would have to write the code as follows:

```
Debug.Print "Name:", _
    ActiveProject.ProjectSummaryTask.Name
Debug.Print "Duration:", _
    ActiveProject.ProjectSummaryTask.Duration
Debug.Print "% Complete:", _
    ActiveProject.ProjectSummaryTask.PercentComplete
```

If you compare the two preceding versions of the same code, you can clearly see that the With statement gives you less to read and makes a more logical block of code. Project VBA finds the ActiveProject.ProjectSummaryTask object in the With statement, which means that it keeps that result and reuses it for the rest of the code block. This makes the code slightly faster to execute.

Hands On Exercise

Exercise 2-1

Use Parameters in your VBA code.

1. Open a new project file and enter a task named "Hi".

2. Save and close the project as C:\Delete Me.mpp.

3. Press the Ctrl+N keys to create a new project.

4. In the VBE, press Ctrl+G to display and select the Immediate Window.

5. Enter the following code in the Immediate Window and then press the Enter key:

   ```
   fileopen "C:\Delete Me.mpp",,,,,,,,,,,,pjDoNotOpenPool
   ```

6. Close the Delete Me project then type the following code on the next blank row (type it all on one line):

   ```
   fileopen Name:="C:\Delete Me.mpp",
   OpenPool:=pjDoNotOpenPool
   ```

7. Close then delete the Delete Me.mpp file.

Notice that the named parameter version is much easier to type and understand. The version with placeholders can cause problems if you delete one of the commas by mistake or if you insert an extra comma.

Using the MsgBox Function

At some point, your macro may need to display a message to the user and get some feedback in response. For example, you might need to display the message, "There has been an error opening the file, do you want to proceed?" in a dialog with a Yes and No button for the user to click. If the user clicks No, then your code needs to detect that response and end the macro. The MsgBox method lets you display a dialog such as this, and does much more as well. For example, to display the error message above, insert the following VBA code into your module:

```
If MsgBox("There has been an error opening the file, " _
    & "do you want to proceed?", vbYesNo) = vbNo Then
    MsgBox "Macro Cancelled by User", vbInformation
    End
End If
```

Notice that the first line of code is too long to fit on a single line, so I added a " _" (space underscore without the double quotes) at the end of the code line, which means that the line continues to the next row. For readability, if a line extends past the screen's edge, break it into two or more lines by typing " _" and then press the Enter key for a new line and continue typing. The **&** symbol is a concatenation character that the system uses to concatenate strings together.

Notice that I used the MsgBox method twice in the code sample. I used it the first time to display a message and get a response from the user. I used it the second time just to provide information to the user.

The first call treats MsgBox as a Function because it passes a value (the message text) and a setting (vbYesNo), which in this case tells MsgBox that I want the system to display a dialog with Yes and No buttons. The MsgBox function returns a value that indicates whether the user clicked the Yes or No button.

A long message will automatically wrap onto separate lines. However, if you want to add a line break yourself, use the following code:

```
If MsgBox(Prompt:="An error occurred opening the file. " _
    & "Do you want to proceed?" & vbCrLf _
    & "Error: " & Err.Description, Buttons:=vbYesNo) = vbNo
Then
```

In the preceding code example, vbCrLf is a built-in VBA constant that represents a Carriage Return and Line Feed to create a new line. The second line starts with the text "Error: " and then has the VBA Error description appended to it. I explain how to manipulate text in the Handling Text section of Module 03.

There are actually a number of different ways to display message boxes with this very useful function. To learn more about the MsgBox function, click the word MsgBox in your VBA code and then press the F1 function key to read about the different formats you can use with the MsgBox function.

Prompting the User for Inputs

Receiving input from the user is another common requirement. One way to do this is using the MsgBox function described above. This works fine if all you need is two buttons (Yes and No); but if you want to request text input, you need to use the InputBox function. The InputBox function has a number of parameters, but we focus on the first three: Prompt, Title, and Default.

The Prompt parameter is the message displayed in the Input Box, while the Title parameter is what the system displays in the title bar of the Input Dialog. The Default parameter is an optional value you can provide as the default entry value in the Input dialog. For example, the following VBA code produces the result shown in the Figure 2-1.

```
InputVal = InputBox (Prompt:="Please Enter the Delivery " _
    & "Date", Title:="Delivery Date Entry", Default:=Date + 14)
```

**Figure 2-1: InputBox result
(notice the default value)**

If the user presses the *Cancel* button in the Delivery Date Entry dialog shown in Figure 2-1, then the system returns an empty string "" (two double quotes). You need to test for this result as follows:

```
Dim InputVal as String
Dim DeliveryDate as Date
InputVal = InputBox (Prompt:="Please Enter the Delivery " _
   & "Date", Title:="Delivery Date Entry", Default:=Date + 14)
If InputVal ="" Then
   MsgBox "Date entry cancelled by user, macro ended"
   End   'This exits the macro
Else
   'Process Delivery Date
   DeliveryDate = CDate(InputVal)
End If
```

Finally, the InputBox function always returns a String value, so to use the input value as a Date you must convert the returned String into a Date. I describe this conversion procedure in the Converting between Variable Types section of Module 03.

Understanding Functions and Procedures

You can use MsgBox as either a Function or a Procedure (sometimes called a Method). Whenever a value is expected from the MsgBox, then this use is as a Function; otherwise, it is a procedure. An example of using MsgBox as a procedure is:

```
MsgBox "Macro Cancelled by User", vbInformation
```

An example of using MsgBox as a Function is:

```
If MsgBox("There has been an error opening the file, " _
   & "do you want to proceed?", vbYesNo) = vbYes Then
```

Notice that there are two differences between how I use MsgBox in the preceding examples:

- As a Function, there must be something to consume the returned value. In the example, the test part of the IF statement compares the result with the value vbYes.

- A Function always needs its parameters enclosed in round brackets.

Hands On Exercise

Exercise 2-2

Explore the MsgBox function by completing each set of steps.

1. In the VBE, press Ctrl+G to display and activate the Immediate Window.

2. Type: MsgBox "My Prompt", (include the comma at the end of the line)

After typing the comma, you should see IntelliSense display a pick list of all possible actions.

3. Scroll up and down the IntelliSense list to see what actions are available, select the vbYesNo option, and then press the Enter key.

The system displays Microsoft Project temporarily, and displays the dialog with the My Prompt text and with the Yes and No buttons.

4. Click the Yes or No button to close the MsgBox dialog and return you to the VBE.

5. Type: Msgbox "My Prompt", (include the comma).

6. Select vbCritical, type a + (plus sign), select vbOKOnly, and then press the Enter key.

7. Click the OK button to close the dialog window and return you to the VBE.

Using the + sign lets you select more than one option. You cannot select vbOkOnly and vbYesNo at the same time as they conflict with one another.

8. Type MsgBox then press F1 to display and read Help on the MsgBox function.

9. Experiment with other MsgBox options, as you desire.

Using Help to Learn More about VBA

The Help system has full descriptions on using all the code described in this book. Some versions of Project VBA have slightly more capability than others, and produce slightly different results. For example, default behavior might change between Microsoft Project 98 and 2003. Refer to the Help system to learn how Microsoft Project VBA works in your version of the software. The quickest way to find help on a function for any version of Project is to do the following:

1. Close Help if it is already open.

You must complete step #1 because in older versions of Project, if a Help file is open, VBE only searches that Help file rather than all Help files. Closing Help means the system searches all Help files (for Project VBA and other referenced libraries) when you press the F1 key.

2. Press Ctrl+G to go to the Immediate Window.

3. Enter the Method, Property, or Function for which you want help.

4. Press the F1 function key.

You can use the *See Also* links to find related features, and you can use the *Example* link to copy working code into your own macro. There are also many code examples in Help, so use it. Help is a great learning reference tool.

Hands On Exercise

Exercise 2-3

Learn more about VBA from the Help system.

1. In the VBE, click Help ➤ Microsoft Visual Basic Help.

2. In the Table of Contents section, click *Microsoft Visual Basic Documentation*.

3. Click *Visual Basic Conceptual Topics*.

4. Explore and read any topic of interest to you.

 Warning: These instructions apply to Project 2003 Help. Earlier versions have slightly different structures, so you may need to search for conceptual topics. The Table of Contents may even be selectable from the Help menu in some versions of Project.

Module 03

Using Variables and Constants

Learning Objectives

After completing this module, you will be able to:

- Understand and use variables

- Understand and use constants

- Understand the different types of variables

- Convert data between different types of variables

- Safely save data to and read data from the Application area of the Registry

Using Variables to Store Data

In Module 02, I used a variable called InputVal to store the value returned from the InputBox function. I must save the returned value from InputBox; otherwise, I would have to prompt the user for the date every time I need to use that value. Of course, this would frustrate even the most angelic user! You use variables to store pieces of information so that you can reuse the information later.

You cannot use spaces in variable names, so by capitalizing the first letter of each word you make the name much easier to read, such as those shown in Table 3-1.

Using This	Is better than this
DeliveryDate	Deliverydate
DeliveryDate	dtdel
DeliveryDate	D

Table 3-1: Variable Naming Conventions

Declaring Variables

You use variables to hold values temporarily or until the project file is closed. The scope of a variable determines:

- How long a variable survives
- From where the system can read the variable
- From where the system can alter the variable

If you declare the variable within a procedure (like the DeliveryDate variable shown previously), then its scope is as follows:

- The system destroys the contents of the variable as soon as the procedure exits.
- Only the current procedure can read the variable (no other procedure can read the variable).
- Only the current procedure can alter the variable (no other procedure can alter the variable).

If you declare a variable at the top of the module before any Sub or Function statements, we call this a Global variable, and it retains its value until you recompile the code or you close the project file.

There are three variants to the Dim statement, which are as follows:

- Private DeliveryDate as Date

  This statement makes the variable DeliveryDate visible to all procedures in its module only (when declared at the top of the module).

- Public DeliveryDate as Date

  This statement makes the variable DeliveryDate visible to all procedures in all modules (when declared at the top of the module).

- Static DeliveryDate as Date

  This statement means the variable DeliveryDate retains its value when the procedure exits and is available the next time you call the procedure until you recompile the code or you close the project file. You should use the Static version in procedures, as Global variables always hold their values when a procedure exits.

Rod Gill recommends that you never assume the current value of any variable. Instead, always force the variable to a known value. For example, when you first use a count, set the variable to zero so you know it starts at zero, such as setting TaskCount = 0.

Tip: Always declare your variable names in upper and lower case, as in my examples, but type them in lower case only. When you move your cursor to another row, the VBE autocorrects the capitalization of the variable name, exactly as typed in the Dim statement. If you type the name incorrectly, it stays in lower case, which is a quick way to spot a typo that will either prevent your code compiling or cause other problems.

Using a Naming Convention for Variables

A popular naming convention for variables starts the name of the variable with characters denoting the data type. For example, dtDeliveryDate indicates the Date data type. Personally, I find this creates code that is difficult to interpret and read, and it costs more time than it saves. With carefully named variables, such as DeliveryDate, it is obvious that the variable is (or should be) a date value. Whatever approach you take to your naming convention, make sure that it is easy to understand and universal throughout your organization.

Using Constants to Store Fixed Values

Constants are variables that cannot be changed. Refer to the following code to see a constant at work:

```
InputVal = InputBox(Prompt:="Please Enter the Delivery " _
    & "Date", Title:="Delivery Date Entry", Default:=Date + 14)
```

The number 14 in the above code represents the number of days for delivery. Imagine that you use that number in three or four different procedures in a module, and then in the future, you need to change the delivery period to 10 days.

Murphy's Law suggests that you will forget one or more of the places where you used the number 14, and that in your hunt to later change the number 14, you may change an unrelated value 14, even if it does not represent the delivery period. In relying upon search and replace to change embedded values like this, you introduce one or more opportunities to create bugs in your code. Remembering the axiom that you spend more time maintaining code than writing it, you can reduce your maintenance time by using constants.

From the above example, I can declare the following constant at the top of the module:

```
Const DeliveryPeriod = 14
```

In all procedures where I need the delivery period value of 14, I use the following code:

```
InputVal = InputBox(Prompt:="Please Enter the Delivery " _
    & "Date", Title:="Delivery Date Entry", _
    Default:=Date + DeliveryPeriod)
```

Using a good constant name makes code more understandable. If the delivery period value changes from 14 to 10, simply edit the Const statement and all statements using that constant change immediately. This makes for a quick and accurate edit.

Best practices suggest that you never use numbers or even text strings in your code; instead, always use Const statements. To create a text constant from the previous example, I use the following code:

```
Const DeliveryPeriod = 14
Const PromptDeliveryDate = "Please Enter the Delivery Date"
Const PromptDeliveryDateTitle = "Delivery Date Entry"
```

I now use the following code:

```
InputResult = InputBox(Prompt:=PromptDeliveryDate, _
    Title:= PromptDeliveryDateTitle, _
    Default:=(Date + DeliveryPeriod))
```

The Const statement can also have a Private or Public qualifier, just like the Dim statement. Beyond those constants that you define using the Const statement, VBA includes a number of built-in constants whose names begin with vb or pj. Constants starting with the prefix "vb" are common to all VBA implementations. Earlier, I showed you the vbYesNo constant that defined a parameter to the MsgBox function to show yes and no buttons in the dialog. The vbYesNo constant actually represents the number 4, which is the value that VBA uses internally for the vbYesNo constant. Obviously, vbYesNo is much easier to remember and understand than a number.

Built-in constants always have a two-letter code at the beginning of the name that explains their source. The following list describes the most common ones:

- **vb** constants are common VBA constants. For example, use the vbYesNo constant wherever you need a yes or no response, such as in the MsgBox function.

- **pj** constants are unique to Microsoft Project VBA. For example, the pjCustomTaskText1 constant represents a number in the Text1 field used internally by Project VBA.

- **xl** constants are unique to Excel. For example, the xlTop constant refers to the top border of a cell.

Controlling Variable Scope

The Scope of a variable defines its visibility. For example, a variable defined in a Sub procedure cannot be read or altered by code in a different Sub procedure. A variable declared at the top of its module can be read and altered by all procedures in the module.

If you make all variables global and give them Public qualifiers, you run a larger risk that unrelated code could change a variable unexpectedly. Each of us tends to reuse our naming syntax in the code we write, so this is a real risk. Think about how difficult it is to determine what code affects what variables within the scope of a large macro or program. If you declare a variable within a procedure, only code in that procedure can affect it.

Forcing Declared Variables

Scope control is about writing secure code that works and continues to work after many changes to code. The first step in creating secure use of variables is to force their declaration using Dim statements. If you do not force declared variables, MyVariable and the typo MyVarible become two different variables, making it difficult to find bugs. If you force declared variables, the system would generate a compile error in the case of the misspelled MyVarible, allowing you to catch and resolve the error very quickly and easily. To force declared variables:

1. In the VBE, click Tools ➤ Options

2. Click the *Editor* tab and select the *Require Variable Declaration* option.

3. Click the *OK* button.

All new modules will now have **Option Explicit** as the first row. For safety, insert this statement at the top of all existing modules. The compiler will now create an error for every undeclared variable.

Rod Gill recommends that you always use the minimum possible scope. If you use or duplicate the name of a variable in one procedure, you do not want it to change the same variable in another procedure. Ignoring this best practice can cause bugs that are very difficult to track down.

Protecting Variables from Unwanted Change

Now that you have forced declared variables, the next step is to secure the use of variables by limiting their scope. For example, consider containing all procedures that need to share a set of variables in one module. Scope can then be limited to just that module rather than having public variables that can be changed by any code in any module.

Tip: Because it can be difficult to find where you initially declared Global variables and to determine their data type, consider using a separate module just for Global variables in larger macro solutions. Start the name of all Global variables with **glbl**, such as glblDeliveryPeriod. This way you know immediately that the variable is Global and that you declared it in the GlobalVariables module.

Sharing Variables with Another File

To see variables used in another .mpp file, you must set a reference to the file. This is not a robust solution, as file names tend to change and move around, breaking your code references. A better way of sharing small amounts of data between files, and even between Office programs, such as Project and Excel, is to write the data to the Windows Registry in the safe Applications area.

Storing Data in the Registry

The VBA SaveSetting, GetSetting, and DeleteSetting commands allow you to save, retrieve, and delete values in the Windows Registry. The functions use a safe Application area in the Registry that cannot interfere with any other program's settings. These statements are completely safe to use and you cannot do any damage to the Registry by using them. You cannot read or change any Registry settings other than those created in the VBA application area.

For example, suppose you want to save the path of a particular file for use by another application, such as Excel. In Project VBA, use the following code to save the path to the Registry:

```
SaveSetting "MyProject", "Files", "Weekly Report File", MyPath
```

MyPath needs to be a String variable holding the path. In Excel, use the following code to retrieve the path from the Registry:

```
MyPath = GetSetting("MyProject", "Files", "Weekly Report " _
    & "File")
```

Again, MyPath needs to be a String variable. Use the following code to delete the Registry setting created with SaveSetting:

```
DeleteSetting "MyProject", "Files", "Weekly Report File"
```

You can use these registry settings to store values for the next time you run a program. If you want to save more than half a dozen pieces of information, then I recommend you use a text file or a database to store your information. It is not a good idea to store lots of data in the registry, and it is easier to review and update data in a text file or a database.

For example you can save file paths, user preferences, lists of tasks, and much more in a text file. Module 05 provides an example of creating, writing to, and reading from a text file. You can use the sample code directly to create a text file that stores and shares data for you.

Working with Data Types

In this part of the module, I teach you how to work with date, text, and number data. I also show you how to convert variable data from one type to another, such as converting date data to text data.

Handling Dates

Date data is very common, especially in Microsoft Project. As with Excel, the system stores dates in two parts: a whole number representing the number of days since 1900, and a fraction representing the time. For example, .5 represents 12:00 Noon, while .75 represents 6:00 PM. You declare a Date using the following code:

```
Dim DeliveryDate as Date
```

VBA provides a number of functions to manipulate dates. If you want to add 14 days to a date, you can use the formula Date + 14, as in the Constants example earlier in this module. To add a month or a number of weeks to a date, it is better to use the DateAdd function. The following example adds 2 months to today's date:

```
DeliveryDate = DateAdd("m", 2, Date)
```

You can use the DatePart function to return any part of the month. The following example returns the current month as a number from 1 to 12:

```
MonthNumber = DatePart("m", Date)
```

You can use the DateDiff function to calculate the number of periods between two dates. Use this function carefully, as the period you choose affects the result. In fact, I recommend that you carefully read the Help article on the DateDiff function before you actually use it. The following code calculates the number of days between two dates:

```
DaysDifference = DateDiff("d", Date1, Date2)
```

VBA for Project offers the DateAdd and DateSubtract functions that add or subtract dates using a specified calendar. You might use the DateAdd function to calculate a Finish date for a task using a Start date, a duration value, and a specific calendar.

Note that Project's DateAdd and DateSubtract methods belong to Project's Application Object. There is a DateAdd function in VBA and another DateAdd function in Project VBA. To use the Project VBA DateAdd, use the following code:

```
Application.DateAdd(StartDate, Duration, Calendar)
```

You can search for help from the VBE on all of these date functions to learn more about them and to see example code for them.

Handling Text

Many VBA macros need to manipulate text (strings), to create displayed messages or to manipulate strings in fields. To declare a Text variable, use the following code:

```
Dim MyStringVariable As String
```

To create a message string that results in "The Delivery Date is: May 1, 2006" you will need to do two things:

- Create a string out of a date and then display that date in a specific format.

- Concatenate the formatted date and delivery date strings together.

To concatenate two strings together, use the & (ampersand) character, as in the following code:

```
Result = "My result= " & NextString
```

You can use the Format function to convert numbers and dates into strings using a specific format. For example, you can convert a number to a specific currency format, or convert a date to a specific date format.

 Tip: To avoid confusion when communicating with international audiences, format dates using three letters or the full month name. To create a date with a 3 letter month use the Format function as follows:

Format (MyDateVariable, "mmm d yyyy")

The Format function allows you full format control over your variables. Search in the Help topics for details on how to format numbers and dates exactly as you want them.

To create the delivery date message I referenced above, use the following code:

```
DeliveryMessage = "The Delivery Date is: " _
    & Format(DeliveryDate, "mmm d yyyy")
```

If you need to split text into separate strings, you can use the Left, Right, and Mid functions. The Left and Right functions read a specified number of characters from the left or right end of the string, while the Mid function returns a specified number of characters from a starting point within the string. To determine the length of a string, use the Len function.

In the string "Task Name: My Task; Resource Name: My Resource; Start Date: 10 Jun 2006", I could use the following code to split the single string into three separate strings:

```
Sub SplitString()
'This Sub splits the MyString string into 3 parts
'Each part is separated by a ;

Dim strTask As String
Dim strResource As String
Dim StartDate As Date
Dim Pos1 As Long, Pos2 As Long

Const MyString = "My Task;My Resource;10 Jun 2006"

'Get the Task Name
Pos1 = InStr(MyString, ";")
strTask = Left(MyString, Pos1 - 1)
Debug.Print strTask

'Get the Resource Name
Pos2 = InStr(Pos1 + 1, MyString, ";")
strResource = Mid(MyString, Pos1 + 1, Pos2 - Pos1 - 1)
Debug.Print strResource

'Get the Start Date
StartDate = CDate(Right(MyString, Len(MyString) - Pos2))
Debug.Print StartDate

End Sub
```

In the preceding sample code, I declare three variables to hold the result of splitting the string. Note that I save the StartDate variable as a date rather than as a string.

The next statement is the Const statement that holds the original string. Finally, the code splits the string into three parts based on the semicolons used as separators, with the result saved and displayed in the Immediate Window.

Pos1 and Pos2 are both numeric variables to hold the character number of the two semicolons in the string. For example, the first semicolon is at position 8, or the eighth character in the string.

Pos1 = InStr(MyString, ";") makes use of a string function that returns the numeric position of one string within another. In this case, it returns the character position of the first semicolon.

strTask = Left(MyString, Pos1 - 1) returns the left most characters. As Pos1 is 8, it returns the leftmost 7 characters (Pos1-1).

Debug.Print prints the content of the indicated variable (or list of variables and strings separated by a comma) into the current cursor location in the Immediate Window. This is a great tool for debugging and testing.

Pos2 = InStr(Pos1 + 1, MyString, ";") is a slightly different version of Instr function as it has a starting position (Pos1+1). The net effect finds the second semicolon after the first (marked by Pos1).

strResource = Mid(MyString, Pos1 + 1, Pos2 - Pos1 - 1) The Mid function statement specifies the string (MyString), the starting position (Pos1+1), which is the first character after the first semicolon, and the number of characters to copy (Pos2-Pos1-1), again ignoring the semicolons.

StartDate = CDate(Right(MyString, Len(MyString) - Pos2)) The Right function reads the rightmost number of specified characters. The calculation is the total number of characters minus the position of the second semicolon.

If you put the SplitString code into Project's VBE and run it, the Immediate Window displays the following:

> My Task
>
> My Resource
>
> 10/06/2006

Tip: You can single-step through your VBA code using the F8 function key while in the VBE. You can even float your mouse pointer over each variable after the system performs each instruction to read the variable's current value.

Tip: To speed up your code execution, use Long variables rather than the variable types Byte or Integer. Modern PC's use 32-bit words, so the Long variable (which is 32 bits) uses a whole word in memory, which is slightly faster to process.

Using Numbers

Numbers have different types. Refer to Table 3-2 for a complete explanation of the different types of numeric variables.

For almost all whole numbers, I recommend you use Long variables. For all numbers with a fractional part, I recommend you use Single variables. I recommend you use the Currency type for all monetary calculations because it suffers fewer rounding errors with only four decimal places.

As mentioned in the preceding tip, most current 32-bit CPU's process the 32-bit Long variables faster than the Integer or Byte variables. This is because the Integer and Byte variables need extra CPU cycles to use only the required number of bits, instead of using the whole 32-bit word. So simplify your code by using only Long variables for any number that does not need a fractional part, and use Single variables if you do need a fractional part.

Type	Storage Size	Number Range
Byte	1 Byte (8 bits)	0 to 255
Integer	2 Bytes	-32,768 to 32,767
Long	4 Bytes	-2,147,483,648 to 2,147,483,647
Single	4 Bytes	-3.402823E38 to -1.401298E-45 for negative values; 1.401298E-45 to 3.402823E38 for positive values
Double	8 Bytes	-1.79769313486231E308 to -4.94065645841247E-324 for negative values; 4.94065645841247E-324 to 1.79769313486232E308 for positive values
Currency	8 Bytes	-922,337,203,685,477.5808 to 922,337,203,685,477.5807
Decimal	14 Bytes	+/-79,228,162,514,264,337,593,543,950,335 with no decimal point; +/-7.9228162514264337593543950335 with 28 places to the right of the decimal; smallest non-zero number is +/-0.0000000000000000000000000001

Table 3-2: Numeric Variables

Using Variant Variables

If you declare a variable using Dim DeliveryDate, and do not specify a data type, the system sets the variable type to Variant. Variants may sound attractive because they can hold any type of data, including strings, numbers, and more; but behind the scenes the system has to test the variable to determine what type of data it currently holds, consuming more system resources. Using the Variant type creates slower code. Rather than using the Variant type, use specific variable types, such as Date, so that the system flags an error when the code compiles and you attempt to store any other type of number or text into the variable. This can save you debugging time later.

 Rod Gill recommends that you declare all your variables using suitable data types. Only use the Variant data type if specifically required by the system.

Converting Between Variable Types

In the SplitString sample code shown previously, I converted a date in string form into a numeric date format so that I could save it into a Date variable. The code to do this was:

```
StartDate = CDate(Right(MyString, Len(MyString) - Pos2))
```

CDate is one of the functions that allows you to convert data types. There is one function for every data type, including CByte, CInt, CSng, CDbl, CCur, CDec, and more.

Sometimes, you do not need to use these conversion functions as VBA can convert the data for you. For example, consider the following code:

```
"My Number is: " & 10
```

Using the above code produces the following result:

    My Number is: 10

The system automatically converts the number 10 into a string. If you want a large number formatted with a thousands separator or with any other formatting, then use the Format function.

With string concatenations like "My Number is: " & 10, it is obvious that the system converts the data automatically. To be certain of a conversion, it is better to declare the data conversion process using a conversion function. This way, you know precisely what VBA is doing in the background, rather than assuming it is doing what you want it to do!

 Warning: The system truncates the fractional part of any number when you convert from a Single to a Long data type, or from any data type with a fractional part to any data type with no fractional part. For example, CLng(10.9) returns 10, truncating the .9 fraction.

To round a number to the nearest whole number, use the Round function instead. For example, CLng(ROUND(10.9,0)) returns 11 because the conversion rounds to 0 decimal places.

Type Cint into the Immediate Window then press the F1 function key. The Help window shows you a list of all available conversion functions. Make sure you close any help window before pressing the F1 key.

 Tip: A great way to find help is to type the name of a function, object, property, or method in the Immediate Window and then press the F1 function key.

Compiling Your Code

When you write a macro, the system saves all of your code internally as Opcodes and displays them as text in the Code window. This allows you to interpret and edit your code on the fly. Opcodes, sometimes called Pcodes, are machine independent so they can run on Macintosh computers, PC's, etc.

When you run your code, or you click Debug ➢ Compile VBAProject, the system creates Excodes from the Opcodes. Excodes are machine dependent codes that the system saves with your file. This speeds up the execution the next time you run your code.

Whenever you type a line of code and move your cursor to the next line, VBA automatically converts the line of code into Opcode. If the system finds a bug, such as an undeclared variable name, it immediately displays a message to explain the error. You must fix all errors before the system can compile your code.

Hands On Exercise

Exercise 3-1

Single step through the Sub routines in a module.

1. Open the Module 3 Sample Code.mpp file.

2. Click anywhere in the first Sub routine.

3. Press the F8 function key repeatedly to single step through each line of code.

4. Float your mouse pointer over each variable in the active row (highlighted in yellow) and the previous row to watch the code execute.

5. Repeat steps #3-4 for each Sub routine.

6. In the third Sub routine, change Dim strTask As String to Dim strTask As Long.

7. Press the F8 function key to single step through the code again.

Changing the strTask variable to Long produces a type mismatch error.

8. In the error dialog, click the *End* button.

9. Restore the strTask data type to String.

Exercise 3-2

Explore useful Help topics and write some VBA code.

1. In the VBE, press Ctrl+G to activate the Immediate Window.

2. In a blank row, type *cLng.* and then press the F1 function key for Help.

3. In the Immediate Window, use the Format function to print today's date, displayed using the full name of the month, the date, and the 4-digit year (such as March 18, 2006).

Answer: ? Format(Date, "mmmm dd, yyyy")

Module 04

Using Conditional Statements and Loops

Learning Objectives

After completing this module, you will be able to:

- Format blocks of code
- Use conditional statements
- Write code to perform loops in different ways

Structuring Your VBA Code

Structuring your VBA code is a two-step process:

1. Lay out your code so that it is easy to read.
2. Create and edit structural blocks of code.

If you do not indent your code, it becomes difficult to read. Poor layout costs you time when you try to read and comprehend your old code.

In this module, I present one way of laying out your code. You may choose another, but the key is to make your code consistent and easy to read. If you work with a number of VBA developers, you should all adopt the same layout format.

To make your code easier to read, use indenting similar to the sample code in this workbook. The Sub statement should always be in the leftmost column of your code window.

Indent logical blocks between If…Then statements and Do…Loop statements to show clearly the start and finish of each code block, as illustrated below:

```
Sub MyProcedure()
'Variable Declarations
Dim MyInput As String
Dim MyDate As Date
Dim MyLong As Long

    'Prompt for a date
    MyDate = InputBox("Prompt", "Title", Date)
    If MyInput <> "" Then
        MyDate = CDate(MyInput)
    End If

    'Increment date to the next Monday
    Do Until Weekday(MyDate) = vbMonday
        MyDate = MyDate + 1
    Loop
    Debug.Print Format(MyDate, "ddd mmm d yyyy")
End Sub
```

Consider inserting a blank row to separate variable declarations from code. After variable declarations, tab in once for the main code and twice for the body of the If and Do Statements, and again for If or Do statements nested inside the outer ones.

When you tab, the Visual Basic Editor (VBE) replaces the tab with the number of spaces specified in the *Tab Width* field on the Editor page of the Options dialog, accessed by clicking Tools ➢ Options (in VBE). By default, this value is 4 spaces.

If you position your cursor at the beginning of the row, or just before the first non-space character in the row, and then press the Tab key, the system indents four spaces. If you press Shift+Tab, the system out-dents four spaces. To indent multiple rows, select the rows and then press the Tab key. To out-dent multiple rows, select the rows and then press Shift+Tab.

Note in the previous code example that I added a blank row between the logical blocks of code, followed by a comment describing what the next block **should** do. Comments that simply describe what the code does, such as "add one to the count," do little to help your future understanding. Instead, describe what each block of code **should** do. Consistent use of indenting and comments makes your code much easier to read (for you and others) and saves you much time and money maintaining your macro over its lifetime.

Using the Conditional IF Statement

When you write VBA code, you often need to test a value and then do one of several options, depending on the tested value result. In the following code example, if the InputBox function returns an empty string (because the user clicked the *Cancel* button), warn the user and then end the macro; otherwise continue with processing the code.

```
Sub TestIF()
Dim Answer As String
    Answer = InputBox("Enter Task", "Enter Task Title", "")
    If Answer = "" Then
        MsgBox "No Name entered, Macro ended", vbCritical
        End
    Else
        'Remaining Code
    End If
End Sub
```

If you read the Help article about the If statement, notice that there is an ElseIf part of the statement as well. This means you can have code such as the following:

```
If Test1 Then
    ' Code if Test1 is True
ElseIf Test2 Then
    ' Code if Test2 is True
ElseIf Test3 Then
    ' Code if Test3 is True
ElseIf Test4 Then
    ' Code if Test4 is True
Else
    ' Code if none of the tests are true
End If
```

You can write as many ElseIf statements as you like. However, after one or two ElseIf statements, your code becomes more difficult to understand and maintain. If you have one test that can have a number of different results, then use the Select Case statement instead. Use the Select Case statement as follows:

```
Select Case TestValue
    Case "Define"
        'Code if Answer string = "Define"
    Case "Design"
        'Code if Answer string = "Design"
    Case "Develop"
        'Code if Answer string = "Develop"
    Case "Test", "Debug"
        'Code if Answer string = "Test" or "Debug"
    Case Else
        'Code if none of the above Case's match
End Select
```

In the previous code example, TestValue is a variable, a calculated value, or a function that returns a value.

Refer to Microsoft Project VBA Help for all the details about what the Select Case statement can and cannot do, and find some useful variations of the Select Case statement. If you need to match multiple results against one variable or test, the Select Case statement is the neatest and easiest technique to use. However, if you have multiple tests to make, then you must use the If, ElseIf, End If structure instead.

Tip: As a shortcut when typing **End If**, type **endif** as one word. As soon as you press the Enter key, the VBE converts this to End If for you.

Working with Loops

You frequently need to code to loop through all tasks or resources in a project, or to loop through other Object Collections. Available VBA code loops include the **Do loop**, the **For Next** loop, and the **For Each Next** loop. Refer to Microsoft Project VBA Help to see more loop examples and variations.

Using the Do Loop

The most commonly used loop code is Do loop. The following code loops through every project file name in a selected folder:

```
Sub ListFiles()
Dim MyString As String
Const FLDR = "G:\Projects\*.mpp"

    MyString = Dir(FLDR)
    Do Until MyString = ""
        Debug.Print MyString
        MyString = Dir
    Loop
End Sub
```

The **Dir** function shown above is an extremely useful function and is available in all VBA implementations. Call the Dir function with a folder path and file filter (in this case *.mpp) and it returns the name of the first file found. Call it again without the path (str = Dir) and it returns the next file, and so on. Finally, after Dir returns all filenames, Dir returns an empty string ("").

The Do loop above continues until Dir returns a "". If you forget the MyString = Dir statement, Dir is not called repeatedly and MyString always holds the name of the first file. This means it is never reset to "" so the loop never exits. If you're debugging and your code does not end, press Ctrl+Break to force a break so you can either end the procedure, edit existing code, or add extra statements. Make sure you always understand exactly what conditions should exit your loops and then test them.

Debug.Print MyString prints the current value of MyString to the Immediate Window.

Another way to control Do loop termination is to test for the end of the loop in the loop itself, and then to exit the loop forcibly using Exit Do, as shown in the following code example. Typically the previous version is easier to understand and maintain.

```
Sub ListFiles()
Dim MyString As String
Const FLDR = "G:\Projects\*.mpp"

   MyString = Dir(FLDR)
   Do
      If MyString = "" then
         Exit Do 'Forcibly exit Loop, last file found
      Else
         Debug.Print MyString
         MyString = Dir
      End If
   Loop
End Sub
```

Yet another type of Do loop termination is to put the test at the end in the Loop statement so that the code is always executed at least once. This does not work for this sample code because there may not be a .mpp file in the folder, however, I include the code for comparison purposes. Again, the first version is easier to understand and maintain.

```
Sub ListFiles()
Dim MyString As String
Const FLDR = "G:\Projects\*.mpp"

   MyString = Dir(FLDR)
   Do
      Debug.Print MyString
      MyString = Dir
   Loop Until MyString = ""
End Sub
```

You typically use the Do loop to continue processing until a variable reaches a certain condition, unknown at the start. For example, you may not know how many files are in the folder. If you do know the exact number of times you want to loop through your code, then instead use the For Next loop.

Using the For Next Loop

The For Next loop is useful when you know in advance or can calculate how many loops you want to perform. For example, if you know there are 10 objects and you want to process all of them, then use code similar to the following:

```
Dim Count as Long
   For Count = 1 To 10
      'Do something that uses the value of Count
      Debug.Print Count
   Next Count
```

In Project VBA, this is probably the least commonly used loop construct.

Using the For Each Next Loop

The For Each Next loop is very useful for looping through all Objects in a collection of Objects. The most common example is looping through all Tasks in an ActiveProject object:

```
Dim Tsk as Task
   For Each Tsk in ActiveProject.Tasks
      'Code for each Task
      Debug.Print Tsk.Name
   Next Tsk
```

In the above code example, Tasks represents a Property of ActiveProject and it returns the collection of all Tasks in the active project. Tsk is a variable of type Task and is set in turn, to every task in the active project.

The loop in the preceding code fails if your schedule has a blank task in it. See Module 12 (Looping through your Schedule) for a way of handling blank tasks.

Hands On Exercise

Exercise 4-1

Use If and Loop statements.

1. In the VBE's Immediate Window enter If and then press F1 for Help to explore the different variations for the If statement.

2. Enter the sample code for If into a new module (or open the sample file for Module 4 from the web site).

3. Single step over the code and make sure you understand the logical sequence of steps.

4. Enter the word Select and press F1 to learn the different variations of the Select Case statement.

5. Enter the word Do and press F1 to learn the different variations of the Do statements.

6. Enter the Loop sample code into the Module and edit the FLDR Constant to a path containing .mpp files on your PC or network. **Note:** You may also edit the string to look for Word Documents (*.Doc) instead.

7. Single step through your code to understand how it executes.

Note: Remember to float your mouse over variables to see their values.

Module 05

Using Classes

Learning Objectives

After completing this module, you will be able to:

- Create a Class
- Write VBA code in Classes

Creating a Simple Class

You commonly use Classes in professional programming languages. In VBA, Classes are less common, but the code behind a User Form is automatically in a Class. The example we use in this module is a Class created to read a text file. The advantage of doing this in a Class is that all operations we use to manipulate the text file exist in one place, making them easy to find and use.

 A good way to use a text file is to store information for transfer from Project to other programs (such as Excel) or to hold data until the next time you open the project and run the macro again.

Classes have Methods and Properties. Methods **do** things; Properties come in Read only, Write only or Read and Write flavors. While you can pass arrays of data (an array is like a collection of variables) or collections of Objects, typically Properties read or write single pieces of information.

For our example in this module, we want to read and write several pieces of information as follows:

1. Provide the Path for the .txt file.

2. Open the file for Reading.

3. Read the next line of text and return it.

4. Read the next word and return it.

5. Close the file.

In a Class Module, every Sub becomes a Method. Properties are special statements that start with **Property**.

To store data for the Class, declare your variables at the top of the Class. To declare a Class variable use a statement such as the following:

```
Private MyVariable as DataType
```

 To prevent code from outside the Class reading or writing to a variable within the Class, declare it as **Private**.

65

To read ten variables, you need ten **Property Get** procedures; to write to ten variables, you need ten **Property Let** procedures. To prevent reading or writing, simply omit the Get or Let procedure for that variable.

A Class Module provides all code required for the Class Object. To use the Class you must create a variable for it in a procedure in a different module. Set the variable to equal a **New** copy of the class to copy it into memory. This automatically triggers a built-in initialize routine. When you close the class a built-in terminate procedure runs.

The result is that you can have as many Class variables (txt in the sample below) as you like. In the following text file example you can open as many text files as you like, each one with its own copy of the Class in memory without interfering with each other. Without Classes, you need to anticipate the number of files you want open and have a separate set of variables for each file. Classes provide a powerful solution for this problem.

For a text file reader Class, start with the code below and add more functionality, if needed. The goal is to demonstrate the use of a Class and provide a structure for you to copy. Copy this code into a new Class Module you create by clicking Insert ➤ Class Module in the VBE. You can also find this code in the file Module 5 Sample Code.mpp.

```
Option Explicit

'Privately declared variables to hold data start with prv
Private prvPath As String
Private prvLine As String
Private prvLinePos As Long
Private prvEOF As Boolean
Private prvLastWord As Boolean

Private Sub Class_Initialize()
'There is nothing to initialize in this class
    Debug.Print 'Blank line
    Debug.Print "Text file Class Initialized"
End Sub

Property Let FilePath(path As String)
    'Store the file path
    prvPath = path
End Property

Property Get FilePath() As String
    'Return the File Path
    FilePath = prvPath
End Property
```

```
Property Get NextLine() As String
   Line Input #1, prvLine
   NextLine = prvLine
   If EOF(1) Then
      prvEOF = True
   End If
End Property

Property Get NextWord() As String
Dim pos As Long
Dim Word As String
   If prvLine = "" Then
      Line Input #1, prvLine
      NextWord = prvLine
      If EOF(1) Then
         prvEOF = True
      End If
   End If

   If prvLine <> "" Then    'prvLine could still be empty
      pos = InStr(prvLine, " ")
      If pos = 0 Then
         Word = prvLine
         prvLine = ""
      Else
         Word = Left$(prvLine, pos - 1)
         prvLine = Mid$(prvLine, pos + 1)
      End If
   'Remove trailing characters such as . and ,
   'You can add more Replace's as needed
      Word = Replace(Word, ",", "")
      Word = Replace(Word, ".", "")
      NextWord = Word
   Else
      NextWord = ""
   End If

   'Test for Last word and set flag if true
   If prvEOF And prvLine = "" Then
      prvLastWord = True
   End If
End Property

Property Get ISEOF() As Boolean
   ISEOF = prvEOF
End Property
```

```
Property Get ISLastWord() As Boolean
   ISLastWord = prvLastWord
End Property

Sub FileOpenReadOnly()
   If Dir(prvPath) <> "" Then
      Open prvPath For Input As #1
      prvEOF = False
      prvLastWord = False
   Else 'File not found. Set End of file and last word flags
to TRUE
      prvEOF = True
      prvLastWord = True
   End If
   prvLine = ""
End Sub

Sub FileClose()
   Close #1
End Sub

Private Sub Class_Terminate()
'Close the file in case it hasn't already been closed
   Close #1
   Debug.Print "Text file Class Terminated"
End Sub
```

In a Module, use the following code to read a text file. Edit the path to match the path for a suitable text file. Make sure the text file is not too long!

```
Sub ClassExample()
Dim txt As New clsTextFile
   txt.FilePath = "C:\Test Class File.txt"
   txt.FileOpenReadOnly
   If txt.ISEOF Then
      Debug.Print " Text file empty or doesn't exist"
      Exit Sub
   End If

   Debug.Print "Line by Line"

   Do Until txt.ISEOF
      Debug.Print "  "; txt.NextLine
```

```
Loop
   txt.FileClose

   Debug.Print "Word by Word"
   txt.FileOpenReadOnly
   Do Until txt.ISLastWord
      Debug.Print "  ", txt.NextWord
   Loop
   txt.FileClose
   Set txt = Nothing  'Finished with the Class
End Sub
```

When you run this code, the system displays the results in the Immediate Window (press Ctrl+G to display it). The figure below shows how the Properties and Methods coded above appear in IntelliSense. The pick list in Figure 5-1 appears as soon as you type a period character after the class variable's name (in this case txt.)

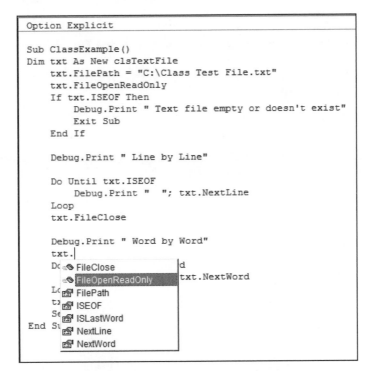

**Figure 5-1: IntelliSense shows
Class Methods and Properties**

This Class holds all code relevant to Text files and provides a neat way of accessing it by IntelliSense. All you have to do is type the class object name, type a period, and the system displays all Properties and Methods for your selection, along with a popup menu showing parameters.

Hands On Exercise

Exercise 5-1

Experiment with Classes.

1. Enter the Class and Module code above into a new project or download the Module 5 Sample Code.mpp file.

2. Download the Module 5 Sample.txt file or create a small text file with 4 or 5 lines of text in it.

3. Edit the path in the ClassExample Sub to match the name and path of your text file.

4. Run ClassExample.

5. Add your own VBA code to count the number of words as they are read.

6. Add a Property to return the number of words already read.

7. Add Methods to open a file in Write mode and write a line of text to the text file.

 Tip: Search Help on the VBA Open statement to learn how to open text files in write mode.

Module 06

Working with Other Applications

Learning Objectives

After completing this module, you will be able to:

- Reference other Office applications such as Excel in your Project macros
- Add a self-signed digital certificate to a project

Understanding VBA Automation

VBA Automation is the concept that VBA code (or VB or C#. etc.) can control any application that is an Automation Server. An Automation Server allows other applications to control its host application. Just about all Office Applications, including Microsoft Project are Automation Servers, so other applications can control each of them.

Automation Clients are applications that can control other applications with an Automation Server. All Office programs, including Microsoft Project, are Automation Clients.

This means that Microsoft Project can control Excel, and Excel can control Microsoft Project. By "control," I mean that one application can do anything in the other application as if the code was running in the other application.

To make all the Objects, Methods, and Properties of an application visible in another application, you need to set a reference to the other program's Object Library.

Adding References to Other Applications

All VBA implementations allow you to add a reference to other applications so that you can control those other applications from your VBA macro. Module 21 describes a macro that exports data from Microsoft Project to create a report in Excel. This module simply describes the code common to all VBA implementations.

To add a reference to another application, complete the following steps:

1. Open the VBE.
2. Click Tools ➤ References.
3. From the list of all installed applications, select the application to which you want to set the reference.
4. Click the *OK* button.

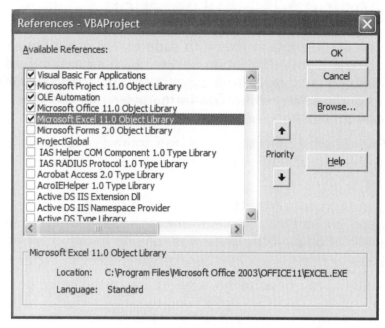

**Figure 6-1: References dialog after adding
a reference to Excel**

 In Figure 6-1, the numbers associated with each
Reference or Library refers to the application's version.
The Microsoft Excel 11.0 Object Library is for Excel 2003.

There are several points to keep in mind regarding references:

- The VBE puts all selected references at the top of the reference list.

- All Microsoft applications start with the word Microsoft and are therefore under M in the alphabetically sorted list.

- By default, there are several Libraries required by VBA, which the system references automatically and which you should not deselect.

- When you open a file from an older version in a newer version of a program, the system automatically upgrades all selected references to the latest versions for you. However, if you open a file for a newer version on a PC with an older version of the program, the references do not update automatically. In this case, you must update the references manually.

Tip: When distributing a file, save it in the format for the oldest version you need to support. So if you have Microsoft Project 2003 and Excel 2003, but some of your team members have Project 2000 and Office 2000, then save the project in 2000 format with a reference to Excel 9 (Excel 2000).

Managing VBA Security

Each version of Microsoft Office has introduced stricter security that may or may not be effective in protecting you. By default, later versions have Macro Security set to Very High so you cannot run macros except from trusted locations.

Until you sign your VBA Projects, you need to set Macro security to medium or lower. To set macro security to medium:

1. Click Tools ➤ Macro ➤ Security.

The system displays the Security dialog, as shown in Figure 6-2.

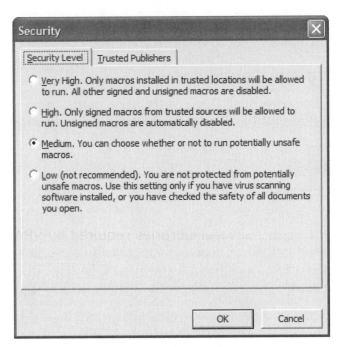

**Figure 6-2: Security dialog
from Project 2003**

2. Select the *Medium* security option.

3. Click the *OK* button.

When you open any project file containing a VBA macro, the system displays the dialog shown in Figure 6-3. (You must set macro security to Medium before you can see this warning message!)

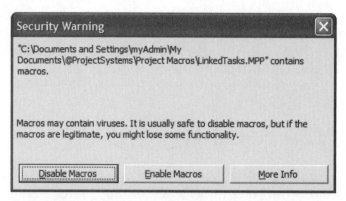

**Figure 6-3: Security Warning dialog appears
when you open a file containing macros**

To run a macro you need to click the *Enable Macros* button. To open a file and prevent any macro from running automatically on opening:

1. Click File ➤ Open and then click once to select the file you want to open.

2. Press and hold the Shift key and then click the *OK* button.

3. Release the Shift key after the system opens the file.

Creating a Digital Certificate

For development purposes, you can create your own digital certificate. To create a self-signed digital certificate, complete the following steps:

1. Open Windows Explorer and navigate to C:\Program Files\Microsoft Office\OFFICE11.

2. Double-click the SELFCERT.exe file.

 The file location is correct for a default installation of Microsoft Project 2003 or Microsoft Office 2003. Earlier versions will have differently named Office folders.

If you do not find the Selfcert.exe program, then you must reinstall Microsoft Project. On the page Custom Installation options, expand Office Tools item, and then select Digital Signature for VBA projects. Click the pick list arrow button to the left of this item and select the *Run from My Computer* option. Setup then installs Selfcert.exe.

3. In the Create Digital Certificate dialog, enter the developer's name for the certificate name then click the *OK* button as shown in Figure 6-4.

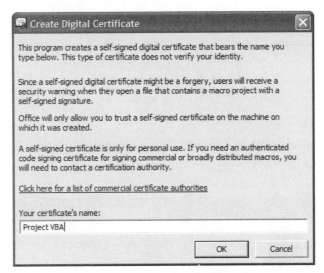

**Figure 6-4: Create Digital
Certificate dialog**

To sign a project file with your certificate, complete the following steps:

1. Open the VBE.

2. Select Tools ➢ Digital Signature.

3. In the Digital Signature dialog shown in Figure 6-5, click the *Choose* button and select the certificate you created.

**Figure 6-5: Apply a Self Cert
to a VBA project**

4. Save the project and close it.

When you reopen the project file, the system displays the Security Warning dialog shown in Figure 6-6.

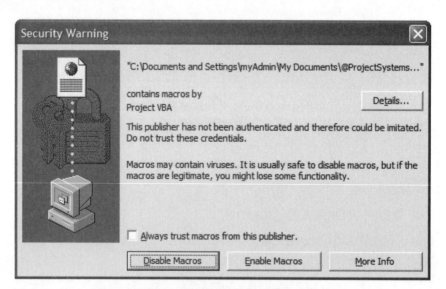

**Figure 6-6: Security Warning dialog
after signing a VBA Project**

5. Select the *Always trust macros from this publisher* option and then click the *Enable Macros* button.

From this point forward, the system no longer displays the Security Warning dialog when you reopen the project.

Because no formal certification authority issued the digital certificates you create, macro projects you digitally sign display as self-signed projects. Highest security settings may not allow you to run self-signed macros. A more complete solution is to acquire a digital certificate from a formal certification authority, but this involves an annual cost.

Self-signed certificates work fine for development purposes. Other people can edit your VBA code, but when they save the project, Microsoft Project cancels the certificate. This causes the security dialog to reappear, telling you someone has probably edited your code.

Hands On Exercise

Exercise 6-1

Work with References.

1. Open the VBE in a new project.
2. Add a reference to Excel.

Exercise 6-2

Work with digital certificates.

1. Create a Self-Signed digital certificate for yourself.
2. In a project, assign the certificate in the VBE.

Module 07

Writing and Debugging Your Code

Learning Objectives

After completing this module, you will be able to:

- Use a simple approach to developing macros
- Predict how long it might take to develop the final product
- Understand basic debugging features
- Write code that is easier to understand and debug

Using a Simple Approach to Create a VBA Macro

Writing your first macro may seem very daunting, but a simple game plan makes all the difference in the world. There are many approaches to writing code, but for VBA code, the following process works well for a beginner:

1. Write down everything the macro has to achieve.

2. Code features with similar functionality at the same time so you can share common code.

3. Make sure you know how to perform manually your code's objective in Microsoft Project. If you cannot do it manually, it may not be possible to automate in VBA.

4. Focus on the 20% of features that deliver 80% of the desired outcomes, and then code and debug them first. Occasionally, you may be surprised to find that you finished in 20% of the time expected!

5. Structure your macros by asking yourself the following questions:

   - What variables need to be Global (changeable by all procedures in all modules)?

   - What code is best grouped into one or more Classes?

   - What inputs does the code macro need to accept, and how can they be stored and maintained?

   - What other programs does the macro need to use? For example, do you need to create reports in Excel?

   - What test data do you need? How will you prove each macro is working as expected?

   - What test procedures do you need to use to test all code with your test data? For example if you have a sample .mpp file and a sample Excel report created manually from the test .mpp file, then running the macro to create the report should produce the same result. Make sure you have a second set of Project and Excel reports for final testing as well.

   - What calculations fit better in formulas?

   - What custom fields do you need? Define these custom fields, and then keep a list of all custom fields and the names you give them.

   - What Views, Tables, and Filters do you need to create and manage to support the macro?

   - How will you run the macro: by toolbar, shortcut keys, or remotely from other applications?

6. Define what small utility functions are useful. For example, write code to return task updates for a certain week from your corporate database. Put these utility functions in separate modules so they are easier to copy and reuse in other macros.

7. Write brief descriptions of what each procedure needs to do. Copy these as comments for each procedure when you create them.

8. Create the following sections for each macro:

   - A Declaration area where all variables are declared with suitable types

   - An Initialization area where all variables are initialized and setup code done (for example to clear a custom field)

   - A Body area for the bulk of your code

   - A Shut Down area where any objects you created are set to Nothing to play safe

9. To write difficult code, such as creating a Table or Filter, record a macro while you do it manually. Edit the recorded code to make it more readable and flexible as required.

The smaller the blocks of code you need to write, the easier your coding will be. In Section 2 of this book, I present some complex macros, which I created using principles from the preceding list.

Estimating Development Time

There is only one reliable way of predicting how long it takes you to write any software code: predict your estimated development time, measure your actual development time, and then learn from variances. To get started, define what the macro has to do, then break the work into small blocks, as in the following example:

- Clear custom Fields.

- Loop through tasks updating custom fields.

- Start new Excel application and create Report headings.

Each of these blocks should be small and reasonably easy to predict in minutes or hours. Add them all up, add 30% for overall testing, and add another 20% to the total to handle change requests from your users (this could be you!). Initially, the percentages you add to the total estimate may need to be larger. Again, you need to predict, measure, and learn what margin of time you need for testing.

Running and Debugging Your VBA Code

Your code can fail to work in infinite ways, notwithstanding Murphy's Law to complicate matters! Eventually, you will need to debug your VBA code. The Visual Basic Editor (VBE) has a number of useful tools for code debugging.

For example, to debug the following sample code, type it into a new module or copy the Module 7 Sample Code.mpp file.

```
Sub SplitString()
Dim strTask As String
Dim strResource As String
Dim StartDate As Date
Dim Pos1 As Long, Pos2 As Long

Const MyString = "My Task;My Resource;10 Jun 2007"

    Pos1 = InStr(MyString, ";")
    strTask = Left(MyString, Pos1 - 1)
    Debug.Print strTask
    Pos2 = InStr(Pos1 + 1, MyString, ";")
    strResource = Mid(MyString, Pos1 + 1, Pos2 - Pos1 - 1)
    Debug.Print strResource
    StartDate = CDate(Right(MyString, Len(MyString) - Pos2))
    Debug.Print StartDate
End Sub
```

When debugging the preceding sample code, you may need to run your macro a number of times. When you need to run a macro repeatedly, consider assigning it to a shortcut key. The system provides only eight available shortcut keys because the system reserves the rest. The available keys are A, E, J, L, M, Q, T, and Y. To assign one of these keys to a macro:

1. In Microsoft Project, click Tools ➢ Macro ➢ Macros (or press Alt+F8).

2. Select the macro to which you want to assign a shortcut key.

3. Click the *Options* button.

4. In the Macro Options dialog, enter a letter in the *Shortcut key* field and then click the *OK* button.

85

Rod Gill recommends that you always save the file with your macro first before you run your code. This is easier when you develop your code in an .mpp file and not the Global.Mpt file.

Using VBA's Debugging Features

Use the following instructions with the preceding sample code to get a quick walkthrough of the basic debug features:

1. In VBE, click anywhere on the strTask = Left(MyString, Pos1 - 1) instruction line and click Debug ➢ Toggle Breakpoint (or press the F9 function key).

This highlights that row of code in Red.

2. While the cursor is anywhere in the procedure's code, press F5 to run it.

Running the macro executes the subroutine in which you located the cursor. Your Red line will turn Yellow to indicate that it is the next instruction to execute, and that execution temporarily halted at the breakpoint.

3. Float your mouse pointer over the Pos1 variable.

The system displays the value 8 as a tooltip, as shown in see Figure 7-1. This indicates that the first semicolon is the eighth character in the MyString string.

```
Option Explicit

Sub SplitString()
Dim strTask As String
Dim strResource As String
Dim StartDate As Date
Dim Pos1 As Long, Pos2 As Long

Const str = "My Task;My Resource;10 Jun 2007"

    Pos1 = InStr(str, ";")
    [Pos1 = 8]sk = Left(str, Pos1 - 1)
    Debug.Print strTask
    Pos2 = InStr(Pos1 + 1, str, ";")
    strResource = Mid(str, Pos1 + 1, Pos2 - Pos1 - 1)
    Debug.Print strResource
    StartDate = CDate(Right(str, Len(str) - Pos2))
    Debug.Print StartDate
End Sub
```

**Figure 7-1: Hover over a variable
to see the variable value**

4. Click and drag with your mouse to select the Left(MyString, Pos1 - 1) code in the breakpoint line.

5. Press Shift+F9.

This code contains the Left function in it so it cannot display a value. Pressing Shift+F9 displays the Quick Watch dialog, as shown in Figure 7-2, to calculate the result of the selected code and display it. The Quick Watch dialog is a very powerful tool. If the result is not what you expected you can edit the code, select it again, and then view the new result.

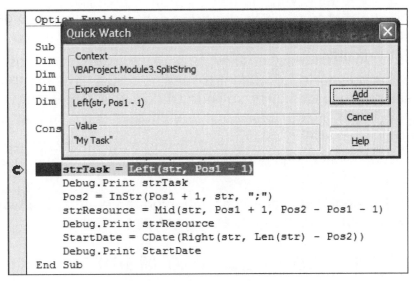

**Figure 7-2: Quick Watch dialog
displays the value for strTask**

6. Copy the selected text then press Ctrl+G to display the Immediate Window.

7. Type a question mark character, paste the copied code, and then press the Enter key.

VBA again displays the result but now you can use the Immediate Window as a testing place for editing code. Figure 7-3 shows the results in the Immediate Window. Once you do this, copy the edited code into the Code Window and proceed to your next bug!

```
Immediate
?Left(str, Pos1 - 1)
My Task
|
```

Figure 7-3: Immediate Window

8. Press F8 once to single step to the next instruction. Hover you mouse over the strTask variable to confirm it has the correct result.

Notice that in the gray border on the left of the Code Window, there is a yellow arrow representing the next statement to execute and that the Breakpoint has a red spot. Click on the spot to turn the breakpoint off or on, or click on the code line and press F9 again. You can also click and drag the yellow arrow to move the yellow line to the next executable instruction.

You can press F5 at any time to run the macro to the next Breakpoint or to the end of the subroutine. Alternatively, continue pressing F8 to step from one instruction to the next, which is a great debugging procedure as you can inspect variables and sweep across to Project to see the cumulative effect of the code as it executes.

If you want to stop your code while it is running, press Ctrl+Break. This action pauses the code execution so you can debug or force your code to end. Typically, this is most useful when you encounter a continuous loop that does not terminate as expected.

To end your code processing completely when paused in debug mode, click Run ➤ Reset in the VBE.

Once again, Help contains useful information on more advanced ways of debugging your code. The methods above get you going.

Making Your Code Easier to Maintain

Following are some tips to help you improve the readability of your VBA code:

- Capitalize the first letter of each word.

- When you have a complicated coding challenge, first write a comment to describe what the code **should** do, then code what the comment describes.

- Include in a comment for complex code a way of testing the code and what makes for a successful test. For example:

```
'The following code must return a date in the future
'for a Monday
```

- Restrict all procedures to no more than one screen full of code in the Code Window. If a procedure is so long that you have to scroll up and down to see it, this makes understanding the code more difficult. If a Module gets too big, split it into several smaller modules. Then call one module from the other, or call them from a new high-level module, as in the following example:

```
'Global variables shared by both procedures
Dim GlobalVariable as VariableType

Sub Main
    Macro1
    Macro2
End Sub

Sub Macro1
    ' Code
End Sub

Sub Macro2
    ' Code
End Sub
```

- Separate small blocks of repeated code into a separate procedure and then call this utility procedure when needed. It can be very confusing seeing the same code a number of times. It is also cheaper and quicker to maintain code in only one place, rather than duplicated in different parts of your code.

- When maintaining a file (making changes or additions to a macro already in use), always add a comment starting with the current date or version number above each edit. This lets you see when, where and why code changed, such as in the following example:

```
'Nov 11 2006 or 'V1.3
    Modified Code
```

Making Your Code Easier to Debug

The first rule for easy debugging is readability, but I have harped on that enough. Beyond readability is the structure of the code, where the following tips are helpful:

- Rather than doing a number of calculations all in one statement, break the statement into separate lines and store partial results in variables. This way you only have a small piece of code to understand and debug one line at a time.

- If you get a compilation error when moving your cursor from one line to another, fix the error as soon as possible. Errors tend to compound, so fix them when you find them. This applies to all bugs.

- Use typed variable names, not variants. This makes sure that you use correct data format and avoids unexpected type conversion errors. For example, Dim TaskCount as Long is a better practice than Dim TaskCount or Dim TaskCount as Variant. Defining TaskCount as Long makes sure it can only have a number (with no decimal places) and no strings.

- Keep procedures shorter than one screen in length so they are easier to understand.

- Before writing a macro, create a test plan so you know what your code should do. A high-level test plan could be a sample .mpp file and a sample report created manually in Excel, explicitly showing the report that the macro must produce based on the sample Project file. When your code successfully duplicates the sample report in Excel, you know that your macro works correctly!

- Record, create, and save macros in separate .mpp files before moving them to the Global.Mpt file. Do this for macros that need to be available to all your projects. Filling the Global.Mpt file with recorded macros, partially complete macros, and macros that do not work is confusing. At worst, this could damage your schedules if you run an uncompleted macro by mistake.

- When adding code to a macro, save a copy of the original macro so you can revert back to it later, if necessary. Yes, you need to back up macro files, too!

Hands On Exercise

Exercise 7-1

Use the debug features of VBA in the SplitString code from Module 3 (duplicated in the Module 7 Sample Code.mpp file).

1. Click anywhere within the Sub procedure and click on the following line:

   Debug.Print strTask

2. Press F9 to set this line as a break point (it should show a red background.

3. Press F9 again to toggle to break point off, and then press F9 yet again to restore the break point.

4. Press F5 to run the code, it should stop execution at the break point.

5. Hover your mouse over the MyString variable to see its contents, and then hover over the strTask variable as well.

6. Select the Left(MyString, Pos1 - 1) code then press Shift+F9. This displays the result in a popup dialog and offers an *Add* button. Click the *Cancel* button for now.

7. Select the variable strResource then press Shift+F9. This time click the *Add* button to add the variable strResource to the watch pane.

8. Press F8 to single step three times and watch the strResource variable in the Watches Window each time. This is a good technique to keep track of the contents of multiple variables as you debug.

Hands On Exercise

Exercise 7-2

Practice making your code more readable.

1. Take any code you have already created and test it for readability.

2. Replace any numbers in the code with Constants.

3. Make your variable names both easy to understand and meaningful.

4. Add comments that describe what your macro **should** do.

5. Break long routines that do not fit on one screen into shorter routines that do fit into one screen.

SECTION 2

MICROSOFT PROJECT VBA ESSENTIALS

Learning Objectives

After completing the Modules in this Section, you will be able to:

- Use formulas to replace some of your VBA code
- Write Project VBA code to control Microsoft Project
- Write Excel VBA code to control Microsoft Project

Introducing Project VBA

Project VBA is Microsoft's implementation of VBA into Microsoft Project. All the common VBA code is available in Project VBA, as is the common Visual Basic Editor (VBE).

Section 2 of this book assumes that you know the basics of VBA, because this section concentrates on how Microsoft implemented VBA in Microsoft Project. If you do not understand or are not sure about the basics of VBA, please study Modules 01-07 in Section 1 of this book.

Rather than repeating what is in the Help files (and that may vary slightly from version to version), I teach the basics by creating a number of useful macros. My goal is to create something that may already do some of what you want to do, and provide you basic blocks of working code that you can copy into your own macros. You will learn by example and will end up with lots of useful working code. This gives you a great head start in writing your own macros.

First of all, you need to make sure that you make good use of formulas in custom fields. It does not make sense to write event code and a loop to calculate data for each task if a formula can do it for you without code. The first module in this section, therefore, deals with custom fields and writing formulas. Module 10 then delves into where the system stores your code, and then you need to get dirty digging into how Project VBA structures its Objects (such as Projects, Tasks etc.) Finally, the fun starts as you learn to create productive macros in Project VBA!

Downloading the Sample Files

You can download the Microsoft Project sample files containing all of the sample code in this workbook at the following URL:

http://www.projectvbabook.com/dl

Microsoft Project 98 uses a different file format, so if you do have Project 98, make sure you download the Project 98 zip file. The Project 2000-2003 file format is suitable for use with any recent version of Microsoft Project, from 2000 to 2003.

Warning: Microsoft Project 2007 uses a different file format, so if you have Project 2007, you must open and re-save the files in Project 2007 format. Check the URL above for a Project 2007 zip file available with the 2007 release.

Module 08

Defining and Using Custom Fields

Learning Objectives

After completing this module, you will be able to:

- Use formulas in custom fields to complement Microsoft Project VBA macros
- Define custom fields and outline codes to track task and resource information
- Define custom fields using value lists, formulas, and graphical indicators
- Create custom views, tables, and filters using custom fields
- Use AutoFilter to easily create custom filters

Overview of Custom Fields

Microsoft Project offers custom fields to store your unique project data. As Project users find more uses for custom fields and demand extra capacity, Microsoft has steadily increased the number of fields and field types available. Microsoft introduced unlimited custom fields in Project 2007.

In pre-2007 versions, the software includes a number of custom fields that you can use to capture additional project information about tasks and resources. Project Server 2002 and 2003 users may also use Enterprise fields representing a doubling of available fields in the system as well as project-level fields not available in the stand-alone application.

Table 8-1 lists the local custom fields available in Microsoft Project 2003 (earlier versions have fewer than those shown in Table 8-1). Project 2007 has an unlimited number of custom enterprise fields.

 In addition to the custom fields listed in Table 8-1, Microsoft Project Professional 2002 or newer, when connected to Project Server, offers additional enterprise custom fields. Enterprise fields come in three types: Task, Resource, and Project. While many standard (non-enterprise) custom task fields carry a discrete value at the assignment level, enterprise task fields cannot contain unique values at the assignment level. The system stores enterprise field definitions in the Enterprise Global file and only Project Server administrators can create and edit these field definitions.

Field Type	Number Available	Data Type
Cost	30 (10 task, 10 resource, and 10 assignment fields)	Cost data formatted in Dollars
Date	30 (10 task, 10 resource, and 10 assignment fields)	Date data formatted using the formatting specified in the Options dialog
Duration	30 (10 task, 10 resource, and 10 assignment fields)	Duration data formatted in Days
Finish	30 (10 task, 10 resource, and 10 assignment fields)	Date data formatted using the formatting specified in the Options dialog
Flag	60 (20 task, 20 resource , and 20 assignment fields)	Yes or No only
Number	60 (20 task, 20 resource , and 20 assignment fields)	Unformatted number data
Start	30 (10 task, 10 resource, and 10 assignment fields)	Date data formatted using the formatting specified in the Options dialog
Text	90 (30 task, 30 resource , and 30 assignment fields)	Unformatted text data
Outline Code	20 (10 task and 10 resource fields only)	Outline data formatted using an Outline Code definition

**Table 8-1: Custom fields available
in Microsoft Project 2003**

Microsoft Project displays fields as data columns in task and resource Tables. The software includes user-defined custom fields in only a few of the default Tables. For example, the PERT Analysis data stores user-defined Duration, Start, and Finish fields. The software provides the remaining custom fields for your personal project management use.

To become truly knowledgeable about Microsoft Project, Rod Gill recommends that you learn as much as you can about default and custom fields. Gaining more knowledge about Fields also increases your knowledge about Views, Tables, Filters, Groups, and Reports.

Microsoft Project manages data in both standard and custom fields in one of three ways:

- **Calculated** – Microsoft Project calculates the values in the field and you cannot change the value.

- **Entered** – You must manually enter the values in the field.

- **Calculated/Entered** – Microsoft Project calculates the values in the field, but allows you to edit or enter a value as well.

 The Duration field is a good example of a standard Calculated/Entered field. The software calculates the Duration of a task when you assign resources to a task using Units and Work values for the assignment. On the other hand, you can enter your own Duration value for the task forcing the software to recalculate either Units or Work.

For the most part, data in user-defined fields is user-entered. The fields in the PERT Analysis tables and the Rollup table are the only exceptions to this rule of thumb.

Using Formulas to Support Project VBA

You can use formulas in custom fields to replace or complement Project VBA macros. For example, if you want to use a text field to display a Duration value converted to 8 hour working days, then use the following formula:

Format([Duration]/60/8,"0\d")

The preceding formula does everything you need, eliminating the need for a macro.

Use a combination of a custom field and a macro when you need to report on a subset of tasks for different management reports by completing the following steps:

1. Create a custom Flag field for each report, such as the Flag1 field, and set it to Yes for each task you want to include in the report.

2. Write your VBA macro code to do the following:

   - Create a filter for the Flag field used with the report.

   - Apply the filter.

   - Print the report.

If you want a result displayed in a custom field and the result uses data for only the current task, then a formula is likely to get the job done. If you need to read data across tasks, such as predecessors and successors, use VBA code. Custom fields can often act as very useful intermediary steps. The simplest solution to a reporting problem might include both formulas and VBA code.

 To discover how to write VBA code to add formulas to a field, simply record a macro while you manually create a formula in a custom field.

Defining Custom Fields

Before you define any custom fields, you must understand your organizational reporting needs. Based on your knowledge of project stakeholders, you can define custom fields for use in the reporting process through custom Views, Tables, Filters, Groups, and Reports.

To define a custom field, open a project and then click Tools ➢ Customize ➢ Fields. The Customize Fields dialog opens as shown in Figure 8-1.

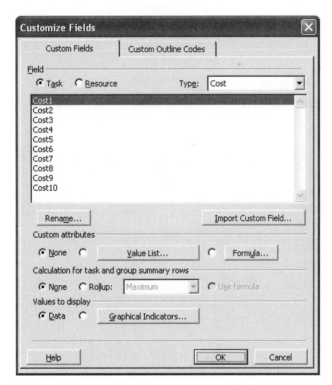

**Figure 8-1: Customize Fields
dialog**

Figure 8-1 shows that each field has it own set of custom attributes, including Value Lists, Formulas, and Graphical Indicators. Assume that as a part of your organization's project management methodologies, you must assign a Cost Center number to each task in every project. To create a custom field to capture this information, complete the following steps:

1. Select the *Task* option at the top of the dialog.

2. Click the *Type* pick list and select the *Text* field type.

3. Select an unused Text field, which is the Text1 field in this example.

4. Click the *Rename* button.

The system displays the Rename Field dialog shown in Figure 8-2.

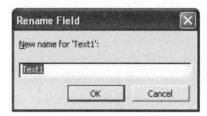

**Figure 8-2: Rename
Field dialog**

5. Enter the name Cost Center in the Rename Field dialog and click the *OK* button.

Figure 8-3 shows the Customize Field dialog after renaming the new Cost Center field.

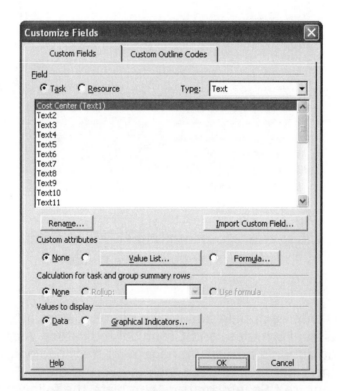

**Figure 8-3: Customize Fields dialog
shows custom Cost Center field**

Using a Value List in a Custom Field

Assume that as a part of your organization's project management methodologies, you must categorize the date slippage risk as High, Medium, or Low for each task in every project. Assume also that the default risk on every task is Low unless you specify otherwise. To create a custom task Text field with a value list, complete the following steps:

1. In the Customize Fields dialog, select the Text2 field and rename the field as Risk.

2. Click the *Value List* button.

The software opens the Value List dialog shown in Figure 8-4. Notice in the dialog title bar that the name Risk is contained in quotes, indicating that this is the new name for the Task Text2 field.

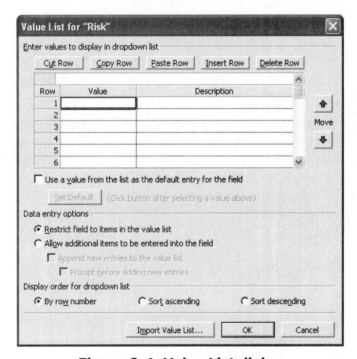

Figure 8-4: Value List dialog

3. Enter High, Medium, and Low values in the *Value* column.

4. Enter an optional description for each value in the *Description* column.

5. Select the option to *Use a value from the list as the default entry for the field.*

6. Select the Low value and click the *Set Default* button.

7. Select the *Restrict field to items in the value list* option in the Data entry options section.

8. Select the *By row number* option in the Display order for dropdown list section.

The software uses your selected options in the Data entry options section of the dialog to validate values entered in your new Risk field. By selecting the Restrict field to items in the value list option, you force the software to limit values in the Risk field to only those values in the value list. Other options in this section include:

- Allow additional items to be entered in the field

- Append new entries to the value list

- Prompt before adding new entries

The first option allows you to type additional values in the field for a single task. The second option forces the software to add new values to the value list as you or others enter them. The third option causes the software to warn you before adding a new value to the value list when you type a new value, allowing you to decide whether to append the value at the time you enter it.

The option you select in the Display order for dropdown list section determines how the software displays your value list in the project. The software displays value list items either by row number, in ascending order, or descending order.

When you define a new field and want to use a value list from an existing field, click the *Import Value List* button at the bottom of the Value List dialog. The system displays the Import Value List dialog shown in Figure 8-5.

Figure 8-5: Import Value List dialog

Click the *Project* pick list button and select one of the project files that you currently have open. Select the *Field type* for the field containing the value list. Click the *Field* pick list button and select the field containing the value list you want to import. Click *OK* to complete importing the existing value list into your current field.

In the case of the Risk field, there is no need to import a value list, so click the *OK* button in the Value List dialog. The software displays a warning message shown in Figure 8-6.

Figure 8-6: Value List warning dialog

The software warns you that if you previously entered values in this field before defining the value list, it may invalidate any or all of those pre-existing values. Click the *OK* button to return to the Customize Fields dialog shown in Figure 8-7.

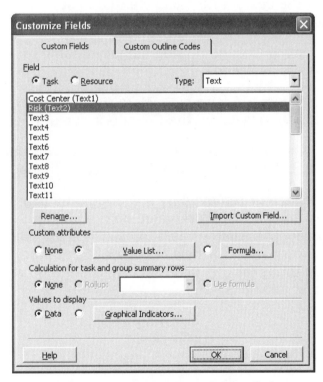

**Figure 8-7: Customize Fields dialog
shows two custom Text fields**

Hands On Exercise

Exercise 8-1

As a part of your organization's change control methodologies, you need to track the change request number of each Task added as a result of the change request.

1. Add a custom field called Change #. If your change numbers are numeric use a Number field, otherwise use a Text field.

2. Close the Customize Fields dialog.

3. Insert the custom field you created in step #1 to the Gantt Chart view of any project.

4. Enter some Change numbers against some tasks that have resources assigned.

5. Click Project ➢ Group by ➢ More Groups and then create a new Group that groups by the Change # custom field.

6. Apply the Work table then apply your new custom Group to see subtotals for extra Work added by each change.

For work changed or removed by a change, you can use a custom Number field to hold the Work value before you apply the change. Use a formula in another custom field to calculate the difference between the original Work (zero for new tasks for the change) and current Work. Group totals for this difference field will then reflect changes to Work, not just additions.

Using a Formula in a Custom Field

Microsoft introduced the use of formulas in custom fields in Project 2000, therefore, Project 98 does not allow you to use formulas.

Assume that as part of your organization's project management methodologies, you must show the percentage of cost over budget for every task in each project. This requires a custom Number field containing a formula. To define this custom field, complete the following steps:

1. In the Customize Fields dialog, click the *Type* pick list and select the *Number* fields.

2. Select an available Number field and rename it as Percent Over Budget.

3. Click the *Formula* button.

The software opens the Formula dialog shown in Figure 8-8.

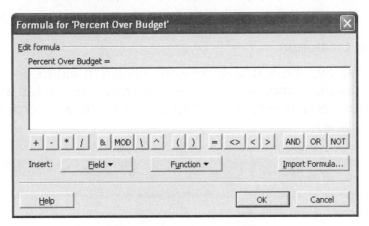

Figure 8-8: Formula dialog

The Formula dialog provides graphical tools for building formulas. You can use the *Field*, *Function*, and various operand buttons to build your formula, or you can type your formula manually. The software displays the resulting formula in the text area of the dialog.

4. Using the *Field* pick list button and operand buttons, create the following formula to calculate the percent of cost variance:

IIf([Baseline Start]=ProjDateValue("NA"), 0 ,[Cost Variance]/[Baseline Cost])

Notice in the preceding formula that I used the ProjDateValue("NA") function as a part of a test to determine whether I have saved a baseline for each task. I discuss the use of the function in the Testing for an NA Date Value section later in this module.

Notice that the formula for the percentage of cost over budget is simply the Cost Variance divided by the Baseline Cost. If the current Cost for a task is $50,000 when the Baseline Cost is only $45,000, then the Cost Variance is $5,000 (Cost – Baseline Cost). Applying the percentage of cost over budget formula, the task is 10% over budget ($5,000 ÷ $50,000).

If you created a formula in another field, you can import it into the current field by clicking the *Import Formula* button. The formula can be in a field in the active project, or in another project, but the project containing the formula must be open before you can import it.

5. Click the *OK* button.

The software displays the warning message shown in Figure 8-9. The warning indicates that, upon acceptance, the software deletes any pre-existing values in the Percent Over Budget field because a formula now calculates the values.

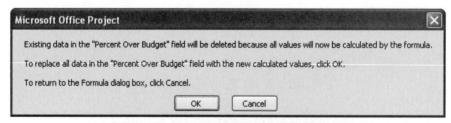

**Figure 8-9: Warning dialog for the
Percent Over Budget field formula**

6. Click *OK* to close the warning dialog.

Microsoft Project formats all values in user-defined Number fields as a decimal. To display the % Over Budget field values with percentage formatting, enter the following formula in any user-defined Text field:

Format([Cost Variance]/[Baseline Cost],"0%")

The Format function takes a number and formats it as a text string just like the VBA Format function.

Figure 8-10 shows the Customize Fields dialog with the new custom field containing the formula.

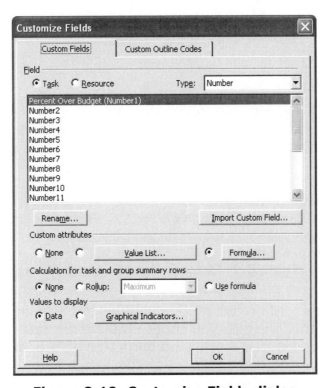

**Figure 8-10: Customize Fields dialog
shows Percent Over Budget field**

When you define a custom field with a formula, you must determine how the software uses the formula for summary tasks and group summary rows by selecting options in the Calculation for task and group summary rows section of the dialog. If you want Microsoft Project to apply the formula directly to both summary tasks and group summary rows, select the *Use formula* option. For the Percent Over Budget field, select the *Use formula* option to apply the formula to all summary tasks and subtasks in the project.

If you want to apply the formula in a different manner, select the Rollup option and then select a rollup value from the pick list. Rollup options apply to all custom fields except Text fields. Table 8-2 lists the field types and their rollup capabilities.

Rollup Type	Cost	Date	Duration	Flag	Number
Average	X		X		X
Average First Sublevel	X		X		X
Count All					X
Count First Sublevel					X
Count Nonsummaries					X
Maximum	X	X	X		X
Minimum	X	X	X		X
Sum	X		X		X
And				X	
Or				X	

Table 8-2: Custom Field Rollup Types

Now that you know which rollup method applies to each specific field type, the following explanations help you choose the appropriate method for your new field. Keep in mind that there is no particular right or wrong answer. The choice you make must follow the function that you intend for the field.

- **Average**: Causes the rollup to be an average of all non-summary values beneath the summary row.

- **Average First Sublevel**: Causes the rollup to be an average of both the non-summary and summary values on just the first level of subtasks or grouped tasks.

- **Count All**: Causes the rollup to be a count of all summary and non-summary items beneath the summary row.

- **Count First Sublevel**: Causes the rollup to be a count of both the summary and non-summary tasks on only the first level beneath the summary row.

- **Maximum**: The rolled up value is the maximum value of values beneath the summary row.

- **Minimum**: The rolled up value is the minimum value of all values beneath the summary row.

- **Sum**: The rolled up value is the sum of all non-summary values beneath the summary row.

- **AND**: The rolled up value is the logical AND of all the flag values appearing beneath the summary row. If all flags in the subtasks are set to Yes, then the rollup in the summary task is Yes. If any flags in the subtasks are set to No, then the rollup in the summary task is No.

- **OR**: The rolled up value is the logical OR of all flag values appearing beneath the summary row. If any flags in the subtasks are set to Yes, then the rollup is Yes.

Testing for an NA Date Value

When there is no date in a Date field such as Baseline Start, then Microsoft Project displays an NA value in the field. The system stores the NA value internally as the largest possible number the Date field can hold. One test for an NA date value is to test for the date being a large number. However, this method does not always work.

A more reliable method is to test for the value returned by using the function ProjDateValue("NA"). For example, to use the Text1 field to display whether a date exists in the Baseline Date field, use the following formula:

IIf([Baseline Start]=ProjDateValue("NA"),"No Date",[Baseline Start])

Using Graphical Indicators in a Custom Field

Using graphical indicators with a custom field offers you the ability to create a graphical presentation of the data in the field. It is easiest to apply graphical indicators to a field that already contains a Value List or a Formula.

Assume that as a part of your organization's project management methodologies, you must use stoplight indicators to display the data in the Percent Over Budget field. Assume your organization's criteria for displaying stoplight indicators in the Percent Over Budget field are as follows:

- If the % Over Budget is less than 5%, then display a green smiley face icon.

- If the % Over Budget is greater than or equal to 5% but less than 10%, then display a yellow neutral face icon.

- If the % Over Budget is greater than or equal to 10%, then display a red unhappy face icon.

In addition, you want to see the underlying value in this field for any task by floating the mouse pointer over the graphical indicator while in a task view. To define graphical indicators in the Percent Over Budget field, complete the following steps:

1. In the Customize Fields dialog, select the Percent Over Budget field.

2. Click the *Graphical Indicators* button.

The system opens the Graphical Indicators dialog shown in Figure 8-11. Notice in the Indicator Criteria For section of the dialog, the system accepts the criteria for displaying graphical indicators for three types of tasks: Nonsummary tasks (subtasks), Summary tasks, and the Project Summary Task (Row 0). Because of this, you can set completely different criteria for each of the three types of tasks, and define whether the summary rows inherit criteria from the non-summary rows.

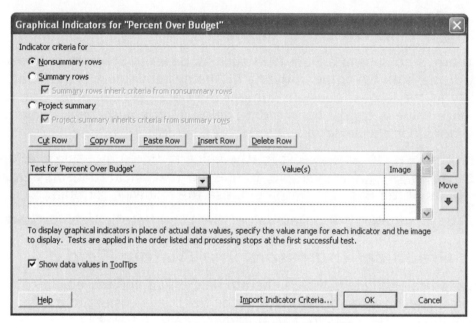

**Figure 8-11: Graphical Indicators dialog
for the Percent Over Budget field**

3. Select the *Nonsummary rows* option.

4. Set the Test, Value(s), and Image values as follows:

Test	Value(s)	Image
Is greater than or equal to	.10	Red unhappy face
Is greater than or equal to	.05	Yellow neutral face
Is less than	.05	Green happy face

5. Click the *OK* button.

 In Figure 8-11 the *Show data values in ToolTips* option is located in the lower left corner of the Graphical Indicators dialog. When you select this option, the software displays the underlying value in the field as a tooltip when you float the mouse pointer over the graphical indicator.

 If you previously created graphical indicators in a field, you can import them into the current field by clicking the *Import Indicator Criteria* button. The indicator criteria can be in a field in the active project, or in another project, but the project containing the indicator criteria must be open before you can import them.

To set the criteria used to determine the graphical indicator for each task, you must specify multiple tests using the available pick lists in the grid. The Test column offers the following tests:

- Equals
- Does not equal
- Is greater than
- Is greater than or equal to
- Is less than
- Is less than or equal to
- Is within
- Is not within

- Contains
- Does not contain
- Contains exactly
- Is any value

 The "Is any value" test yields a positive result in all cases. This makes it useful as a "catch all" test to include at the bottom of the criteria list, as it will display an indicator to represent any value not otherwise defined.

The tests you select in the Test field apply to the values you select or enter in the Value(s) field. In the Value(s) field, you can select any standard or custom field, or you can enter a literal value. In the Image field, select a graphical indicator for each test.

Table 8-3 shows the types of multi-colored graphical images available and the number of each type of image.

Image Type	Number
Blank indicator	1
Stoplights	13
Flags	8
Solid color squares	5
Plus signs	5
Minus signs	6
Solid color diamonds	3
Blue arrows	5
Semaphores	7
Light bulbs	2
Miscellaneous	5
"Smiley face" icons	6

Table 8-3: Graphical Indicators

How does Microsoft Project determine which graphical indicator to display for each task? The software processes the graphical indicator test criteria from the top down. If the first test results in a "False" condition, the system processes the second test, and continues processing each test in the list until a test results in a "True" condition. The software displays the graphical indicator for the first test that results in a "True" condition and then stops processing the list of tests. If none of the tests results in a "True" condition, the system does not display a graphical indicator for that task. You should keep this in mind while structuring your tests and, at the same time, use it to your advantage.

 Microsoft Project displays a blank graphical indicator in any cell in which a formula generates an error, such as when the software generates a division by 0 error.

Hands On Exercise

Exercise 8-2

As a part of your organization's project management methodologies, you need to define a custom field to calculate the percentage of Work that exceeds your original Baseline Work budget for every task in your project.

1. Open any project file you have baselined that contains tasks, resources, and assignments.

2. Click Tools ➢ Customize ➢ Fields.

3. Select the task Number1 field and rename it as Percent Work Over Budget.

4. Create a formula in the field that calculates the percentage of Work in excess of your original Baseline Work budget.

5. Apply the formula to every task in the project, including summary tasks and group summary rows,

6. In the % Work Over Budget custom field, display graphical indicators according to the following criteria:

   • If the task is on or below its original Baseline Work budget, display a green smiley face indicator.

   • If the task is greater than 0% and less than or equal to 5% over its original Baseline Work budget, display a green indicator.

   • If the task is greater than 5% and less than or equal to 15% over its original Baseline Work budget, display a yellow indicator.

   • If the task is greater than 15% and less than or equal to 25% over its original Baseline Work budget, display a red indicator.

   • If the task is greater than 25% over its original Baseline Work budget, display a black indicator.

7. Close the Customize Fields dialog.

8. Save and close your project file.

Defining Custom Outline Codes

Custom outline codes differ significantly from custom fields in the following ways:

- Outline codes can accommodate either a flat value list or hierarchical outline structure.

- Outline codes do not contain formulas or graphical indicators.

- When defining a custom outline code, you must first define a code mask that determines the allowable structure of an outline code value.

Assume that as a part of your organization's resource management information, you need to track each resource's primary job skill. To create a custom resource outline code for this purpose, complete the following steps:

1. In the Custom Fields dialog, select the *Custom Outline Codes* tab.

Figure 8-12 shows the Custom Outline Codes page of the Customize Fields dialog.

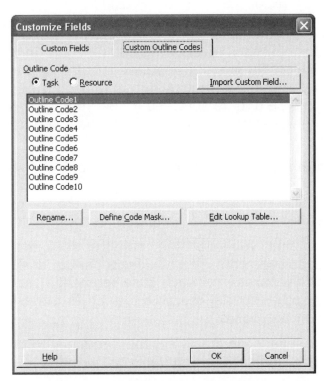

**Figure 8-12: Custom Outline Codes page
in the Customize Fields dialog**

2. Select the *Resource* option.

3. Select the *Outline Code1* field and rename it as Primary Skill.

4. Click the *Define Code Mask* button.

The software opens the Outline Code Definition dialog shown in Figure 8-13.

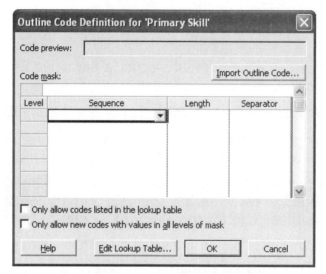

**Figure 8-13: Outline Code
Definition dialog**

To define the outline code mask, you must specify the Sequence, Length, and Separator values for each level of the outline code. In the *Sequence* column, you may select Numbers, Uppercase Letters, Lowercase Letters, or Characters. When you select a Sequence, the values for each code segment must adhere to the type of data specified in the Sequence. Selecting the Characters option gives you the most flexibility, as you may use any character to define your values.

In the *Length* column, you have the choice of limiting the segment to a number value on the list (between 1 and 10) or to a number you type into the field. You may also choose the Any selection from the pick list to allow any number of defined characters for the outline code segment.

In the *Separator* column, you select the character used as the separator between outline code segments. You can use a period, dash, plus sign, or a forward slash as the separator for each code segment. The system also allows you to enter other special characters, such as those found above the number keys on your keyboard.

5. Define a two-level code mask, set the Sequence to Characters, set the Length to Any, and set the Separator as periods.

Figure 8-14 shows the completed code mask for the Primary Skill outline code in the Outline Code Definition dialog.

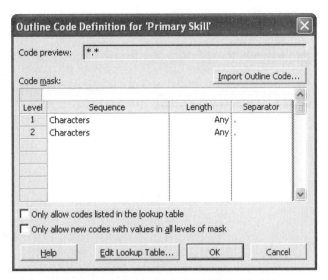

**Figure 8-14: Completed Code mask in
the Outline Code Definition dialog**

The Outline Code Definition dialog presents you with two additional options
for defining the code mask:

- Select the *Only allow codes listed in the lookup table* option to restrict
  the selection of code values to only those values defined in the outline
  code

- Select the *Only allow new codes with values in all levels of the mask*
  option to allow the entry of additional outline codes, but to restrict the
  new outline codes to only those that conform to the code mask

 Warning: Microsoft Project allows ad hoc entry of **any
type** of additional code values that do not conform to the
code mask **unless** you restrict this by selecting one of
these two additional options.

6. Click the *Edit Lookup Table* button.

The system displays the Edit Lookup Table dialog shown in Figure 8-15.

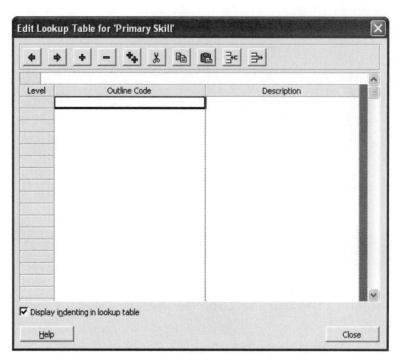

Figure 8-15: Edit Lookup Table dialog

7. Enter the outline code information for each segment in the Outline Code column, using the Indent and Outdent buttons as necessary to build the outline code structure.

 You can enter an optional description for each outline code segment in the Description column.

Figure 8-16 shows the completed outline code structure for the resource Primary Skill outline code.

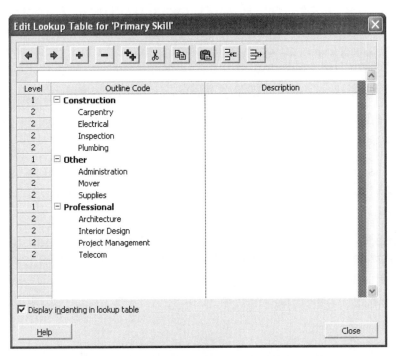

Figure 8-16: Completed outline code

Figure 8-16 shows that you can display indenting by selecting or deselecting the *Display indenting in lookup table* option in the lower left hand corner of the dialog.

 Tip: Although you can select a sort order for custom fields, outline codes always observe a descending sort. If you want the system to display an outline in a specific order, prefix your codes with numbers, or with alphabetic characters such as "a-," "b-," etc.

8. Click the *Close* button to return to the Outline Code Definition dialog.

9. Click the *OK* button to return to the Customize Fields dialog.

Deleting a Custom Field or Outline Code

The only way to delete a custom field or outline code is to use the Organizer tool and complete the following steps:

1. Open a project containing the custom field or outline code.

2. Click Tools ➢ Organizer to display the Organizer dialog.

3. Select the *Fields* tab.

4. In the list of custom fields on the right side of the dialog, select the custom field or outline code you wish to delete.

5. Click the *Delete* button.

6. If you previously copied the custom field or outline code to your Global.mpt file, select it from the list on the left side of the dialog and click the *Delete* button.

7. Click the *Close* button.

8. Save the project.

Hands On Exercise

Exercise 8-3

You need to report on the likelihood of your project completing its main deliverables on time.

1. Include a summary task at the top of one of your schedules with a milestone to represent every deliverable in your project.

2. Link those deliverable milestones to the last task that completes them.

3. Double-click each milestone, click the *Advanced* tab, and enter a deadline for its delivery date in the *Deadline* field.

 To add Deadline dates to your tasks, you can also insert the Deadline column temporarily in any Task view.

When you add a Deadline date for a task, the system displays a hollow green arrow on the Gantt Chart representing the Deadline date for each task. If the task slips past its Deadline date, the system displays a red diamond in the Indicator column.

4. Create a custom Text field and name it RAG (RAG stands for Red, Amber and Green).

5. Create a formula in the RAG field to do the following:

    *   Display a G if the task's Finish date is 5 working days ahead of the Deadline date.

    *   Display an A if the task's Finish date is less than 5 days ahead.

    *   Display an R if the Task's finish date is later than the Deadline date.

    *   Display a blank value if there is no Deadline date on the task.

125

Module 09

Using Objects, Methods, and Properties

Learning Objectives

After completing this module, you will be able to:

- Understand and use Microsoft Project Objects, Methods, and Properties
- Use the Object Browser to find different Objects, Methods, and Properties in Project

Understanding the Project Object Model

The Object Model is at the heart of VBA for Microsoft Project. Because there are hundreds of Objects, Properties and Methods, I describe only the ones most commonly used in this book. However, pay close attention to the **Using the Object Browser to Locate an Object, Method, or Property** section of this module to learn ways of finding the information you need to write that extra little bit of code.

To see a diagram in Project Help on all Objects in Project VBA, complete the following steps:

1. In the VBE, click Help ➤ Microsoft Visual Basic Help.

2. If the Table of Contents section is not visible, display it.

3. At or near the top of the Table of Contents click the topic *Microsoft Office Project Visual Basic Reference.*

4. In the expanded list is the link *Microsoft Office Project Object Model* (versions earlier than 2002 call it *Microsoft Project Object Model Overview*). Click this link to see the Object model, as shown in Figure 9-1.

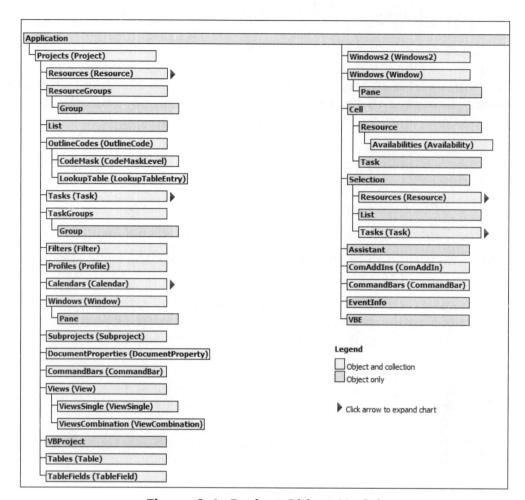

Figure 9-1: Project Object Model

5. Click any yellow box (with a small red arrow to the right of them) to expand that part of the hierarchy (for example the Tasks Object has an arrow and expanding it shows all Objects below it).

Objects are in hierarchies and the topmost Object is the Application Object.

Using Application-Related Objects, Methods, and Properties

The Application Object represents Microsoft Project itself, so anything that you want to do with the application rather than with a project belongs to the Application Object. Classic methods for the Application Object are **FileOpen**, **FileClose**, and **SaveBaseline**. All of these actions are independent of a project or you can perform them only on the active project, so they belong to the Application Object.

The following code opens a project, sets the Header to the project name and the current date, turns off the Legend section, and then displays a Print Preview for tasks for the next two weeks. Finally, it closes and saves the project so the Header settings are preserved.

```
Sub PrintProject()
Const DaysToPrint = 14
    FileOpen "C:\My Schedule.mpp"
    FilePageSetupHeader Text:="&[Project Title] - &[Date] "
    Application.FilePageSetupLegend LegendOn:=False
    FilePrint FromDate:=Date, ToDate:=Date + DaysToPrint, _
      Preview:=True
    FileClose pjSave
End Sub
```

Four important objects belong to the Application Object: ActiveCell, ActiveProject, ActiveSelection, and ActiveWindow. Use them as follows:

- **ActiveCell** provides a pointer to the active cell in the current View. You typically use this Object to reference the current task or resource where the cursor is located. The following code displays the name of the currently selected task in a task View such as the Gantt Chart:

```
MsgBox ActiveCell.Task.Name, vbInformation, _
    "Current Task's Name"
```

  ActiveCell.Task returns the Task Object for the selected task on task Views and ActiveCell.Resource returns the Resource Object for the selected resource in resource Views.

- **ActiveProject** returns an Object for the current project. Use this Object when you want to refer to the current project rather than a named project. Macros that use ActiveProject work with the currently active project. The following code sets an Object variable for the active project, opens a new project then reselects the original one.

131

```
Sub ActiveProjectSample()
Dim FirstProject As Project
Dim SecondProject As Project
    Set FirstProject = ActiveProject
    FileOpen "Second Project.mpp"
    Set SecondProject = ActiveProject
    FirstProject.Activate
End Sub
```

 In the preceding code sample, notice that I must use the Set statement when setting an object variable to point to an Object.

I can use the Objects FirstProject or SecondProject (instead of ActiveProject) to access any task in either project without first making them active, and without moving the cursor.

- **ActiveSelection** is a collection of all tasks or resources currently selected. Use it for macros that need to operate on selected cells only in task or resource Views. ActiveSelection.Tasks only works when a task View is active and returns a Task collection containing all selected tasks. You don't need to select the whole task by clicking its row ID number; selecting only one cell is enough. The following code displays the number of tasks selected:

```
MsgBox "Number of tasks selected is: " & _
    ActiveSelection.Tasks.Count
```

- **ActiveWindow** returns a Window Object and you mostly use it to select, close, or refresh the current window.

The following list contains other useful Application level Objects and Methods:

- **Projects** is a collection of Project Objects that point to all open projects.

- **FileOpen**, **FileClose**, and **FileSave** are Methods that do the same as their namesakes under the File menu.

- **Select Methods** – The system provides a variety of Select Methods, such as SelectCellDown, that move the cursor. However, you do not need to move the cursor when you work with tasks. Preferred practice is not to use these Select methods unless you want to leave the cursor in a specific place at the end of your macro.

- **EditGoto** duplicates the F5 Go To (or Ctrl+G) functionality in Microsoft Project. This Method can accept a task ID number; or in a View with a Timescale, you can pass a Date to scroll the Timescale.

- **ViewApply**, **TableApply**, and **FilterApply** do the same as selecting a View, Table, or Filter from the *View* menu or the *Project* menu.

In the Immediate Window, type Application followed by a period character. IntelliSense displays a list of all Objects, Properties, and Methods that belong to the Application Window. To learn more about each one, select it and then press the F1 key for Help.

To be precise, your code should use Application.ActiveProject. However, if you search Help for ActiveProject (or many other Objects and Methods), you will note that Help either says the parent Object (in this case Application) is optional, or the example does not use Application.Object. Instead, it just uses the Object. There is no best practice here. You may either write Application.ActiveProject or just ActiveProject, whichever is easier for you and your team to read and understand, but be consistent.

Using Project-Related Objects, Methods, and Properties

You use the Project Object in most macros, most often as ActiveProject. If your macro always works with the ActiveProject Object rather than using Projects ("My Project") to select a specific project, then your macro will work for any active project. This obviously makes your code much more flexible.

The following sections explain the more useful Objects, Methods, and Properties belonging to the Project Object.

Using Project Objects

Tasks and Resources are two very important collections of Objects that belong to the Project Object. Module 11 describes how to iterate through all tasks and resources in your project file using Project Objects.

In Microsoft Project, you click Tools ➤ Options, select the *View* tab, and then select the *Show Project Summary Task* option to display the Project Summary Task (Row 0) that summarizes your entire project. ActiveProject.ProjectSummaryTask is a Task Object that represents this Project Summary Task. You can use it to read project totals, as shown in the following example:

```
MsgBox "Total Work for Active Project is: "& _
    ActiveProject.ProjectSummaryTask.Work / 60 / _
    ActiveProject.HoursPerDay & " days"
```

The preceding code displays the total work for the project, expressed in days. The Work Property returns the amount of Work in Minutes, so dividing by 60 returns hours. The Property HoursPerDay returns the current Hours Per Day option setting, accessed by clicking Tools ➢ Options and then selecting the Calendar tab.

The ActiveProject.BuiltInDocumentProperties returns a collection of Document Properties. Use them to access the values in the Properties dialog when you click File ➢ Properties. For example, the following code displays the Author name in the Properties dialog:

```
MsgBox "Author: " & _
    ActiveProject.BuiltInDocumentProperties("Author")
```

The final Collection of Project Objects is the Calendars collection. A common use for the Calendars collection is to reference the Standard calendar and set company holidays. I offer sample code to do this in Module 23.

Using Project Methods

Methods do things; and they are the "verbs" of the VBA language. Using Methods, there are not many things that you can do to a project, except for the following:

- **Activate** – If you have several project files open, then you can use the following code:

```
Projects("My Other Project").Activate
```

- **Save, SaveAs,** or **Close** – Use these when you want to work with a project that is not active, such as in the following example:

```
Projects("My Other Project").SaveAs "My Other Project Backup"
```

Using Project Properties

Unlike Project Objects, there are many Project Properties. The previous example for Project Objects used the HoursPerDay property. Many properties are read-only, but the rest are read/write, like the HoursPerDay property. VBA Help will tell you which Properties are read-only and which are read/write. To force the ActiveProject to its default of 8 hours per day, for example, use the following code:

```
ActiveProject.HoursPerDay = 8
```

There is a batch of Properties starting with "Current" that let you read the currently-applied View, Table, Filter, or Group. The following code stores the current task and View name then returns to them after some other code executes, and presumably has changed them:

```
Sub CurrentViewExample()
Dim Tsk As Task
Dim strView As String
    Set Tsk = ActiveCell.Task
    strView = CurrentView
    'Code that changes the Task and View
    ViewApply strView
    EditGoTo ID:=Tsk.ID
End Sub
```

In the preceding example, I use the variable name, strView, to emphasize that it holds the string name of the View and is not a View Object. I also used the EditGoto command to reselect the original task.

Two very useful Project Object Properties are **Name** and **FullName**. Name contains the file name only while FullName includes the full path of the .mpp file, once saved.

You can read and set many of the properties editable via Tools ➤ Options through VBA. The HoursPerDay property is just one example. Follow the instructions on the Object Browser at the end of this module to find the correct property name and whether the property is read-only, read/write or write-only.

Using Task-Related Objects, Methods, and Properties

Task Objects come in Collections, such as ActiveProject.Tasks. To access any Task Object within a Task Collection, you can take three basic approaches:

- ActiveProject.Tasks(1) – Returns a Task Object for the first task (row 1).

- ActiveProject.Tasks("My First Task") – Returns the task named My First Task.

- ActiveProject.Tasks.UniqueID(1) – Returns the task whose Unique ID is 1.

In the preceding three examples, an error occurs if there are no tasks in the schedule, no task called My First Task, or no task with a Unique ID of 1 (such as when it has been deleted).

A task contains three important Objects:

- **Assignments** – A collection of all resource assignments for the task.

- **TaskDependencies** – A collection of all Predecessors and Successors for the task.

 Module 25 describes a macro that works with the TaskDependencies Object to show all tasks linked to the selected task.

- **TimeScaleData** - Returns the data you see in the Usage Views in the timephased grid on the right side of each View.

 I explain the use of the TimeScaleData Collection Object with sample code in Module 20.

Task Objects also contain a few Methods, including:

- **Delete** – To delete the task.

- **Add** – To add a task (Add belongs only to the Tasks Collection).

Each task has hundreds of Properties. For example, there is a Property for every task field, including those added in the enterprise versions.

Unique ID is a little-known field in Project that guarantees to provide a Unique ID number for every task, resource, and assignment in a project. The ID numbers change whenever you delete or add rows or apply sorting; however, Unique ID numbers never change. Therefore, to guarantee that your code can find a specific task, resource, or assignment, save its Unique ID for later use.

The following code shows how to read and write to task fields:

```
ActiveProject.Tasks("My Task").Flag1 = True
MsgBox "Duration = " & ActiveProject.Tasks(1).Duration / 60 _
    & "h"
ActiveProject.Tasks.UniqueID(1).Duration = 8 * 60
```

Note that Duration and Work are always stored in minutes.

Using Resource-Related Objects, Methods, and Properties

Resources are similar to tasks and you access resources exactly the same way as tasks. Resource Objects come in Collections, and ActiveProject.Resources is the main one. The system provides you with three ways to access any one Resource Object within a Resources Collection:

- ActiveProject.Resources(1) – Returns a Resource Object for the first Resource (row 1).

- ActiveProject.Resources("My First Resource") – Returns the resource named My First Resource.

- ActiveProject.Resources.UniqueID(1) – Returns the resource whose Unique ID is 1.

As with tasks, if no object meets any of the three above criteria, the system generates an error. Resource names rarely change (unlike task names) so Resources("Resource Name") is a good way to refer to a specific resource. However, for tasks and assignments, the most reliable access uses their Unique ID.

A resource has only two important Objects that belong to it:

- **Assignments** – All assignments for the resource.

- **TimeScaleData** - Returns data you see in the Usage Views.

Likewise, resources have only a few Methods, including the following:

- **Delete** – To delete the resource.

- **Add** – To create a new resource (Add only belongs to the Resources Collection).

As with tasks, there are hundreds of Properties for each resource, such as a Property for every resource field, including the additional fields added in the enterprise version.

 Important Note: If you Copy/Cut and then Paste a task or resource, the newly pasted task or resource gets a new Unique ID number. This is not a recommended practice when working with Enterprise Projects saved in a Project Server database.

Tip: If you want to be able to update task or resource tracking status in another system, then export current task and resource Unique ID's to that system to track data linked to the Unique ID's. This guarantees that you can find the appropriate task or resource in your update code, even if the task or resource name or row number has changed.

Using Assignment-Related Objects, Methods, and Properties

Assignments belong to tasks and resources. The Assignments collection for a task is all resources assigned to that task. An Assignments collection for a resource is all tasks assigned to that resource. Each assignment is unique, but it appears in both the Tasks collection and Resource Assignments collection.

An assignment has only one Object, the **TimeScaleData** object, which returns the data you see in the Usage views. Assignment objects have several Methods, including the following:

- **Delete** – To delete the resource assignment.

- **Add** – To create a new assignment (Add belongs only to the Assignments Collection).

As with tasks and resources, the system provides more than a hundred Properties for each assignment, including a Property for every assignment field, plus those properties added in the enterprise version.

Using the Object Browser

A common dilemma when writing code is determining the name of a particular Property and determining the Object to which it belongs. This is especially true when you reference another program such as Excel and you need to find something in Excel VBA. There are two approaches that work well in resolving this challenge:

- Record a macro and examine the recorded code.

- Use the Object Browser.

The Object Browser provides a complete list of all Objects, Methods, Properties, and Constants available in any of the linked Libraries for your code. To see all the linked libraries, complete these steps:

1. In the VBE, click Tools ➢ References.

The checked Libraries (they will all be at the top of the list) are the ones you selected, along with some default Libraries such as Office and Project, as shown in Figure 9-2.

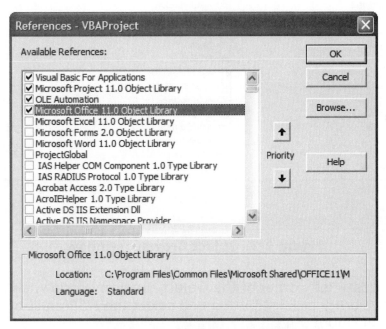

**Figure 9-2: References dialog
shows selected Libraries**

2. Click the *OK* button to close the References dialog.

3. Click View ➢ Object Browser (or press the function key F2).

The system displays the Object Browser window as shown in Figure 9-3.

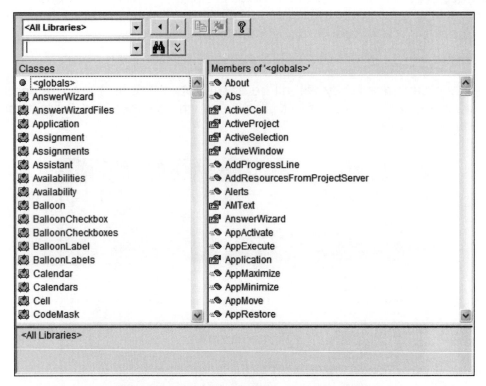

Figure 9-3: Object Browser window

4. In the upper left corner of the Object Browser window, click the *Project/Library* pick list button and select the *MSProject* option, as shown in Figure 9-4.

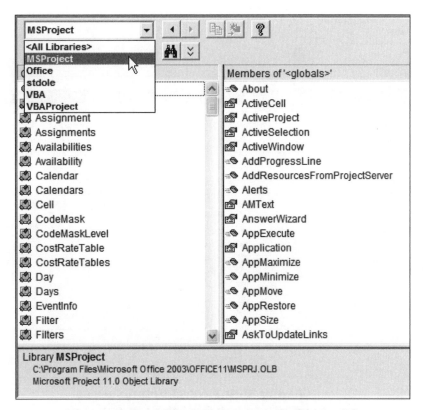

**Figure 9-4: Object Browser window with
MSProject library selected**

The Object Browser now displays only the Objects, Methods and Properties for Microsoft Project VBA.

5. In the upper left corner of the Object Browser window, enter text in the *Search Text* field and then click the *Search* button.

For example, if you want to find the HoursPerDay Property for a project, you might type Hours into the Search Text field. The Search Results pane shows everything related to Hours. In fact, the HoursPerDay Property is the first item on the list, as shown in Figure 9-5.

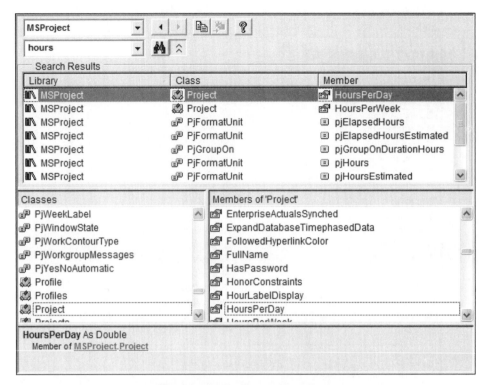

**Figure 9-5: HoursPerDay
Property in the Object Browser**

6. Select an item in the upper pane to see Class and other Object members in the lower pane.

For example, click the HoursPerDay item in the upper pane and notice that the system selects the same item in the lower pane. You can also see that the main Class is the Project Object. Notice the HoursPerWeek Property.

7. Select your item of interest and press F1 to view the Help article on that item.

You should experiment with the Object Browser because it provides a great way to search for Objects, Methods, and Properties within all linked libraries.

Hands On Exercise

Exercise 9-1

Explore the Project Object Model.

1. In the VBE, click Help ➢ Microsoft Visual Basic Help.

2. Display the Table of Contents section, if necessary.

3. At or near the top of the Table of Contents, click the topic *Microsoft Office Project Visual Basic Reference.*

4. In the expanded list is the link *Microsoft Office Project Object Model* (versions earlier than 2002 call it *Microsoft Project Object Model Overview*).

5. Explore the object model and click on different object boxes to see help on what they do. Be sure to explore project, task, resource and assignment objects.

Exercise 9-2

Explore the Object Browser.

1. In the VBE, press the F2 function key to display the Object Browser.

2. In the upper left corner of the Object Browser window, click the *Project/Library* pick list button and select the *MSProject* option.

3. In the *Search Text* box enter the word "Current" (without the quotes) and then press the Enter key or click the *Search* button.

4. Browse the *Search Results* list to see the current Properties.

5. Click the *CurrentView* Property then click the *Help* button or press the F1 function key for Help to read about this Property.

6. Search for other topics such as Task, HoursPerDay and Calendar to explore the Project Object Model further.

Module 10

Recording Macros

Learning Objectives

After completing this module, you will be able to:

- Record a macro in Microsoft Project VBA
- Understand what types of macros are the most useful to record
- Understand macro recording limitations
- Modify recorded macros
- Store your VBA modules in your desired location
- Control file bloating
- Repair corrupted files

Understanding When to Record a Macro

With Microsoft Project, you can record macros, in addition to writing them. Recording a macro is useful, for example when you want to create a macro to edit a Table, but recording a macro definitely has its limits. For example, you cannot record a loop to do the same thing to all tasks, but you can record what to do to one task and then manually add Loop code around your recorded code.

Recording a Macro

To record a macro, complete these steps:

1. Click Tools ➤ Macro ➤ Record New Macro.

The system displays the Record Macro dialog shown in Figure 10-1.

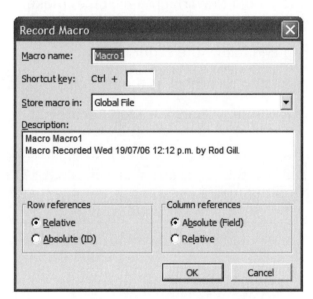

**Figure 10-1: Record Macro
dialog**

2. In the *Macro Name* field, edit the name to give it a meaningful label.

 Because the system does not allow you to use spaces in the macro name, Rod Gill recommends that you capitalize the first letter of each word in the name.

3. Click the *Store macro in* pick list and select the *This Project* option. Do not save your macro in the Global.mpt file until you complete testing the macro and determine whether you wish to share it with all projects.

4. Enter a description in the *Description* field to describe the function of your macro.

5. Click the *OK* button.

Recording macros works better if you execute your manual actions correctly; otherwise, your recorded code includes all your corrections and mistakes as well! To properly prepare for recording a macro, I recommend you do the following:

1. Write down the steps in the form of a script. To create the script, practice the steps manually and write them down as you go.

2. If you want the macro to work on a new file, make sure the first recorded operation is to create the new file.

3. Start recording and follow the script.

4. Do not forget to stop recording at the end of the script!

To stop recording, click Tools ➤ Macro ➤ Stop Recording.

 You can use the keyboard shortcut of **Alt+T, M, R** to start and stop the macro.

Hands On Exercise

Exercise 10-1

Assume that you need to record a macro to show all current tasks for the next two weeks. By our definition, current tasks meet the following criteria:

- Progress < 100%
- Start Date < Today's date + 14d

Record a macro to create this new Filter.

1. Open a project with at least one task that is not complete within the next 2 weeks.
2. Click Tools ➤ Macro ➤ Record New Macro.
3. Change the name in the *Macro name* field to CurrentTasks.
4. Click the *Store Macro in* pick list and select *This Project*.
5. Click the *OK* button.

Record the following actions:

1. Click Project ➤ Filtered For ➤ More Filters, and then click the *New* button.
2. In the Filter Definition dialog, create a new Filter to match the specifications displayed in the following table:

Name	Current Tasks		
Show in menu	Selected		
And/Or	**Field Name**	**Test**	**Value(s)s**
	% Complete	is less than	100
And	Start	is less than or equal to	Enter a date 2 weeks into the future
Show related summary rows	Selected		

3. Click the OK button.

4. Click the Apply button.

5. Click Tools ➤ Macro ➤ Stop Recorder.

To see VBA code for the macro you just recorded, complete the following steps:

1. Open the VBE and press Ctrl+R to activate the Project Explorer.

2. In the Project Explorer pane, expand the project in which you recorded the macro, expand the Modules folder, and locate the newest module (its name is likely to be Module1 or Module2).

The code you see should be similar to the following:

```
FilterEdit Name:="Current Tasks", TaskFilter:=True, _
  Create:=True, OverwriteExisting:=True, _
  FieldName:="% Complete", Test:="is less than", _
  Value:="100%", ShowInMenu:=True, _
  ShowSummaryTasks:=False
FilterEdit Name:="Current Tasks", TaskFilter:=True, _
  FieldName:="", NewFieldName:="Start", _
  Test:="is less than or equal to", Value:="6/6/06", _
  Operation:="And", ShowSummaryTasks:=False
FilterApply Name:="Current Tasks"
```

There are a few points worth noting about this recorded code:

- The software records the code as one line per action. You need to break the long lines up using the "space underscore" continuation characters (_) to read the code without needing to scroll horizontally.

- Some Parameters, such as OverwriteExisiting for which there were no options in the Filter window, will contain no values.

- You will need to modify the preceding recorded code to make it survive the test of time, and to be more readable and easier to maintain.

Modifying a Recorded Macro

If you run the recorded code from Exercise 10-1, it works as expected. If you run the code a day later, however, the results are incorrect because the Macro Recorder hard coded today's date into the macro (6/6/06 in the previous code example). This problem is inherent when recording macros, but luckily, it is easy to fix.

To change the macro so that it will always work with a date 14 days from today, you would need to edit the date value from "6/6/06" to become Date + DeliveryPeriod. You should also set a constant called DeliveryPeriod and set the constant equal to 14. The final code from Exercise 10-1 (including indenting for readability) should appear as follows:

```
Sub CurrentTasks()
Const DeliveryPeriod = 14

    FilterEdit Name:="Current Tasks", TaskFilter:=True, _
        Create:=True, OverwriteExisting:=True, _
        FieldName:="% Complete", test:="is less than", _
        Value:="100%", ShowInMenu:=True, _
        ShowSummaryTasks:=False
    FilterEdit Name:=" Current Tasks ", TaskFilter:=True, _
        FieldName:="", NewFieldName:="Start", _
        Test:="is less than or equal to", _
        Value:=Date + DeliveryPeriod, _
        Operation:="And", ShowSummaryTasks:=False
    FilterApply Name:="Current Tasks"
End Sub
```

 Tip: Always indent any continued lines. It makes them much more readable and therefore easier to understand and maintain.

Recording macros can be very useful and can save you a lot of time when you do not know how to write the required code in Project VBA. With a little bit of editing, you can create very useable and efficient code.

The most important manual action **not to record** is moving the cursor from task to task because your schedules change over time and you cannot predict future task sequencing. If you record cursor movements, delete them. Replace them with Task Objects pointing to your Tasks, and then work with those Objects.

Hands On Exercise

Exercise 10-2

Modify a recorded macro.

1. In a new project, record a macro to create and apply a new Table in an existing project.

2. Break up long lines of code using the underscore character so that all code can be read without needing to scroll.

Storing Your VBA Code

Typically, the system stores VBA macros in the .mpp file where you first create them and most can easily stay there. However, if you want a macro to work in all projects without needing the original .mpp file, then do one of the following:

- Copy or move the module into the Global.mpt file.

- If your organization uses Microsoft Project Server, ask your Project Server administrator to copy or move the Module into the Enterprise Global file, making your macro available to all Project Server users.

The Global.mpt file stores all default objects that ship with Microsoft Project, including Views, Tables, Filters, Groups, Macros, etc. Should you desire, you can also use the Global.mpt file to store your custom personal objects, including any macros you write or record. To copy Modules to and from your Global.mpt file, or between any open files, or to rename or delete Modules, do the following:

1. Click Tools ➢ Organizer.

2. Click the *Modules* tab.

Figure 10-2 shows the Organizer dialog after I select the *Modules* tab.

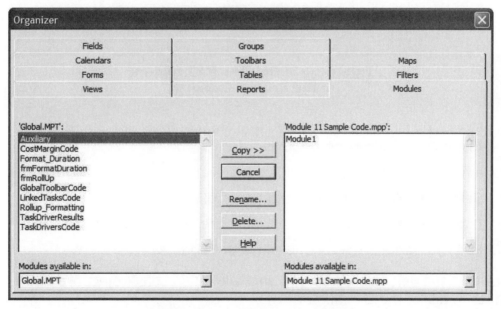

Figure 10-2: Organizer dialog

3. Select the Module name from the list on the right side of the dialog and then click the *Copy* button.

4. To delete a Module, select the Module name and click the *Delete* button.

5. To rename a Module, select the Module name and click the *Rename* button.

6. Click the *Close* button when finished.

To copy or rename Modules you can also use the Project Explorer by completing the following steps:

1. Open the VBE then press Ctrl+R to open and activate the Project Explorer.

2. Expand all the folders for the open projects and for the Global.mpt file. You should see something similar to Figure 10-3.

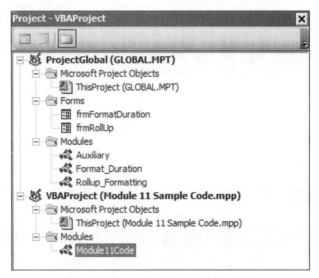

**Figure 10-3: GLOBAL.MPT folders
in the Project Explorer**

3. To copy a Module, click and drag a Module from one file to another, just as you do in Windows Explorer.

To rename a Module using the Project Explorer, complete the following steps:

1. Select the Module you want to rename.

2. Press the F4 function key to display the Properties window.

3. Edit the *Name* property and press the Enter key.

Notice that the default macros that ship with Microsoft Project are in the Modules folder of the Global.mpt file.

The **ThisProject (Global.mpt)** file is very special. Store macro code here that needs to run automatically when certain events occur, such as when you open a file.

 Rod Gill recommends that you store macros in individual files if you intend to use the macros for one or two projects only. Use the Global.mpt file only for macros needed by many different projects. This keeps the Global.mpt file less cluttered and more manageable.

Controlling the Size of Project .MPP Files

If you do a lot of code editing, especially if you add and remove Modules, or if the code adds and deletes a lot of tasks, your Project .mpp file size may bloat. The reason is because Microsoft Project keeps deleted material in the file to save time, and because new tasks added into the project are written into new file sectors at the end of the file. The result is a fragmented and bloated file. To correct this problem, use the following steps:

1. Close the .mpp file.
2. Re-open the .mpp file.
3. Immediately save the file before performing any other action.

 Microsoft Project compacts a file only when you save the file immediately after opening it, or when you perform a Save As. The compacting process shrinks .mpp file sizes by removing blocks of data left over from deletions and by putting all Tasks together sequentially, thus making the file smaller and more efficient.

Repairing Corrupted Files

Occasionally .mpp files can become corrupt, especially if you have links between files, have linked master projects or resource pools, and you do one of the following to one of the linked files:

- Overwrite it

- Rename it

- Delete it

- Move it

Any of these actions will eventually cause a corruption. Symptoms of file corruption include:

- You cannot open the file.

- The file does not calculate properly.

- The file displays unusual behavior.

If you can open a file that you suspect is corrupt, one way to repair the corruption is to do the following:

1. Save the file with a different file type, preferably as an .mpd or .xml file (try both).

2. Close your project.

3. Reopen the project from the new file type.

4. Save the file as the original file type, preferably with a different name in case the process loses anything.

Tip: You will probably save many copies of your projects. To avoid breaking hyperlinks and links, never rename your master copy; only add dates to the names of master file **copies**.

Tip: If you want to create a temporary file, name it Delete Me.mpp so you know you can safely delete it when next you see it.

Module 11

Looping Through Your Schedule

Learning Objectives

After completing this module, you will be able to:

- Create code to loop through your schedule
- Prevent blank rows from interfering with looping through your project

Looping Through All Tasks in a Project

Looping through all tasks is a common chore for Project VBA macros. Usually looping works well, but there is one common problem that stops code "dead in its tracks" unless your code handles it. The problem is blank task rows in your project schedule.

It is a best practice to increase row height to create blank space in your project rather than using empty rows, but you must plan to handle blank rows in your VBA code nonetheless. In Project VBA, if you try to set a Task Object to a blank row, it gets the special value: **Nothing**.

Nothing is a VBA value that refers to any Object that has not been or cannot be initialized. Therefore, you should always test for blank rows, as the sample code below demonstrates.

To loop through all tasks and ignore blank rows use the VBA code in the following example:

```
Dim Tsk as Task

For Each Tsk in ActiveProject.Tasks
   If Not Tsk is Nothing Then 'Test for blank row
      'Code to run on all tasks
   End IF
Next Tsk
```

The same situation applies to all resources. The following code copies the Text1 field for each task into the Text1 field for each assignment:

```
Dim Tsk as Task
Dim Assign as Assignment

For Each Tsk in ActiveProject.Tasks
   If Not Tsk is Nothing Then 'Test for blank row
      For Each Assign in Tsk.Assignments
         Assign.Text1 = Tsk.Text1
      Next Assign
   End IF
Next Tsk
MsgBox "Assignment Text1 fields updated", vbInformation
```

The For Each command is the easiest to use to loop through collections of Objects. It can be used to loop through Objects such as Tasks, Resources, Assignments, Calendars, etc.

Clearing a Custom Field for Non-Summary Tasks

The following code is another example that loops through all tasks, and if the task is not a Summary Task, it clears the Text1 field. In addition, this code example loops only through all **selected** tasks using the ActiveSelection.Tasks collection.

```
Dim Tsk as Task

For Each Tsk in ActiveSelection.Tasks
    If Not Tsk is Nothing Then  'Test for blank row
        If Not Tsk.Summary Then       'If not a Summary Task
            Tsk.Text1 = ""
        End If
    End IF
Next Tsk
```

 This form of looping (For Each) does not affect the location of the cursor, but instead, points the Task object Tsk to each task in turn. There is rarely any need to move the cursor from task to task. For performance and simplicity reasons, you should not loop through tasks by moving the cursor.

Using Loops to Set Custom Field Values

There may come a time when you need to report the summary task name for every task. You can record this information for each task in a custom text field. To identify and ignore top level tasks (which have no parent task), use the OutlineLevel property of a task. The OutlineParent property of each task is a Task Object of its Summary Task, so you can use its Name Property. Write the VBA code to copy Summary Task names as follows:

```
Sub SummaryNameCopy()
Dim Tsk As Task
    For Each Tsk In ActiveProject.Tasks
        If Not Tsk Is Nothing Then      'Test for blank row
            If Tsk.OutlineLevel = 1 Then
                Tsk.Text2 = ""          'No parent
            Else
                Tsk.Text2 = T.OutlineParent.Name
            End If
        End If
    Next Tsk
End Sub
```

Again note that the code does not move the cursor, the code tests for blank rows, and if the task is at level 1 it clears the Text2 value by setting it to an empty string (""). By using the ActiveProject Object, you have a procedure that works with any project, and is easy to copy and modify to perform a range of other tasks.

Hands On Exercise

Exercise 11-1

Module 11 Sample Code.mpp has some tasks with the Number1 field set to be the required Outline level for the tasks. Practice with this file to loop through all tasks in a project.

1. Write a macro to indent all tasks until their OutlineLevel Property equals the value in Number1.

2. Write code to do one loop through all tasks and then do a second loop to keep indenting the task until its OutlineLevel equals the value in the Number 2 field.

You need to use this code if you ever want to import tasks and their Outline level from a database or from a Microsoft Excel workbook. Given the required Outline level, you can then indent tasks using the OutlineIndent method.

The solution for this Exercise is in the Module 11 Sample Code.mpp file and is shown in Figure 11-1 below.

Task Name	Number1
Planning and Control	1
Business plan identifying project opportunity	2
Define project objective and information needs	3
Identify industry standards for project objectives	2
Develop preliminary conceptual schedule and staffing	2
Initial planning complete	2
Develop appropriation strategy	3
Develop management model and staff plan	2
Site Assessment	1
Identify potential sites	2
Define infrastructure requirements	2

**Figure 11-1: Test tasks for
Exercise 11-1**

Module 12

Creating New Objects in Microsoft Project

Learning Objectives

After completing this module, you will be able to:

- Understand how to create new Microsoft Project objects, such as custom Views, Tables, and Filters
- Write code to create new toolbars and menus

Safely Creating New Objects

In Module 10 you learned that recording a macro is a powerful way to generate base code for your macro projects. It's always a good practice to assume that the custom View, Table or Filter that you need to reference in your macro does not exist or that the user has changed it. To guarantee that objects such as Tables, Filters, and Views exist when you want them, always re-create them before applying them.

 The exception to this rule is when you work in the Project Server environment where Views, Tables and Filters in Project Server can be changed only by the Project Server administrator.

Creating New Views, Tables, and Filters

The simple way to create new Filters and Tables is to record a macro while creating them manually. To avoid adding these to lists of Tables and Filters available in Project, do not select the *Show in Menu* option (remember that every Table appears in the More Tables dialog and every Filter appears in the More Filters dialog).

When you create a new Table or Filter, use meaningful names, such as Weekly Report – Milestones. You can use the same name for a Filter and a Table, so the following code will work well for a Weekly Report:

```
Sub WeeklyReport
    ViewApply "Weekly Report - Milestones"
    TableApply "Weekly Report - Milestones"
    FilterApply "Weekly Report - Milestones"
    FilePrintPreview
End Sub
```

By forcing the application of the View, Table, and Filter in the preceding code, you know exactly what you will get as a result. Better still, if your code re-creates the View, Table, and Filter first, your can be certain that no one changed it previously, thus guaranteeing the results.

Creating a New Toolbar

Recording a macro while you manually create a toolbar is the easiest way to get started using VBA to create new toolbars. There are two basic Objects with which you work to create a new toolbar: **CommandBars** and **CommandBarButtons**. A CommandBar is a toolbar and appears in Toolbar lists. A CommandBarButton is a button on the toolbar to which you can add a picture or text, and to which you can assign an action that the button performs.

The following code creates a toolbar with one button. When a user clicks the button, the following macro (called RunMyMacro) runs:

```
Sub AddToolbar()
Dim MyBar As CommandBar
Dim MyButton As CommandBarButton
   On Error Resume Next
   Set MyBar = CommandBars("My Bar")
   If MyBar Is Nothing Then
      Set MyBar = CommandBars.Add(Name:="My Bar", _
         Position:=msoBarFloating, Temporary:=True)
      MyBar.Visible = True
   End If

   Set MyButton = MyBar.Controls("MyButton")
   If MyButton Is Nothing Then
      Set MyButton = _
         MyBar.Controls.Add(Type:=msoControlButton)
      With MyButton
         .Style = msoButtonCaption
         .Caption = "My Macro"
         .OnAction = "RunMyMacro"
      End With
   End If
End Sub
```

Run this code either as an individual macro, or in the Project_Open event. (Refer to Module 15 to learn how to automatically run code when you open a project.)

The preceding code introduces you to some basic error handling. The intent is that if the MyBar Commandbar does not exist, then the error does not stop the code. Instead the next statement tests whether the MyBar variable has been set up correctly. If not then the variable myBar equals the special value Nothing. If MyBar is Nothing equates to True, then the bar does not exist, so the code creates it. MyButton is then tested the same way and if it is Nothing, the code creates it as well.

Rod Gill recommends that you never assume that Views, Tables, Filters, toolbars, and buttons exist in a project. Make sure your code always tests for their existence or always recreates them.

Creating a New Menu

One way to make your macros accessible to end users and to make the macros easy to run is to add your macros to a menu. The following code creates a menu with three items on it:

```
Sub AddMenu()
Dim MyMenu As CommandBarControl
Dim MyButton As CommandBarButton
   On Error Resume Next
   Set MyMenu = CommandBars("Menu Bar") _
      .Controls("My Menu")
   If MyMenu Is Nothing Then
      Set MyMenu = CommandBars("Menu Bar") _
         .Controls.Add(Type:=msoControlPopup, _
         ID:=1, Before:=9, Temporary:=True)
      MyMenu.Caption = "My Menu"
      Set MyButton = MyMenu.Controls.Add( _
         Type:=msoControlButton, ID:=1, Before:=1)
      With MyButton
         .OnAction = "AddToolbar"
         .Style = msoButtonCaption
         .Caption = "Add Toolbar"
      End With
      Set MyButton = MyMenu.Controls.Add( _
         Type:=msoControlButton, ID:=1, Before:=2)
      With MyButton
         .OnAction = "DeleteBar"
         .Style = msoButtonCaption
         .Caption = "Delete Toolbar"
      End With
      Set MyButton = MyMenu.Controls.Add( _
         Type:=msoControlButton, ID:=1, Before:=3)
```

```
        With MyButton
            .OnAction = "DeleteMenu"
            .Style = msoButtonCaption
            .Caption = "Delete Menu"
        End With
    End If
End Sub
```

The preceding code is similar to the code that creates a toolbar, but use a CommandBar instead of a CommandBarControl. The menu bar is a standard CommandBar that always represents the main menu.

In Microsoft Project, the ninth menu from the left is the *Window* menu, therefore the Before:=9 parameter inserts My Menu immediately to the left of the *Window* menu. Another routine you need is the DeleteMenu macro code as shown below:

```
Sub DeleteMenu()
    On Error Resume Next
    CommandBars("Menu Bar").Controls("My Menu").Delete
End Sub
```

The following Code includes one procedure to add a toolbar with one button on it and a separate procedure to delete the bar:

```
Sub AddToolbar()
Dim MyBar As CommandBar
Dim MyButton As CommandBarButton
    On Error Resume Next
    Set MyBar = CommandBars("My Bar")
    If MyBar Is Nothing Then
        Set MyBar = CommandBars.Add(Name:="My Bar", _
            Position:=msoBarFloating, Temporary:=True)
        MyBar.Visible = True
    End If

    Set MyButton = MyBar.Controls("MyButton")
    If MyButton Is Nothing Then
        Set MyButton = MyBar.Controls.Add( _
            Type:=msoControlButton)
```

```
        With MyButton
            .Style = msoButtonCaption
            .Caption = "My Macro"
            .OnAction = "DeleteBar"
        End With
    End If
End Sub

Sub DeleteBar()
    On Error Resume Next
    CommandBars("My Bar").Delete
End Sub
```

These examples should provide enough foundation for you to create the toolbars and menus you need.

 Rod Gill recommends you delete or at least hide menus and toolbars when you close the project file containing the macros referenced by the menus or toolbars. No toolbar or menu should be visible if the macros needed are not available because the user closed the file containing the macros.

Hands On Exercise

Exercise 12-1

Create a new menu or toolbar.

1. Record a macro to display the Gantt Chart and then the Tracking table.

2. Use the code detailed earlier in this module to add a menu called Macros and a menu item to run your recorded macro.

3. Use the code detailed earlier in this module to add a toolbar called MyMacros and add a button to it to run your recorded macro.

Module 13

Managing Run-Time Errors

Learning Objectives

After completing this module, you will be able to:

- Understand why run-time errors happen
- Add error handling to your code
- Understand and choose between two main types of error handling

Managing Errors

All VBA code, when first written, works perfectly and continues to work perfectly. Yeah, right! In reality we encounter three types of errors in our code:

- **Compile Errors** can be caused by a spelling mistake or an If statement without an End If.

- **Run-Time Errors** can be caused by code that tries to do something illegal that the compiler did not detect, such as using an Object variable without initializing it.

- **Logical Errors** can be caused by creating a new toolbar called MyToolbar when a toolbar with that name already exists or by trying to open a file that does not exist. The compiler can never trap this type of error and will always create errors when the code runs.

Your code cannot run until Project has successfully compiled it (usually automatically in the background). So, once you correctly enter your code and it compiles, only the second and third error types should concern you at run-time. There are three types of run-time error handling you can use, which are:

- **No error handling** – The system performs no error handling, so each error stops the code and displays a message describing the error. To catch the obvious problems, it can be useful to perform your early testing with no error handling. No error handling is great while you debug your code. It can be useful to allow errors to occur and to display error messages so that you can track down potential problems and write code error handlers for as many errors as possible.

- **Resume Next error handling** – Using this method, errors do not stop the code, but you have to test for errors after every statement that might cause an error, such as opening a file or setting up an application object for another program. This method is the simplest and easiest to use, as all error checking happens immediately after the statement that might cause the error.

- **Goto error handling** – Using this method, an error triggers the system to jump to a specified location in your routine. Obviously, the error handling code at this location needs to manage any error that might occur in the procedure. This method of error handling is more useful if you have a number of statements that might cause the same error.

To force no error handling, use the following code:

```
On Error Goto 0
```

This is not an obvious statement but does the job! To initiate Resume Next error handling, use the following code:

```
On Error Resume Next
```

This statement says that when there is an error, resume executing with the next statement. To initiate Goto Error handling, use the following code:

```
On Error Goto ErrorHandler
```

ErrorHandler is a label in your Sub Procedure. I present an example for using this method of error handling in the Using Goto Error Handling section of this module.

Finally, before you see errors generated in your code, I strongly recommend that you consider preventing errors **before they happen**. For example, before opening a file you should test for the file's existence, as in the following example:

```
Dim MyPath As String
   MyPath = "C:\MyProject.mpp"
   If Dir(MyPath) = "" Then
      MsgBox MyPath & " doesn't exist", vbCritical
      End
   End If
```

In the preceding code example, Dir is a VBA function that searches for all files in a path. C:*.mpp finds all .mpp files in C:\. Testing for a full name as above returns only one name if that file exists. If the file cannot be found, the Dir function returns an empty string (""). When you test for the file's existence before trying to open it, you write code that avoids an error rather than code that handles an error.

 Tip: Search Help for Dir and learn what options it has. Dir is a very powerful file search tool for your VBA code.

Using Resume Next Error Handling

The AddToolBar Sub shown below is a good example of using Resume Next error handling. The first part of the Sub is duplicated here:

```
Sub AddToolbar()
Dim MyBar As CommandBar
Dim MyButton As CommandBarButton
   On Error Resume Next
   Set MyBar = CommandBars("My Bar")
   If MyBar Is Nothing Then
      Set MyBar = CommandBars.Add(Name:="My Bar", _
         Position:=msoBarFloating, Temporary:=True)
      MyBar.Visible = True
   End If
End Sub
```

Set MyBar = CommandBars("My Bar") fails if My Bar does not exist and the system sets the MyBar variable to Nothing. To test for the existence of MyBar, use If MyBar is Nothing Then in your code to force code continuation if the bar does not exist, or use On Error Resume Next.

Using Goto Error Handling

To use Goto error handling, I rewrote the preceding code as follows:

```
Sub AddToolbar()
Dim MyBar As CommandBar
Dim MyButton As CommandBarButton
   On Error GoTo ErrorHandler
   Set MyBar = CommandBars("My Bar")
   'Remaining code for Sub
   Exit Sub

ErrorHandler:
   Set MyBar = CommandBars.Add(Name:="My Bar", _
      Position:=msoBarFloating, Temporary:=True)
   MyBar.Visible = True
   Resume Next
End Sub
```

The main part of the preceding code actually looks simpler, but it assumes there may be only one error, when there might actually be a variety of errors or statements causing errors in the procedure. The error handler needs to be able to handle all possible errors in the procedure, or to run until a Resume Next statement is executed. After executing an On Error GoTo statement, any error causes execution to start at the first line of code after the named label. Resume Next in the error handler code returns execution to the statement after the one that caused the error.

You can of course have a number of error handlers, each with their own label, but using On Error Resume Next quickly becomes simpler and easier to manage. Notice that you need an Exit Sub statement before the error handler code; otherwise the error code runs even when there is no error!

You can get information on handling errors programmatically using VBA's Err Object, as described in the Using the Err Object section later in this module.

Selecting an Error Handling Method

If you want to set an Object variable to an Object (such as a toolbar or application) whose existence is uncertain, use the On Error Resume Next option. If there are a number of similar statements that might create the same or similar errors, then use the On Error Goto ErrorHandlerLabel option. You can swap from one form of error handling to another as often as you like. To turn off error handling entirely, use the following code:

```
On Error Goto 0
```

Using the Err Object

When you use Resume Next error handling to test for an error, use the Err object with the following code:

```
If Err Then
    'Error handling Code
End If
```

Use caution when applying the Err object, as it may still be set from a previous error. The system resets the Err object's properties to zero or to zero-length strings ("") after an Exit Sub, Exit Function, or Exit Property statement.

To manually reset the Err object, use the following statement:

```
Err.Clear
```

Using the If Err statement is the same as using If Err.Number since Number is the Error Object's default property. The other useful property of Err is Description. A general error message using If Err follows:

```
If Err Then
    MsgBox "Error opening file:" & vbCrLf & Err.Description
End If
```

In the previous code example, I use the "& vbCrLf &" string to add a new line so the error message displays on two lines, as shown in Figure 13-1.

**Figure 13-1: Critical error
message using two lines**

Using the Err object makes your error messages more informative, giving you insight into what code caused the error and information on why it occurred. Making sure that each error message is unique helps you here!

Hands On Exercise

Exercise 13-1

Test your VBA code for errors.

1. Using the code to create a Toolbar in Module 13, test the error handling by editing the code from:

   Set MyBar = CommandBars("My Bar")

   To:

   Set MyBar = CommandBars("My Other Bar")

This creates an error as My Other Bar should not exist.

2. Single step through the code to see what happens.

3. Modify the code to use On Error Goto.

Module 14

Creating and Running UserForms

Learning Objectives

After completing this module, you will be able to:

- Understand UserForms
- Create a basic UserForm
- Add code to a UserForm
- Run a UserForm

Understanding UserForms

Occasionally, you want to display a UserForm to gather information from the user. Rather than delving into a comprehensive example, I present the basic concepts and show you how to use the most popular controls. Please note that UserForms in VBA are primitive; you can't do nearly as much with UserForms in Project as you can with forms in Microsoft Access or in programming languages such as Visual Basic. Because of their limited abilities, keep your use of UserForms to a minimum. Keep them simple and do not expect to achieve miracles with them!

Figure 14-1 shows a UserForm created with some basic, popular controls, including a TextBox, a ComboBox (pick list), and a CommandButton. Figure 14-1 shows the Properties window on the left (display it by pressing the F4 function key) with properties for the UserForm, and shows the Toolbox with all available controls.

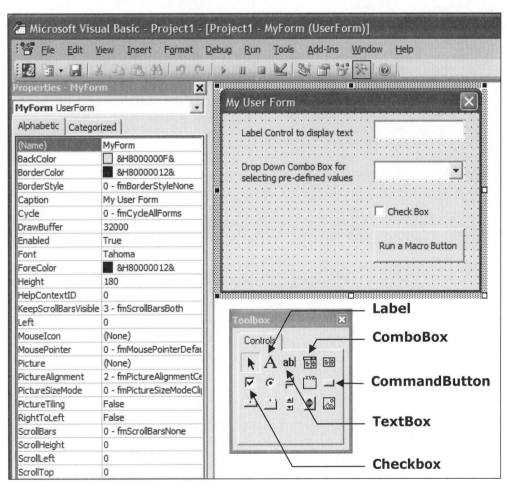

**Figure 14-1: VBE with sample UserForm
and Properties window**

Creating a UserForm

To create a new UserForm, complete the following steps in the VBE:

1. Click Insert ➢ UserForm.

The system displays the new UserForm, along with a floating Toolbox dialog. To add a control to a UserForm, continue with these steps:

2. Select the control you want in the Toolbox window.

3. Drag the control to the UserForm and drop it at the location where you want.

4. Use the resizing handles to change the size of the control.

5. Press Ctrl+R to activate the Project Explorer.

6. Select the UserForm in the Project Explorer.

7. Press F4 to display and activate the Properties window.

8. In the *Name* field, enter a valid and meaningful name for the UserForm.

9. Edit the *Caption* property to change the visible name for each control.

Hands On Exercise

Exercise 14-1

Add sample controls to a UserForm.

1. Click Insert ➢ UserForm.

2. Click and drag the TextBox control from the Toolbox window to the UserForm and drop it at the desired location.

3. Use the resizing handles to change the size of the control.

4. Add a ComboBox, CheckBox, and a CommandButton to your UserForm, as shown in Figure 14-1.

Adding Code to a UserForm

To add code to the UserForm shown in Figure 14-1, use the following steps:

1. Double-click the form in an area where there are no controls to display the correct code window.

2. Enter the following code to initialize the form and add options to the ComboBox control.

```
Option Explicit

Private Sub UserForm_Initialize()
'Macro that runs the first time the form opens
    MyComboBox.AddItem "My First Option"
    MyComboBox.AddItem "My Second Option"
    MyComboBox.AddItem "My Third Option"
    MyComboBox = "My First Option"
    MyTextBox.Text = ActiveCell.Task.Name
    MyCheckBox = True
End Sub

Private Sub RunMyMacro_Click()
'Macro that runs when the Run a Macro button is clicked
   If MsgBox("Do you want to change the Task Name?", _
        vbYesNo) = vbYes Then
      ActiveCell.Task.Name = MyTextBox
   End If
   MyForm.Hide
End Sub
```

The code shows two events. UserForm_Initialize runs when the system displays the UserForm. RunMyMacro_Click runs when the user clicks the RunMyMacro CommandButton. All UserForms must have a UserForm_Initialize procedure regardless of the name of the UserForm.

UserForm_Initialize and RunMyMacro_Click are both Events. This means that when something happens, such as opening the form (the Initialize event) or clicking a command button, (the Click event) you can write code that the system executes when the event happens. I discuss more about Events in Module 15.

The UserForm_Initialize Sub adds three items to the ComboBox control and then sets defaults for each control. The Textbox control gets the name of the current task. I use the CommandButton control to change the name of the Task and to close the form.

To display the UserForm, execute the following code in the Immediate Window or add the following statement in any Sub or Function procedure:

```
MyUserForm.Show
```

Note that MyUserForm is the name entered in the Name Property field in the Properties pane shown in Figure 14-1. You must select the UserForm itself and not any of the controls for the Properties pane to show the Name property for the UserForm.

If you do not have code to close the UserForm, close it by clicking *Close* button (**X**) in the top right corner of the form window.

This module provides only a basic introduction to UserForms. Experiment with the sample form to learn more about UserForms. To see more examples of using UserForms, refer to Module 23.

Hands On Exercise

Exercise 14-2

Create another UserForm.

1. In a new project, create a UserForm to display the Form shown in Figure 14-1 (or load file Module 14 Sample Code.mpp).

2. Edit the code to change the values in the ComboBox and add some new items.

3. Explore some of the properties and methods of a UserForm by copying the name of a UserForm from the Name property into the Immediate Window then typing a period character. Intellisense then displays a pick list for you, so that you can select properties or methods that look interesting, and then press the F1 function key for help on it.

Module 15

Using Events

Learning Objectives

After completing this module, you will be able to:

- Understand what constitutes an Event
- Understand why Events are useful
- Program your own Events

What Are Events?

Events provide a powerful programming tool in VBA and in other programming languages such as dot net languages like VB, C#, and others. I discuss only project and task Events in this module, but Microsoft Project also provides Events for resources and assignments that the system handles in exactly the same way as task Events.

Events allow code to run automatically when they occur in the application. For example, an Event occurs whenever you open a project, close a project, save a project, or create a new task.

When an action occurs that triggers an Event in Microsoft Project, such as opening a file or deleting a task, you can write code that runs when the Event occurs. Some Events happen after the action and some happen before. For example, the File Open event occurs after the file is open and the File Close event occurs before the file closes. That way the file remains available for your code to perform actions against it after the event occurs and before the file actually closes.

Events that occur before an action can actually prevent the action from occurring. These events always have the word **Before** somewhere in their name. For example, if a task edit does not meet certain codified rules, then your code can cancel the task edit action.

Using Project Events

Project events are all related to the whole project (or file). Typical events for a file are:

- File Open
- Before File Close
- Before File Save
- Calculate

To create code for one of these events, complete the following steps:

1. In the VBE, press Ctrl+R to display the Project Explorer.

2. Expand the Microsoft Project Objects folder for your file.

3. Double-click the ThisProject (your file name) file.

4. In the upper left corner of the code window, click the *Object* pick list button and select the *Project* item.

5. In the upper right corner of the code window, click the *Event* pick list button and select the event you wish to use.

Figure 15-1 shows the Object and Procedure pick lists.

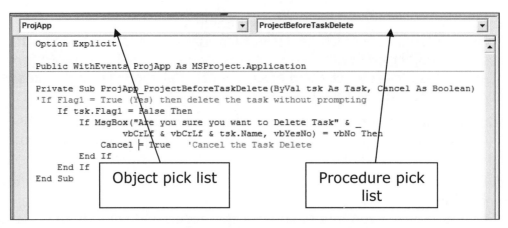

**Figure 15-1: Object and Procedure
pick lists called out**

The following code runs every time the user opens a project and scrolls the timescale to today's date. This is very useful for projects covering a long time frame.

```
Private Sub Project_Open(ByVal pj As Project)
    EditGoTo Date:=Date
End Sub
```

To get all projects to scroll to the current date, copy the above code to the ThisProject object of the ProjectGlobal (Global.mpt) file. Note that your project file must contain at least one task for the Event to trigger when you next open the project.

Using Task Events

Task Events occur when task values change. Unfortunately, they are not as easy to code as project events. To write code for task, resource, and assignment Events, you need code in three different places:

1. The ThisProject object as a Project Open Event to call the enable events code.

2. A Module to hold the enable events code that is in turn called from the Project Open event.

3. A Class Module to hold the code for the Event itself.

Unfortunately these task (and resource and assignment) Events are rather complex to create but provided you follow the steps below they work well.

 Events such as task changes may not be triggered in all cases, or they may trigger other events as well. Sometimes changing one task changes other tasks in the plan, ultimately causing task change events to trigger for a number of other tasks. You need to test your code carefully and thoroughly to make sure that events do what you want them to do; no more and no less!

The instructions below take you through the creation of a Before Task Delete event that displays a confirmation dialog before allowing the user to delete the task. In this code, if the Flag1 field is set to Yes for the selected task, then the code does not display the confirmation dialog and the user can delete the task without prompting. To create this Event, complete the following steps:

1. Go to the VBE (press Alt+F11) and open the ThisProject object.

2. Create a Project_Open event and add this code:

```
Private Sub Project_Open(ByVal pj As Project)

   MsgBox "Hello, you have opened a project with an " & _
      "Open Project and a Before Delete event."

'The following code calls a routine in Module DeleteCode
'To enable the Before Task Delete Event
   EnableEvents
End Sub
```

3. Insert a new Module and rename it from Module1 to DeleteCode.

4. In the new Module, enter the following code:

```
Public Del As New clsDelete
Sub EnableEvents()
   Set Del.ProjApp = MSProject.Application
End Sub
```

In the preceding code sample, Del is a variable and clsDelete refers to the Class Module Name. They can both have other names, but make sure that you make the names the same for the other steps; otherwise the events will not work.

5. Click Insert ➤ Class Module.

6. Press F4 to display the Properties Window and rename the Class to clsDelete

If you start all class names with cls, they all appear together in IntelliSense lists. This is always useful if you cannot remember the exact name and have several Class Modules.

The system calls the EnableEvents procedure from the Project Open Event so that it automatically runs every time the user opens a project file. To add the Delete class code, complete these steps:

1. In the Class Module, enter the following code:

```
Public WithEvents ProjApp As MSProject.Application
```

ProjApp is a variable name. You can use any valid name you wish, but remember it for step 6.

2. You can either type the procedure name and parameters, or you can select it from the class module window. To select the ProjectBeforeTaskDelete declaration from the Procedure pick list, do the following:

2.1. Click the *Object* pick list button and select *ProjApp.*

2.2. Click the *Procedure* pick list button and select *ProjectBeforeTaskDelete*. The list will hold all events available for tasks, resources, and assignments.

3. Enter code for the whole Delete Class as follows:

```
Public WithEvents ProjApp As MSProject.Application

Private Sub ProjApp_ProjectBeforeTaskDelete( _
        ByVal tsk As Task, Cancel As Boolean)
'Only allow the task to be deleted if Flag1 is False
'Or the user says Yes to the MsgBox prompt
    If tsk.Flag1 = False Then
        If MsgBox("Are you sure you want to Delete Task" & _
        vbCrLf & vbCrLf & tsk.Name, vbYesNo) _
            = vbNo Then
            Cancel = True    'Cancel the Task Delete
        End If
    End If
End Sub
```

To test the code, save and close the project and then reopen it.

 If your code did not run at all, your macro security may be set too high. Change it to Medium or Low.

 In the event declaration ByVal tsk As Task, Cancel As Boolean, tsk is a task variable that you can use to get all task information for the task that triggered the event.

Cancel is only available for all Before events. Set Cancel to True to stop the action that triggered the event. In the example above, the system will cancel the Task Delete action.

 Some events are duplicated in the Procedure drop down list, but have a 2 at the end of their name. In Project 2002, Microsoft needed to redo events, so they added the 2 versions for backwards compatibility. You will not need to worry about them, so ignore the event names ending with a 2.

Hands On Exercise

Exercise 15-1

Create a task Event.

1. In a new project file, or one of your own, add an Event that occurs whenever the user creates a new assignment (assigns a resource to a task).

2. Add a message that the system displays only if the user assigns a resource at 100% Units. The message should suggest making the assignment more realistic, since no one really works a full 100% of each working day!

Module 16

Creating the Project Control Center Macro

Learning Objectives

After completing this module, you will be able to:

- Structure and design your macros before writing them
- Understand how the Project Control Center macro works, how to construct it, and how it helps you

Structuring Your Macros

Before I introduce you to the very useful Project Control Center macro, you first need to understand how to structure and design your macros. Doing a little bit of design early in the process can save you hours (if not days) later on.

Structuring your macros is about defining the task your macro must perform and then logically designing your macro in small chunks of code. You can split large macros into separate modules, each performing separate functions. For example, you might have one module for reporting in Excel, one for collecting the data, and another for small utility functions that you copy and reuse in many macros. You might have another module for all code communicating with a database.

Another productive technique for creating large macros is to split the development into several iterations. The first iteration might get all data needed, exporting it to a .csv file that is ready for testing in Excel. A second iteration might get all data from Excel, and the final iteration performs all report formatting. A real world analogy is planning a long walk by splitting it into a number of one-day hikes. Planning each one-day hike is then easy and the entire long walk is then a matter of combining the daily hikes into one long walk.

Try not to reinvent the wheel every time you create a macro. Keep together small utility functions that you might use again. The more working code you can copy, the quicker you develop your new macro. Note what practices and techniques work for you and then learn from them by reusing what works and avoiding what does not work. Excel makes a great reporting tool, but for VBA beginners, automating another program can be a difficult challenge. To make the coding easier, try to reuse someone else's working code (such as the code in this workbook) and then adapt what works for you for future macros.

If you are developing a macro to create project reports in Excel, you have three choices where to put your VBA code:

1. Write all your code in Project VBA.

2. Write all your code in Excel VBA, reading data from Project files.

3. Write code in Project VBA that reads the data and exports it to Excel, and then write code in Excel VBA that does all the report formatting. Excel templates are great tools for holding pre-formatted reports along with the code to run them.

Writing Project VBA code that works only with Project and writing Excel VBA code that works only with Excel is the easiest way to develop code. Code that controls one application from another is more difficult to write, but not impossible. Module 20 contains some great code for working with Excel to provide you with the best start possible for your macros.

Rather than talking theoretically about structuring macros, I want to show you how to use the Project Control Center macro to build a multi-project reporting tool.

Project Control Center Macro Overview

I designed the Project Control Center macro to create basic multi-project reports. You can easily add to it and each addition typically works on all projects linked to in the Project Control Center project file. By the time you reach the end of this workbook, the Project Control Center example will include the following functionality:

- Read summary data for all projects, including resource hours per week for each project.

- Display the driving tasks that affect the selected task's Start date in any project.

- Create an S-Curve report in Excel showing cumulative cost and work against baseline cumulative cost and work over time.

- Create Who Does What When report in Excel.

- Update the Standard Calendar for all projects in the Project Control Center project file.

- Create a snapshot of all projects in one consolidation.

By the time you complete this workbook and practice with your own macros, you will be able to customize the Project Control Center into a powerful and very productive tool. My intention is that the Project Control Center macros will pay for this book many times over in increased productivity.

The remaining topics in this module describe the basic code required to loop through all projects and read basic summary data into the Project Control Center to create a summary report.

Designing the Project Control Center

To design a multi-project reporting tool, set the following high-level goals:

- Report across multiple Microsoft Project .mpp files.

- Easy and simple to use by project and program managers.

- Report on project status, resource usage per week and percent complete. This list should be easy to expand at a later date.

- The tool must be low cost, flexible, and work with many groups of projects where any one project may belong to any one group of projects (programs of projects).

- Must be robust so that renaming or moving a file will not corrupt any file or data.

You are likely to have additional high-level goals, but the preceding goals will suit our purposes for this example.

There are many available solutions on the market that meet or exceed these goals, including Microsoft Project Server. However, what these goals infer is something much simpler than a large commercial solution, and because there are no complicated reporting needs, they are much more basic as well. A tool that sits below the level of advanced tools such as Project Server meets the need nicely for teams and small departments looking for their first multi-project reporting tool. Creating your own small multi-project reporting tool is a very useful step towards implementing a full Enterprise Project Management (EPM) system.

Because this book focuses on Project VBA, I base the design around an .mpp file that contains tasks representing each of the projects in a single program. One of Microsoft Project's features is the ability to include a Hyperlink for each task. We exploit the Hyperlink feature by having tasks representing each project in the program, with each task's Hyperlink pointing to the .mpp file for that project. To add a project, simply add a task with a Hyperlink pointing to the new .mpp file and the macro does the rest.

Hyperlinks are essentially text strings containing the path of a file, with the ability to click the Hyperlink to open the file automatically. Therefore, the first benefit of our special .mpp file is a list of all projects in the program, with the ability to open any one of them just by clicking the Hyperlink. Moreover, we gained this benefit without writing a single line of code!

The Project Control Center structure consists of one .mpp file holding a list of all projects in a program, and we use each task to report on one project. We use a Project VBA macro to open each project individually, using the file path in the Hyperlink, and then read all the project level data.

As I mentioned previously, one productive way to develop new systems is to break a big solution into a number of small chunks and deliver them as a series of iterations. We already know enough to begin writing the first iteration. You will learn to add much more functionality in later modules.

Deliverables for Project Control Center

Now that you have the goals for the code, the next step is to create logical blocks for the code. I do this by writing a list of Comments (including their leading single quotes) so I can copy and paste the list of steps directly into a module ready for coding. Following is a list of my comments, written in a Microsoft Word document, but written in the VBA code format:

```
Sub ReadAllProjectData
'Calculate the date for the start of the week.
'This macro assumes Monday is the start of each week
'Calculate the date for this week's Monday
'Delete any current data such as resources
'For Each Task in the Project Control Center
'Extract File path from the Hyperlink
'Open the project file read only with no updates from
'resource pools or links.
'Make sure the project has its week start on Monday
'Read project level data from the Project Summary Task
'Close the project and don't save any changes
'End of Loop for project
'Tidy up
End Sub
```

After you copy and paste these comments to your Module in the VBE, you now know **what** your code should do and you can focus on writing one chunk of VBA code at a time. By structuring your solutions like this, you gain the following benefits:

- A more logical design for your code.

- The ability to code small chunks of code at one time.

Understanding the Project Control Center Code

Below is the code required for the basics of the Project Control Center macro:

```
Option Explicit

Sub ReadAllProjectData()
Dim StartOfWeek As Date
Dim Tsk As Task
Dim prjPCC As Project
Dim prj As Project
Dim Path As String

'Calculate the date for the start of the week.
'    This macro assumes Monday is the start of each week
'    Calculate the date for this Monday
   StartOfWeek = Date - Weekday(Date) + vbMonday

'Delete any current data such as resources
   'Nothing to do here yet
```

```
'For Each task in the Project Control Center
   Set prjPCC = ActiveProject
   prjPCC.StartWeekOn = pjMonday
   For Each Tsk In prjPCC.Tasks
      If Not Tsk Is Nothing Then      'test for empty tasks

'Extract File path from the Hyperlink
        Path = Tsk.HyperlinkAddress
        Path = Replace(Path, "/", "\")
        Path = Replace(Path, "%20", " ")

'Open the project file read only with no updates from
'resource pools or links.
        FileOpen Name:=Path, ReadOnly:=True, _
           noAuto:=True, openpool:=pjDoNotOpenPool
        Set prj = ActiveProject

'Make sure the project has its week starts on Monday
        prj.StartWeekOn = pjMonday

'Read project level data from the project Summary Task
        With prj.ProjectSummaryTask
           Tsk.Name = .Name
           Tsk.PercentComplete = 0    'Remove actuals
           Tsk.Start = .Start
           Tsk.Duration = .Duration
           Tsk.PercentComplete = .PercentComplete
           Tsk.PercentWorkComplete = .PercentWorkComplete
           Tsk.BaselineStart = .BaselineStart
           Tsk.BaselineFinish = .BaselineFinish
        End With

'Close the project and don't save any changes
        prj.Activate  'Make correct project active
        FileClose pjDoNotSave

'End of Loop for all projects
     End If
   Next

'Tidy up and format time scale on Gantt Chart
   prjPCC.Activate   'Make sure its active
   ViewApply "Gantt Chart"
```

```
    TimescaleEdit majorunits:=pjTimescaleMonths, _
        majorlabel:=pjMonth_mmm_yyy, _
        Minorunits:=pjTimescaleWeeks, _
        minorlabel:=pjWeek_mmm_dd

    EditGoTo Date:=Date

    Set prjPCC = Nothing
    Set prj = Nothing
End Sub
```

If you are overwhelmed at the sight of all this code, then relax, take slow deep breaths, as I explain everything! You are already familiar with the comments, but the code evolved enough so that I added one or two extra Comments. As with the comments, I discuss the code one block at a time.

```
'Calculate the date for the start of the week.
'    This macro assumes Monday is the start of each week
'    Calculate the date for this Monday
    Date - Weekday(Date) + vbMonday
```

Before you can read weekly data, you need to make sure that every project starts its week on the same day. This code ensures consistency across all project files.

Date is a VBA function that returns today's date. Weekday is another VBA function that tests the date (in this case StartOfWeek) and returns the day of the week. vbMonday is a VBA constant representing Monday as a number (2 – Sunday is 1). Date – Weekday(Date) returns the date of last Saturday. Adding vbMonday therefore returns the date of last Monday.

```
'Delete any current data such as resources
    'Nothing to do here yet

'For Each task in the Project Control Center
    Set prjPCC = ActiveProject
    prjPCC.StartWeekOn = pjMonday
    For Each Tsk In prjPCC.Tasks
        If Not Tsk Is Nothing Then    'test for empty tasks
```

Set prjPCC = ActiveProject sets the project variable prjPCC to the active project. By setting a project variable to the Project Control Center project, even when another project is open and active, you can still work with all the Project Control Center's tasks. There is no need to swap from one project to another to copy or read data.

```
'Extract File path from the Hyperlink
        Path = Tsk.HyperlinkAddress
        If Left$(Path, 1) = "." Then
            Path = ActiveProject.Path & "\" & Path
        End If
        Path = Replace(Path, "/", "\")
        Path = Replace(Path, "%20", " ")
```

Each task has a Hyperlink and part of it is the Hyperlink address, available via the HyperLinkAddress property. The system often stores Hyperlinks as paths **relative to** the current project's path. FileOpen cannot always resolve relative paths successfully so you need to precede the relative path with the path to the current project.

All relative paths start with two period characters (..). If they exist, add the current project's path to the front so that FileOpen operation can resolve the address. While this may not be completely clear now, if you look at the value in the path variable as you single step through the code, the results are obvious to you. Experiment with and without different statements in this block of code to see what works and what does not.

Hyperlinks use forward slashes while file paths require backward slashes. Replace is yet another VBA function you can use to swap one string for another within a nominated string. The first Replace function swaps "/" for "\". Another part of Hyperlink addresses is that every space is represented by %20. The second Replace function swaps "%20" for spaces. After these statements, Path should hold a valid address that you can use with the FileOpen command.

You could use the FollowHyperlink method, belonging to the Application Object, to open each project. This works, but if the file is already open or belongs to a Resource Pool, then the system displays various dialogs when opening the project. This is problematic because you want the macro to run without any manual user intervention. Getting the Hyperlink address and then using it in a FileOpen statement gives you much more control over the process.

```
'Open the project file read only with no updates from
'resource pools or links.
        FileOpen Name:=Path, ReadOnly:=True, _
            noAuto:=True, openpool:=pjDoNotOpenPool
        Set prj = ActiveProject
```

FileOpen has a variety of parameters you can learn about via Help. The goal with FileOpen is to open the file without any prompts requiring user input. ReadOnly is self-explanatory, but you do want to open each file in read only mode in case someone already has the file open for editing. The noAuto parameter means that you do not want the system to run any macros set to run automatically on file open. Again, we use this to prevent any possible interruptions or problems when opening the file. The openpool parameter forces the project to open while ignoring any shared resource pool to which it is connected, which again prevents any possible problems.

Set prj = ActiveProject is not really necessary, but it is neater to have a separate variable so there is no confusion about the project methods and properties with which you are working. Sometimes users can swap between projects while macros are running. Saving a variable that points to the newly opened project guarantees that the code still runs with the correct project, even if the user changes the active project.

 Tip: Do not rely on users to do what you want or expect! Always make your code as tolerant as possible to any user actions.

```
'Make sure the project has its week start on Monday
        prj.StartWeekOn = pjMonday
```

Later on we add code to this macro to read time phased data. Forcing the project to have the expected WeekStartingOn value avoids problems where different projects start weeks on different days.

```
'Read project level data from the project Summary Task
     With prj.ProjectSummaryTask
         Tsk.Name = .Name
         Tsk.PercentComplete = 0     'Remove actuals
         Tsk.Start = .Start
         Tsk.Duration = .Duration
         Tsk.PercentComplete = .PercentComplete
         Tsk.PercentWorkComplete = .PercentWorkComplete
         Tsk.BaselineStart = .BaselineStart
         Tsk.BaselineFinish = .BaselineFinish
     End With
```

The preceding code is the "meat and potatoes" of the macro. It reads data directly from the opened project's project summary task and stores it in the task for the project in the Project Control Center's project file. The With statement makes the code cleaner and makes it run slightly faster.

```
'Close the project and don't save any changes
         prj.Activate  'Make correct project active
         FileClose pjDoNotSave
```

Just in case a user swaps projects, this code first makes sure the expected project is active before closing it with the pjDoNotSave Constant. This is a quicker way to close a project than waiting for it to save and makes sure that the macro does not make erroneous changes.

```
'End of Loop for all projects
     End If
  Next

'Tidy up and format time scale on Gantt Chart
   prjPCC.Activate  'Make sure its active
   ViewApply "Tracking Gantt Chart"
   TimescaleEdit majorunits:=pjTimescaleMonths, _
     Majorlabel:=pjMonth_mmm_yyy, _
     Minorunits:=pjTimescaleWeeks, _
     Minorlabel:=pjWeek_mmm_dd
   EditGoTo Date:=Date

   Set prjPCC = Nothing
   Set prj = Nothing
```

The first block of code ends the If and Loop statements. The second block displays the Tracking Gantt view, with the timescale zoomed to months and weeks before moving the timescale to today's date. You want to display the Tracking Gantt so that baseline dates also appear.

Finally, the main Object variables are released by setting them to **Nothing**.

 Rod Gill recommends that you set all Object variables to **Nothing** at the end of each routine. While this is not strictly necessary, failing to do so can cause occasional problems.

Without doing difficult coding yourself, you now have a useful piece of code you can use with your own macros. The next stage is to add more and more functionality to the Project Control Center until you have a productive set of tools to enhance your project reporting and file management productivity. Adding to the Project Control Center is what the rest of this workbook is all about; teaching you new techniques and much more about the "ins and outs" of Project VBA programming.

As far as predicting how long it takes to develop a macro, once you have some practice in developing macros, it should not be too difficult to estimate times for each of the commented chunks in the design step. Then add the required percentages for system testing and a margin for extra features and your estimate should be reasonably accurate. Note that no accuracy is possible without design or without measuring how long each macro actually takes you to develop!

 When running the ReadAllProjectData procedure in Project 2003, if one of the linked projects has VBA code in it, then the system prompts you to enable macros. Because the file is one to which you created a Hyperlink, it should be safe, making this level of security annoying. The only way around it is to set your Macro security level to **Low** before running the Macro, and then resetting it to at least **Medium** afterwards. For security reasons, you cannot reset security levels via VBA. To prevent the prompt you can apply a security certificate. If the projects are all yours, then the SelfCert utility can create a certificate for you as described in Module 6.

Hands On Exercise

Exercise 16-1

Explore the Project Control Center macro code.

1. Open a copy of Module 16 Sample Code.mpp or enter the above code into a blank project.

2. In row 1 of the project, press Ctrl+K to insert a Hyperlink. Browse to any of your Project files and select it.

3. In row 2 add a Hyperlink to another of your project files.

4. Press Alt+F8 to open the Macros dialog.

5. Double-click the ReadAllProjectData macro to run it.

The code runs and fills in all project details. If not, check your code and single step through it to see what does and does not happen. A first check is in the VBE where you can click Compile ➤ Compile VBAProject. If you see any errors, resolve them and then try to run the macro again.

6. Add your own VBA code to read the Cost data and Baseline Cost data as well.

Module 17

Displaying Driving Tasks

Learning Objectives

After completing this module, you will be able to:

- Understand and use a macro to display the tasks driving the Start date of a selected task
- Add a toolbar to a macro to run the file's macros

Designing the Driving Task Macro

A common frustration among many Microsoft Project users is, "Why is my task starting when it is?" The answer is not always easy to determine without the help of a macro that displays the answer for you.

 Microsoft Project 2007 has the capability to display what is driving the active task using one of its built-in features. Therefore, this macro is not very useful to you if you are a Project 2007 user, but it is useful for you to understand how the macro works and how to design it.

You activate this macro by selecting a task and then running the macro by clicking a button on a toolbar you create later. The macro determines what predecessor tasks and other factors drive the selected task start date, and then it displays the answer in a UserForm. So what conditions can control the Start date of a task? The following situations can drive the Start date of any task:

- A task Constraint (usually because the user typed a Start date or Finish date, or dragged and dropped the task's Gantt bar in the Gantt Chart)

- Predecessors you created by linking tasks

- Predecessors on the task's summary task

- An Actual Start date for the task

- Linked Fields from another application

A task's Start date may also have an unexpected value if Microsoft Project's calculation mode is set to Manual (click Tools ➤ Options and select the *Calculation* tab). This provides us with enough information to build the basic Sub procedure that determines what is driving the Start date of any task.

Remembering that I recommend building macros in iterations, for this macro, I use the following iterations:

1. Build the basic task-driving macro and display results to the Immediate Window.

2. Add a UserForm to display the results to users.

3. Add a toolbar to enable the user to run the macro by clicking a button.

Designing the Main Procedure

The main comments for this routine are as follow:

```
Sub WhatsDrivingMyTask
'Declare Variables
'Point to selected Task and read start date
'Test Calculation mode and
'prompt user to allow automatic mode.
'Cancel Macro if permission denied
'Test Task Constraint
'Test Predecessors
'Test Predecessors on Summary task
'Test Actual Start Date
'Test for any Linked Fields
'Tidy Up
End Sub
```

The code to determine task predecessors is the most complex and I suggest putting this code into a separate procedure. A separate procedure is especially useful because it looks like we need to call it once for the selected task's predecessors and once for the predecessors of the selected task's summary tasks. Comments for the Check Predecessors code might be:

```
Function CheckPredecessors(tskCheck as Task)
'Note that predecessors and successors are both dependency
'  Objects, so test From or To property to determine if a
'  Dependency is a Predecessor or Successor.
'Declare Variables
'For each predecessor in tskCheck's predecessors
'If the dependency is a predecessor get link type and Lag
'If FF or FS then get dependency finish date
'Else If SF or SS then get start date
'Return result
End Function
```

Please do not let my example limit the comments you add to code as you go. The more comments you have and the more meaningful they are, the better your code.

The comments now provide enough structure to code the macro and to predict how long it might take you to develop. Knowing that the CheckPredecessors code will work best as a separate Function is something that will come after a little experience. Without that experience, the steps you might conceive are:

1. Write all code as one procedure.

2. Realize that the code is the same to get the active task's predecessors and the active task's summary task's predecessors.

3. Move predecessor code to a separate procedure.

4. Realize that making the CheckPredecessors procedure would work more simply as a Function rather than using a global variable.

With only a small amount of code to create for each comment, this macro is fairly straight forward when you understand how dependencies work in Project VBA.

Understanding Task Dependencies

When you link two tasks in Microsoft Project, the system creates a link record. In Project VBA, the link is called a Dependency and it is an Object. The Dependency Object has a number of useful properties, including:

- **From** is a Task Object representing the task driving the link.

- **To** is a Task Object representing the task driven by the dependency. Using the From and To Task Objects, you can recover the selected and predecessor tasks details.

- **Type** returns a number that represents the link type (such as Finish to Start, Start to Start, etc.). Use project constants in your code (for example, pjFinishToStart) rather than using any number returned.

- **Lag** is the Lag for the link that you specify either as a string, such as "2w", or as a number representing the number of working minutes (8*60 for 8 hours).

Understanding the Task Driver Code

Following is the basic code:

```
Option Explicit

Sub WhatsDrivingMyTask()
'Declare Variables
Dim Tsk As Task
Dim Str As String
Dim StartDate As Date

'Point to selected Task and read start date
    Set Tsk = ActiveCell.Task
    StartDate = Tsk.Start
```

```
'Test Calculation mode and
'prompt user to allow automatic mode.
   If Application.Calculation = pjManual Then
      'Cancel Macro if permission denied
      If MsgBox("Calculation Mode is set to manual, " _
         & "is it okay to set to Automatic?", _
            vbYesNo + vbCritical) = vbNo Then
         MsgBox "Macro cancelled by user." _
            & "Calculation mode needs to be " _
            & "on automatic.", vbInformation
         End
      Else
         Application.Calculation = pjAutomatic
      End If
   End If

'Test Task Constraint
   If Tsk.ConstraintType <> pjASAP Then
      Debug.Print "Constraint is " & _
         Choose(Tsk.ConstraintType, _
         "ALAP", "MSO", "MFO", "SNET", "SNLT", "FNET", _
         "FNLT") & ", Date: " _
         & Format(Tsk.ConstraintDate, "Medium Date")
   Else
      Debug.Print "Constraint is ASAP"
   End If

'Test Predecessors
   Debug.Print "Predecessors: " & CheckPredecessors(Tsk)

'Test Predecessors on Summary task
   If Tsk.OutlineLevel > 1 Then
      Debug.Print "Summary Task Predecessors: " & _
      CheckPredecessors(Tsk.OutlineParent)
   Else
      Debug.Print "No Summary Task Predecessors"
   End If

'Test Actual Start Date
   If Tsk.ActualStart = "NA" Then
      Debug.Print "No Actual Start date"
   Else
      Debug.Print "Actual Start Date: " _
      & Tsk.ActualStart & vbCrLf
   End If
```

```
'Test for Linked Fields
   If Tsk.LinkedFields Then
      Debug.Print "There are linked fields."
   Else
      Debug.Print "No linked fields"
   End If


'Tidy Up
End Sub
```

The above code is the main routine. I explain this before explaining the CheckPredecessors code. The first section with variable declarations should now seem straightforward to you. If not, please revisit earlier modules in this workbook to reinforce your knowledge.

```
'Test Calculation mode and prompt user
'to allow automatic mode.
   If Application.Calculation = pjManual Then
      'Cancel Macro if permission denied
      If MsgBox("Calculation Mode is set to manual, " _
         & "is it okay to set to Automatic?", _
         vbYesNo + vbCritical) = vbNo Then
         MsgBox "Macro cancelled by user." _
            & "Calculation mode needs to be on " _
      & "automatic.", vbInformation
         End
      Else
         Application.Calculation = pjAutomatic
      End If
   End If
```

Calculation is a property of the Application Object and returns the current state as two numbers, again represented by constants. If the returned value is equal to the project constant pjManual, then the macro needs to ask the user's permission to force automatic calculation. With calculation set to Manual, trying to determine what causes the task to start when it does is meaningless. Therefore, the first MsgBox call requests permission and displays a Yes and No button version with the critical icon. Figure 17-1 shows the dialog.

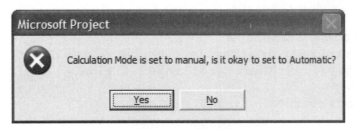

Figure 17-1: First Msgbox

If the user clicks the *No* button, the macro displays a warning message using MsgBox and then the End statement ends all code. If the user clicks the *Yes* button, then the system forces calculation to Automatic and the macro continues.

```
'Test Task Constraint
   If Tsk.ConstraintType <> pjASAP Then
     Debug.Print "Constraint is " & _
     Choose(Tsk.ConstraintType, _
        "ALAP", "MSO", "MFO", "SNET", "SNLT", _
        "FNET", _"FNLT") & ", Date: " _
        & Format(Tsk.ConstraintDate, "Medium Date")
   Else
     Debug.Print "Constraint is ASAP"
   End If
```

Once you remember that all code starting with **pj** is a built-in Project constant, this code becomes easy to understand, with the exception of the Choose statement. Choose is another VBA function that is available to all VBA implementations. Tsk.ConstraintType returns a number and the Choose function returns the value of the relevant parameter. For example, if your task has a Start No Earlier Than constraint, Tsk.ConstraintType returns the value 4. The fourth parameter in the Choose statement after Tsk.ConstraintType is "SNET" so the system returns "SNET" as the result or value, of the Choose function.

If there is no task Constraint, then the default constraint value is pjASAP (As Soon As Possible) so the code Debug.Print "Constraint is ASAP" is executed by the Else part of the IF .ConstraintType <> pjASAP Then statement.

```
'Test Predecessors
   Debug.Print "Predecessors: " & CheckPredecessors(Tsk)

'Test Predecessors on Summary task
   If Tsk.OutlineLevel > 1 Then
      Debug.Print "Summary Task Predecessors: " & _
         CheckPredecessors(Tsk.OutlineParent)
   Else
      Debug.Print "No Summary Task Predecessors"
   End If
```

CheckPredecessors is a function coded below. It returns a string with a list of any predecessors or returns the value "No Predecessors." Your code needs to pass the function the current Task Object Tsk. If the Tsk Object is for a task at Outline Level 2 or greater, then call CheckPredecessors again, this time with the Tsk Object for the current task's Summary task.

```
'Test Actual Start Date
   If Tsk.ActualStart = "NA" Then
      Debug.Print "No Actual Start date"
   Else
      Debug.Print "Actual Start Date: " _
         & Tsk.ActualStart & vbCrLf
   End If

'Test for Linked Fields
   If Tsk.LinkedFields Then
      Debug.Print "There are linked fields."
   Else
      Debug.Print "No linked fields"
   End If

'Tidy Up
End Sub
```

Apart from knowing which properties to use, this is simple to code. For linked tasks, I simply pressed "L" while the system displayed an IntelliSense list for a TaskObject. LinkedFields looked suitable, so I selected it and then pressed F1 for Help (which confirmed its suitability). I am not aware of a property that details to which field a task is linked. In Microsoft Project, look for the small green triangle in the top right corner of a cell that indicates a linked cell.

The CheckPredecessors code is as follows:

```
Function CheckPredecessors(Tsk As Task) As String
'This routine looks at all predecessors of Task T
'Note that predecessors and successors are both
'dependency Objects.
'So test From or To property to determine if a
'Predecessor or Successor.
'Declare Variables
Dim Dep As TaskDependency
Dim Str As String

'For each predecessor in tskCheck's predecessors
'If the dependency is a predecessor get link type and Lag
    For Each Dep In TSK.TaskDependencies
        If Dep.To.ID = TSK.ID Then
            If Dep.Lag = 0 Then
                Str = Dep.From.ID & ", " & _
                    Choose(Dep.Type + 1, "FF", "FS", _
                        "SF", "SS") & ", "
            Else
                Str = Dep.From.ID & ", " & _
                Choose(Dep.Type + 1, "FF", "FS", _
                    "SF", "SS") & Dep.Lag / 60 / 8 & "d, "
            End If

            'If FF or FS then get dependency finish date
            'Else If SF or SS then get start date
            If Dep.Type = pjFinishToFinish Or _
                    Dep.Type = pjFinishToStart Then
                Str = Str & Format(Dep.From.Finish, _
                    "Short Date") & ", " & Dep.From.Name
            Else
                Str = Str & Format(Dep.From.Start, _
                    "Short Date") & ", " & Dep.From.Name
            End If
        End If
    Next Dep

'Return result
    If Str = "" Then
        Str = "No Dependencies"
    Else
        CheckPredecessors = Str
    End If
End Function
```

The first line deserves some explanation.

```
Function CheckPredecessors(Tsk As Task) As String
```

Tsk as Task describes the parameter that the system must pass to CheckPredecessors. For this function, you can now use the Variable Tsk to reference the current task. String states that the CheckPredecessors function returns a string and forces any code that uses the CheckPredecessors function to treat the returned value as a string. This avoids run time errors when a string is forced into a date or number variable because the compiler flags a problem before you run the code.

```
If Dep.To.ID = Tsk.ID Then
    Str = Dep.From.ID & ", " & _
        Choose(Dep.Type + 1, "FF", "FS", "SF", "SS")
    If Dep.Lag = 0 Then
        Str = Str & ", "
    Else
        Str = Str & Dep.Lag / 60 / 8 & "d, "
    End If
```

The loop statement should be familiar to you now so the next interesting bit of code is:

```
If Dep.To.ID = Tsk.Id
```

Dep represents the dependency the macro is currently reading. To is the Task Object for the task driven by the link. This test says that if the ID of the driven task is the same as the task passed to the function, then we have a predecessor rather than a successor.

Dep.Type returns a number so we use the Choose Function again to return a string describing the Task Type. If the Lag is greater than zero, then append the lag to the string. In either case append ", " as a spacer before the preceding task's name is appended.

```
'If FF or FS then get dependency finish date
    'Else If SF or SS then get start date
    If Dep.Type = pjFinishToFinish Or _
            Dep.Type = pjFinishToStart Then
        Str = Str & Format(Dep.From.Finish, _
            "Short Date") & ", " & Dep.From.Name
    Else
        Str = Str & Format(Dep.From.Start, _
            "Short Date") & ", " & Dep.From.Name
    End If
  End If
Next Dep
```

The above code finishes the loop and appends the Finish date of the preceding task and its name to the string. Depending on the type of link, the Start or Finish date is required. The macro retrieves the task Name by getting the From Task Object and reading its Name property.

```
'Return result
   If Str = "" Then
       Str = "No Dependencies"
   Else
       CheckPredecessors = Str
   End If
End Function
```

Finally, if Str is empty (=""), then set it to the No Dependencies string. CheckPredecessors = Str sets the value returned by the CheckPredecessors function to the calling code. Because the Function was defined as returning a string, Str has to be a string as well, otherwise compile errors occur.

Hands On Exercise

Exercise 17-1

Test the Iteration 1 code.

1. Either download Module 17 Sample Code.mpp or enter the code into a Module.

2. Test the code to make sure it works and edit the code, if necessary.

3. Make sure you understand the code. Do not proceed to Iteration 2 until you confirm that all the code works with no known bugs.

4. For an advanced test, add code to test for links to any summary task above the selected task. For example, the selected task could have been indented 4 times and either of the top two summary tasks could have a link which is driving the selected task. You will need to add a loop until you reach a Summary task at OutlineLevel 1.

Adding a UserForm to Display the Results

The first iteration of this macro outputs a string to the Immediate Window to report its findings. In this iteration we add a UserForm to improve the user experience for your macro. There are three steps to adding a UserForm to this macro:

1. Create the UserForm, including its controls.

2. Write code to open and close the UserForm.

3. Write code to enable the Command Buttons.

Figure 17-2 shows the completed UserForm with sample data.

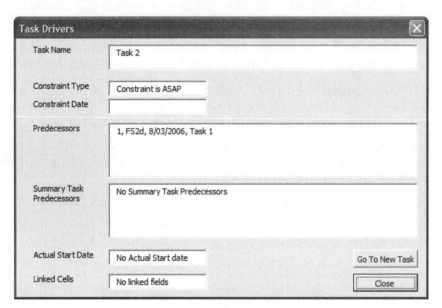

**Figure 17-2: Activated UserForm
with sample data**

A good naming convention for all Text Boxes in a UserForm is to use the two most important words in the text description label. For example, TaskName makes an obvious name for the first field. For the *Summary Task Predecessors* field I used SummaryPredecessors.

```
Sub TaskDrivers()
    TaskDriveResults.Show
End Sub
```

The preceding code is all I need to display the UserForm. Initializing the fields is best left to code in the UserForm class itself. Double-click the UserForm's background or in the Project Explorer right-click the UserForm in your project and click *View Code*.

Figure 17-3 shows all of the Class code for the UserForm. *GotoNewTask* and *Quit* are the names of the two command buttons. You may either type their code manually, or in the VBE select their names from the *Object* pick list (in the upper left corner of Code window). UserForm is active in the Object list in Figure 17-3. The WhatsDrivingMyTask2 procedure is the same as WhatsDrivingMyTask, but contains all code for iteration 2. You do not need different procedures for each iteration; I have numbered them because I want to show you the code for each stage.

```
UserForm                                    ▼   Activate

    Option Explicit

    Private Sub UserForm_Activate()
        WhatsDrivingMyTask2
    End Sub

    Private Sub GotoNewTask_Click()
    Dim str As String
    Dim ID As Long

        str = InputBox("Enter Task ID to Go to")
        ID = Val(str)
        If ID = 0 Then
            MsgBox "Macro cancelled by user or " _
                & "invalid number entered", vbInformation
            Exit Sub
        End If

        If ID > ActiveProject.Tasks.Count Then
            MsgBox "You don't have that many Tasks!", vbInformation
        ElseIf ActiveProject.Tasks(ID) Is Nothing Then
            MsgBox "Task Id you entered is for an empty Task", vbInformation
        Else
            EditGoTo ID:=ID
            WhatsDrivingMyTask2
        End If
    End Sub

    Private Sub Quit_Click()
        TaskDriveResults.Hide
    End Sub
```

Figure 17-3: UserForm Class code

GotoNewTask_Click is worth explaining. I first wrote the procedure for it as follows:

```
EditGoTo ID:= CLng(InputBox("Enter Task ID to Go to"))
WhatsDrivingMyTask
```

This works fine provided you enter a valid ID; the task ID number must exist. Any of the following conditions can make this code fail:

- The user pressed the *Cancel* button in the Input box dialog, so InputBox returned an empty string ("").

- The user selected the ID of a blank row in the schedule.

- The user selected the ID of a row below the last task.

- The user enters characters that cannot convert to a number.

Sometimes it takes a simple version of code plus extensive testing to devise a final, working solution. Never be afraid of using this process as it can often be quick and produces the best quality code. Create a prototype or basic working solution then test, test, and test again! The code I finally developed is:

```
Private Sub GotoNewTask_Click()
Dim str As String
Dim ID As Long

   str = InputBox("Enter Task ID to Go to")
   ID = Val(str)
   If str="" Then
     MsgBox "Macro cancelled by user ", vbInformation
     Exit Sub
   ElseIF  ID = 0 Then
     MsgBox "Invalid number entered", vbInformation
     Exit Sub
   End If

   If ID > ActiveProject.Tasks.Count Then
     MsgBox "You don't have that many Tasks!" _
        , vbInformation
   ElseIf ActiveProject.Tasks(ID) Is Nothing Then
     MsgBox "Task Id you entered is for an empty Task row" _
        ,vbInformation
   Else
     EditGoTo ID:=ID
     WhatsDrivingMyTask
   End If End Sub
```

InputBox always returns a string, and returns an empty string if the user clicks the *Cancel* button. Clng raises a type error if asked to convert an empty or none numeric string to a number, so str is converted by using the Val function. An empty or none numeric string is converted by the VBA Val function as zero. VBA automatically converts the numeric value returned by Val to the Long type required by ID. You now have a valid ID number, so test for blank tasks or an ID greater than the number of tasks in the project.

Next, to open the UserForm which in turn triggers the UserForm_Activate code, add a Sub procedure TaskDrivers shown earlier in this topic. Finally, you need to edit the code in the WhatsDrivingMyTask procedure to display the results in the UserForm rather than the Immediate Window.

Consider commenting out the Debug.Print statements rather than deleting them. You know the Debug code works so if you have difficulties with the UserForm, the Debug code remains available for testing. Once you have the UserForm code working, make a backup and then delete the commented Debug code. The following code shows only the old code commented out with the new code to display results. In the Sample project, there is a new procedure for this called WhatsDrivingMyTask2.

```
'    Debug.Print "Constraint is " _
'      & Choose(Tsk.ConstraintType, "ALAP", "MSO", _
'        "MFO", "SNET", "SNLT", "FNET", "FNLT") _
'        & ", Date: " & Format(Tsk.ConstraintDate, _
'        "Medium Date")
     TaskDriveResults.ConstraintType = _
        Choose(Tsk.ConstraintType, "ALAP", "MSO", _
          "MFO","SNET", "SNLT", "FNET", "FNLT")
     TaskDriveResults.ConstraintDate = _
        Format(Tsk.ConstraintDate, "Medium Date")
   Else
'    Debug.Print "Constraint is ASAP"
     TaskDriveResults.ConstraintType = "Constraint " _
     & "is ASAP"
     TaskDriveResults.ConstraintDate = ""
   End If
   TaskDriveResults.TaskName = ActiveCell.Task.Name
```

TaskDriveResults is the name of the form (entered into Properties while the UserForm is selected). ConstraintType and ConstraintDate are both names for Text Boxes.

```
'      Debug.Print "Predecessors: " & _
          CheckPredecessors(Tsk)
      TaskDriveResults.Predecessors = _
          CheckPredecessors(Tsk)

'      Debug.Print "Summary Task Predecessors: " _
'          & CheckPredecessors(Tsk.OutlineParent)
      TaskDriveResults.SummaryPredecessors = _
          CheckPredecessors(Tsk.OutlineParent)

'      Debug.Print "No Summary Task Predecessors"
      TaskDriveResults.SummaryPredecessors = _
          "No Summary Task Predecessors"

'      Debug.Print "No Actual Start date"
      TaskDriveResults.ActualStart = _
          "No Actual Start date"

'      Debug.Print "Actual Start Date: " _
          & Tsk.ActualStart & vbCrLf
      TaskDriveResults.ActualStart = Tsk.ActualStart _
          & vbCrLf

'      Debug.Print "There are linked fields, check that" _
          & " the Start and Finish fields are not " _
          & "one of them."
      TaskDriveResults.LinkedCells = "There are linked" _
          & "fields"

'      Debug.Print "No linked fields"
      TaskDriveResults.LinkedCells = "No linked fields"
```

You should find this code relatively simple to understand, especially if you remember that CheckPredecessors is a function created earlier in the Module in iteration 1.

Iteration 3 adds a button on a toolbar to run the TaskDrivers procedure which in turn opens the UserForm. The UserForm_Initialize code runs the WhatsDrivingMytask procedure and the *Quit* command button, when clicked, closes the UserForm by running the GotoNewTask_Click event.

Hands On Exercise

Exercise 17-2

Test the UserForm.

1. Set up the UserForm and add the code into the WhatsDrivingMyTask2 procedure.

2. Make sure everything works as you expect.

Running the Macro from a Toolbar

To make it easy for your users to run the code, add a toolbar to the application. You already learned about Events in Module 16, so it should be simple enough to have a toolbar display when you open a macro project, and then hide it when the project is closed. You can do this using the Open and Close project events.

Module 12 introduced you to creating toolbars. Below is the code to automatically create and remove a My Macros toolbar. Add the following code to the Module with all the other code:

```
Sub AddToolbar()
Dim MyBar As CommandBar
Dim MyButton As CommandBarButton
    On Error Resume Next
    Set MyBar = CommandBars("My Macros")
    If MyBar Is Nothing Then
        Set MyBar = CommandBars.Add(Name:= _
            "My Macros", _
    Position:=msoBarFloating, Temporary:=True)
        MyBar.Visible = True
    End If

    Set MyButton = MyBar.Controls("Update Data ")
    If MyButton Is Nothing Then
        Set MyButton = _
            MyBar.Controls.Add(Type:=msoControlButton)
        With MyButton
            .Style = msoButtonCaption
            .Caption = "Update Data"
            .OnAction = "ReadAllProjectData"
        End With
    End If

    Set MyButton = MyBar.Controls("Task Driver ")
    If MyButton Is Nothing Then
        Set MyButton = _
            MyBar.Controls.Add(Type:=msoControlButton)
        With MyButton
            .Style = msoButtonCaption
            .Caption = "Task Driver"
            .OnAction = "TaskDrivers"
        End With
    End If
End Sub
```

Note that the first button added calls the ReadAllProjectData code from
Module 16.

```
Sub DeleteBar()
    On Error Resume Next
    CommandBars("My Macros").Delete
End Sub
```

To the ThisProject file in the Project Explorer window in the VBE, add the
following code:

```
Private Sub Project_Open(ByVal pj As Project)
    AddToolbar
End Sub

Private Sub Project_BeforeClose(ByVal pj As Project)
    DeleteBar
End Sub
```

There should be nothing new to you in this code; it is simply a variation on
code with which you already worked in earlier modules. From this point
forward, the code examples show you code you have seen before and code
you can use as a building block to help you code new macros.

Hands On Exercise

Exercise 17-3

Complete the last Iteration by adding a button to a toolbar.

1. Try adding the event code to display a My Macros toolbar.

2. Test the whole macro again.

3. Save your final macro as a project so that you can use it again as a starting point for a future macro.

Module 18

Distributing Your Macros

Learning Objectives

After completing this module, you will be able to:

- Make your procedures private
- Run a macro from another project
- Distribute your macros to other Microsoft Project users

Making Your Procedures Private

In Module 17, you created a useful macro to show what factors drive a selected task. A little bit of testing quickly shows you that the macro only works for the project in which the macro resides. This module explains how you can make procedures private, call a macro in another file, and share macros across multiple files.

By default, when you declare a Sub or Function procedure, it is visible to all Sub and Function procedures in the same project file. To make them visible only to procedures in your current Module, precede the Sub and Function declarations with the word **Private**, such as in the following examples:

```
Private Sub TaskDrivers()
Private Function CheckPredecessors(Tsk As Task) As String
```

Using the **Private** declaration, you make the procedures hidden to all other Modules and open projects (including using the run statement as shown above).

Calling a Procedure from Another File

To call a Procedure in one open file from another open file, you need to use the Run method as shown in the following code sample:

```
Run "Macro Project File.mpp!MyProcedure"
Run "Macro Project File.mpp!MyProcedure", "My parameter"
```

The second example passes a parameter to the procedure. The project containing the macro to be called needs to be open and the called procedure must not be declared as Private.

You can now call your macros from any open project, but you still must open the project containing the macro. If you need four or five macros, this could mean that you need to open four or five project files, cluttering up your workspace. How can you make this easier?

Using the Global.mpt File

The Global.mpt file contains the default copies of all objects, including Views, Tables, Filters, Modules, Forms, Reports, Maps, Calendars, Fields, Maps, and Groups. In Microsoft Project, if you want to make a new View available to all your projects, use the Organizer (click Tools ≻ Organizer) to copy it from the project to the Global.mpt file. The same holds true for Modules and Forms; copy them to the Global.mpt file and they become visible to all projects.

By default, anything in the Global.mpt file is visible to all of your projects, so you do not need to use the Run method for calling a procedure.

Moving Macros into the Global.mpt File

Before moving macros, you first need a design. In moving macros, your goals are to do the following:

- Move all Modules and Forms to the Global.mpt file.

- Automate the Module and Forms transfer.

- Have a toolbar that is permanently visible for Global.mpt macros.

- Maintain the temporary toolbar for the macro project.

- Make it easy to update Global.mpt code from modified macros in the original project.

Remember that if the goals (deliverables) for your code are not clear, your code gets messy and development frequently takes significantly longer to finish. To achieve these technical goals you need to do the following:

- Write code to move the Modules and Forms.

- Add a button to the macro project's toolbar to run the Copy to Global code.

- Once in the Global.mpt file, the code needs to work with a different Global toolbar. When the macro project closes, the My Macros toolbar deletes. This means you need two sets of toolbars, one for all macros in the Global.mpt file and one for each project file with a macro.

- Move all toolbar procedures into a separate Module so that you can update the main Module easily without needing to edit Global toolbar code each time. This is one example where having multiple Modules saves you time and helps simplify your code.

- Create a Module in the Global.mpt file for all Global toolbar code. You add to this every time you add another macro as you do in the following Modules.

Before doing any of these tasks, you need to tidy up your existing code. You can delete the old lines for Debug.Print code that you commented out and you need to move the toolbar creation code into a separate Module. Module 18 Sample Code.mpp has this work completed for you. For example, I renamed the WhatsDrivingMyTask2 procedure to WhatsDrivingMyTask, and the updated TaskDrivers Form code accordingly.

Because you are creating multiple Modules, it is important to give them meaningful names. A project file with Modules named Module1, Module2, and Module3 provides no clue what code may be contained in them or how the code is structured. You can rename a Module in the VBE by pressing the F4 function key and editing the Name property. Finally re-test everything to make sure your changes did not introduce any bugs.

Copying Modules and Forms to the Global.mpt

The easiest way to create code for this is to record a macro of the steps you need to move a Module manually to the Global.mpt file using the Organizer. The results of a recorded macro should look something like this (I added line continuation characters):

```
OrganizerMoveItem Type:=3, FileName:="My Macro Project", _
    ToFileName:="Global.MPT", Name:="MyModule"
OrganizerMoveItem Type:=3, FileName:=" My Macro Project ", _
    ToFileName:="Global.MPT", Name:="MyUserForm"
```

Type defines the type of object being copied. To improve the code, replace the number 3 with the project Constant **pjModules**.

 Notice in the preceding code that the system considers the UserForm as a Module. This is because the Forms page in the Organizer refers to Microsoft Project Custom Forms and not to VBA UserForms.

The final code should look like the following:

```
Public Sub CopyToGlobal()
   Application.DisplayAlerts = False
   OrganizerMoveItem Type:=pjModules, _
      FileName:="Module 18 Sample Code.mpp", _
      ToFileName:="Global.MPT", _
      Name:="TaskTaskDriversCode"
   OrganizerMoveItem Type:=pjModules, _
      FileName:="Module 18 Sample Code.mpp", _
      ToFileName:="Global.MPT", _
      Name:="TaskDriveResults"
   Application.DisplayAlerts = True
End Sub
```

I use DisplayAlerts to stop warning messages from displaying in Project. If the Module already exists in the Global.mpt file, then Microsoft Project displays a warning dialog. If I set DisplayAlerts to False, then these warning dialogs do not appear and the system overwrites the existing items.

 Warning: You must reset DisplayAlerts to True at the end of the macro so that the user continues to get normal warnings while working in Microsoft Project.

The CopyToGlobal code is best kept in the main Module, or even a separate Module because this code is not needed in the Global.mpt. In Module 18 Sample Code.mpp, the above code is in the Module CopyGlobalCode.

Adding the CopyToGlobal Toolbar Button

To make it easy for users to access your macro, add a button to the My Macros toolbar to give them something to click to perform the copying. I added the following code to the AddToolbar procedure in the ToolbarCode Module in the Module 18 Sample Code.Mpt file:

236

```
Set MyButton = Nothing
Set MyButton = MyBar.Controls("Copy To Global")
If MyButton Is Nothing Then
    Set MyButton = MyBar.Controls.Add( _
       Type:=msoControlButton)
    With MyButton
       .Style = msoButtonCaption
       .Caption = "Copy To Global"
       .OnAction = "CopyToGlobal"
    End With
End If
```

This code must be in the macro file, as it is needed only by the macro project and is not needed in the Global.mpt file. Set MyButton = Nothing is the first statement so that if the Set MyButton = MyBar.Controls("Copy To Global") statement fails because the button does not exist, then MyButton will equal Nothing. Otherwise it will continue to point to the first button and the system doesn't detect and create the missing button. The toolbar for the macro project should look like Figure 18-1. You now have an easy way to distribute macros in a project file to other Microsoft Project Users.

**Figure 18-1: My Macros
toolbar**

Creating a Global Macros Toolbar

The final step is to transfer the Task Drivers macro to the Global.mpt file and to edit the toolbar code in the Global.mpt file and edit the Project Open Event. This edit creates a new Global Macros toolbar. I created a GlobalToolbarCode Module with this code in the following code sample:

```
Sub AddToolbar()
Dim MyBar As CommandBar
Dim MyButton As CommandBarButton
   On Error Resume Next
   Set MyBar = CommandBars("Global Macros")
   If MyBar Is Nothing Then
      Set MyBar = CommandBars.Add( _
         Name:="Global Macros", _
         Position:=msoBarFloating, Temporary:=True)
      MyBar.Visible = True
   End If

   Set MyButton = MyBar.Controls("Update Data")
   If MyButton Is Nothing Then
      Set MyButton = _
         MyBar.Controls.Add(Type:=msoControlButton)
      With MyButton
         .Style = msoButtonCaption
         .Caption = "Update Data"
         .OnAction = "ReadAllProjectData"
      End With
   End If
   Set MyButton = MyBar.Controls("Task Driver")
   If MyButton Is Nothing Then
      Set MyButton = _
         MyBar.Controls.Add(Type:=msoControlButton)
      With MyButton
         .Style = msoButtonCaption
         .Caption = "Task Driver"
         .OnAction = "TaskDrivers"
      End With
   End If
End Sub

Sub DeleteBar()
   On Error Resume Next
   CommandBars("Global Macros").Delete
End Sub
```

The only difference is the name of the toolbar. DeleteBar is not needed anymore (the toolbar displays permanently), but I left it just in case I need it in the future. The Project Open event in ThisProject in the Global.mpt file is as follows:

```
Private Sub Project_Open(ByVal pj As Project)
   ViewApply "Gantt Chart"
   EditGoTo Date:=Date
   AddToolbar
End Sub
```

EditGoto automatically moves the Timescale to today's date. Adding more macros requires extra code in the GlobalToolBar Module.

Hands On Exercise

Exercise 18-1

Automate the transfer of macros to the Global.mpt file.

1. Get the Copy code to work on your system.

2. If you have a macro of your own in a separate .mpp file, add code to automate its copying to the Global.mpt file.

Module 19

Working with Timephased Data

Learning Objectives

After completing this module, you will be able to:

- Understand how the system handles timephased data

- Read and write timephased data

- Create a macro to read timephased data for an S-Curve graph and write it to a .csv file

Understanding Timephased Data

Timephased data is the information you see in Microsoft Project on the right side of the Task Usage and Resource Usage views. Using Project VBA, you can read and write timephased data in exactly the same way you do it manually in either of these Usage views. Once you can handle timephased data programmatically, you can update projects with data from timesheet systems and create all sorts of time-based reports.

Project VBA handles timephased data using the TimeScaleValue object. A TimeScaleValue object holds data for a particular time slice in your schedule, which is the same as a particular cell in a Usage view. TimeScaleValues is a collection of TimeScaleValue objects, and therefore, holds timephased data for a specified date and time range. You fill TimeScaleValues collections using the TimeScaleData method.

 In Project 98, the TimeScaleData method was called TimeScale**d**Data. This can still be used for backwards compatibility, but for future compatibility, you should only use the TimeScaleData syntax.

The TimeScaleData method is available for the following:

- Tasks
- Resources
- Assignments
- Any timescaled data, such as Work, Cost, etc.
- Any date and time range
- Any time units, such as hours, days, weeks, etc.

When providing dates for the TimeScaleData method, Project VBA rounds them up to a whole time unit. For example, if you specify a weekly time interval, but provide a start date halfway through a week, the system returns the value for the whole week.

So, if you want only the last 3 days of a week to start your date range, you either need to use daily intervals and subtotal daily values into weeks or do two separate TimeScaleData calls, one for the first three days and the other for the rest of the time frame in weeks.

Reading Timephased Data

The sample code below reads data for a particular task and resource for every day of the project by day:

```
Sub TimePhasedDataTest()
Dim tsv As TimeScaleValue
Dim tsvs As TimeScaleValues
    'Timephased for Task with a UniqueID of 1
    Set tsvs = ActiveProject.Tasks(1).TimeScaleData( _
        StartDate:=ActiveProject.ProjectStart, _
        EndDate:=ActiveProject.ProjectFinish, _
        Type:=pjTaskTimescaledWork, _
        TimeScaleUnit:=pjTimescaleDays, Count:=1)
    For Each tsv In tsvs
        Debug.Print "Start: " & Format(tsv.StartDate, _
            "Long Date"), "Work: " & Val(tsv.Value) / 60 & "h"
    Next tsv
    Debug.Print    'Blank line

    'Timephased for Resource "Res"
    Set tsvs = ActiveProject.Resources("Res").TimeScaleData( _
        StartDate:=ActiveProject.ProjectStart, _
        EndDate:=ActiveProject.ProjectFinish, _
        Type:=pjResourceTimescaledWork, _
        TimeScaleUnit:=pjTimescaleDays, Count:=1)
    For Each tsv In tsvs
        Debug.Print "Start: " & Format(tsv.StartDate, _
            "Long Date"), "Work: " & Val(tsv.Value) / 60 & "h"
    Next tsv
End Sub
```

The line continuations make the preceding code 12 lines longer than it needs to be, so this sample code is actually quite compact. I wrote the code in two blocks: one to read task data and the other to read resource data. I defined two variables named tsv and tsvs. A good naming convention is to name collections of variables always with a plural name such as tsvs. Therefore, tsv is a single object, not a collection of objects.

Set tsvs = ActiveProject.Tasks(1).TimeScaleData creates the timescale collection of timescale objects based on task ID 1. As parameters for the method, I use the Start and Finish dates of the project. With two tasks in a test project, each with a Duration of 5d, linked with a Finish to Start dependency, and with the same resource assigned on each task at 50% Units, the schedule looks like Figure 19-1.

	❶	Task Name	Duration	Week 1								Week 2							Week 3				
				D-1	D1	D2	D3	D4	D5	D6	D7	D8	D9	D10	D11	D12	D13	D14	D15	D16	D17	D18	D19
1		My task	5 days						Res[50%]														
2		My task	5 days													Res[50%]							

Figure 19-1: Test schedule

The Resource Usage and Task Usage views both show a total of 4 hours per day for the entire 2 weeks of the project. The TimePhasedDataTest procedure prints first the task data, then the resource data to the Immediate Window with the following results (assuming a start date of 1/1/2007):

```
Start: Monday, 1 January 2007          Work: 4h
Start: Tuesday, 2 January 2007         Work: 4h
Start: Wednesday, 3 January 2007       Work: 4h
Start: Thursday, 4 January 2007        Work: 4h
Start: Friday, 5 January 2007          Work: 4h
Start: Saturday, 6 January 2007        Work: 0h
Start: Sunday, 7 January 2007          Work: 0h
Start: Monday, 8 January 2007          Work: 0h
Start: Tuesday, 9 January 2007         Work: 0h
Start: Wednesday, 10 January 2007      Work: 0h
Start: Thursday, 11 January 2007       Work: 0h
Start: Friday, 12 January 2007         Work: 0h

Start: Monday, 1 January 2007          Work: 4h
Start: Tuesday, 2 January 2007         Work: 4h
Start: Wednesday, 3 January 2007       Work: 4h
Start: Thursday, 4 January 2007        Work: 4h
Start: Friday, 5 January 2007          Work: 4h
Start: Saturday, 6 January 2007        Work: 0h
Start: Sunday, 7 January 2007          Work: 0h
Start: Monday, 8 January 2007          Work: 4h
Start: Tuesday, 9 January 2007         Work: 4h
Start: Wednesday, 10 January 2007      Work: 4h
Start: Thursday, 11 January 2007       Work: 4h
Start: Friday, 12 January 2007         Work: 4h
```

In the preceding result, notice the 0h for Saturday and Sunday. The last week of working days for the task Timephased data has 0d of work because it is for Task 1 only does not include work for Task 2. The resource data is for the resource Res who is assigned to both tasks; hence, the system contains work for both weeks.

245

When entering the Type and TimeScaleUnit parameters, IntelliSense displays a complete list of all options, so it is easy to select the one you want and get it right the first time. Note that the Type for the Task block is pj**Task**TimescaledWork while the Type for the Resource block is pj**Resource**TimescaledWork.

A common issue with using timescaled values is that if a timescale range is greater than the source Task, Resource, or Assignment Object, then tsv.Value returns an empty string ("") for time slices outside the object's date range. Val(tsv.Value) converts the empty string to a zero which is much more useful. Timescale value Properties always return Work in minutes, so dividing by 60 gives you hours of Work.

Exporting Timephased Data to a .csv file

In this module, you learn how to export Timephased Data to a .csv file. In Module 21, you will export it to Excel and produce the data for an S-Curve graph. Figure 19-2 shows a sample S-Curve.

In Figure 19-2, if today is week 18 then the project is clearly behind schedule. In fact, it looks like there was no work done for 2 weeks (flat line on the Work graph around week 17). The schedule also shows greatly increased hours per week (the line is steeper) from week 19 onwards and that progress should catch up with the baseline around week 21. The project schedule is finishing 2 weeks late and with more work than predicted.

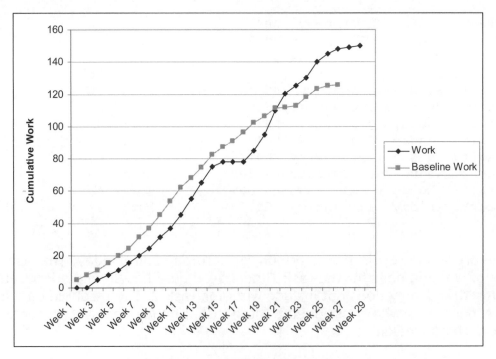

Figure 19-2: Sample S-Curve report

An S-Curve graph is a graph of the cumulative Work or Cost compared against the cumulative Baseline Work or Baseline Cost. You can graph various Earned Value variables as well, but we traditionally use cumulative Cost and Work. The result is a graph that clearly shows progress against the baseline, with the steepness of the curve indicating hours per week usage (the steeper the curve the more hours per week).

This macro exports the basic data and relies on Excel to calculate and plot cumulative hours. Microsoft Project can provide cumulative Work and cumulative Cost data, but not cumulative Baseline Work or cumulative Baseline Cost.

The Code for this macro appears in two parts, with the first part adding two methods to the text Class created in Module 5. The two methods are FileOpenWrite and WriteLine. The added code is as follows:

```
Sub FileOpenWrite()
    Open prvPath For Output As #1
End Sub

Sub WriteLine(strLine As String)
    Write #1, strLine
End Sub
```

Enter this code into the VBE in the Class Module clsTextFile. By clicking on the Open and Write words then pressing F1 for Help, you can quickly find out what these VBA commands do.

By reusing and adding to the Text Class and using the preceding code for timephased data, the macro to export timephased data for a whole project is as follows:

```vba
Sub SCurveCsvFile()
Dim tsv As TimeScaleValue
Dim tsvs As TimeScaleValues
Dim txt As New clsTextFile
    txt.FilePath = "C:\TimeScaleData Work.csv"
    txt.FileOpenWrite

    Set tsvs = ActiveProject.ProjectSummaryTask. _
        TimeScaleData(StartDate:= _
            ActiveProject.ProjectSummaryTask.Start, _
            EndDate:=ActiveProject.ProjectSummaryTask.Finish, _
            Type:=pjTaskTimescaledWork, _
            TimeScaleUnit:=pjTimescaleWeeks, Count:=1)
    For Each tsv In tsvs
        txt.WriteLine Format(tsv.StartDate, _
            "Medium Date") & ", " & Val(tsv.Value) / 60
    Next tsv

    'Tidy Up
    txt.FileClose
End Sub
```

The preceding code sample includes seven lines of code, plus variable declarations and the Text Class! You can edit the file path of the .csv file to be whatever you want. The ProjectSummaryTask property is a Task Object and can therefore return a TimescaleValues collection. The one above is for Work by week from the project's start to finish. txt.WriteLine takes a string as a parameter so your code needs to build the string for the entire row to be saved to the csv file.

Hands On Exercise

Exercise 19-1

Work with TimeScaleData code.

1. Get the SCurveCsvFile code to work by entering the code or using the Module 19 Sample Code.mpp file.

2. Add code to export Baseline Work to C:\TimeScaleData Baseline Work.csv.

3. Add code to export Cost and Baseline Cost to two more .csv files.

Writing Timephased Data

Writing timephased data is slightly more complicated than reading it. If you want to update the timescale values for an assignment that lasts for five days, for example, and you get TimeScaleValues for the five days, then you can easily update those five TimeScale Objects. However, if you have actual data for six days, then a TimeScaleData Object for day 6 does not exist and you need to add one using the tsvs.Add method.

That is the extra complication. Provided you make sure you do not try to refer to a TimeScaleValue Object that does not exist, writing timephased data is as easy as reading it. The following code updates actual hours with the index number of the tsv object, which goes from 1 to 10 for a 10 day task:

```
Sub TimePhasedDataWritetest()
Dim tsv As TimeScaleValue
Dim tsvs As TimeScaleValues
    'Update Task 1 with Actual Data
    With ActiveProject.Tasks(1)
        Set tsvs = .TimeScaleData( _
            StartDate:=.Start, EndDate:=.Finish, _
            Type:=pjTaskTimescaledActualWork, _
            TimeScaleUnit:=pjTimescaleDays, Count:=1)
    End With
    For Each tsv In tsvs
        tsv.Value = 60 * tsv.Index
    Next tsv
End Sub
```

With ActiveProject.Tasks(1) avoids specifying ActiveProject.Tasks(1) for every parameter which makes it simpler to read the code. This code happily assigns Actual Work to Saturday and Sunday, but this is only a test, after all. Day 1 will get one hour, day 2 gets two hours and so on.

If you need to extend the task with two extra days of work, then add the following code at the very end of the procedure:

```
tsvs.Add Value:=(tsvs.Count + 1) * 60
tsvs.Add Value:=(tsvs.Count + 1) * 60
```

Remember that the Value for Work must always be in minutes.

Hands On Exercise

Exercise 19-2

Write TimeScaleData code.

1. Get the TimePhasedDataWriteTest code to work by entering the code or using the Module 19 Sample Code.mpp file. Make sure you have a Task 1 before running the code.

2. Try creating a .csv file with actual values, and then read it into your project and update a task with it. You will need Unique ID's to identify the correct task and match dates in the csv file with tsv.Start dates.

Updating the Project Control Center

In this section, we combine the Project Control Center's Update code created in Module 16 with code to read timephased data for all resources with work in all projects. We do this to get an overall picture of resource usage across all projects. The quality of this information is directly proportional to the accuracy with which you assigned resources to tasks in all projects. If you assigned no resources, no data exists to copy. If you assigned all resources at 100% Units, then you only get an idea of what resources are working on what projects. If you assign resources accurately and realistically on all projects, then you get an accurate picture of total hours of work assigned to all resources across all projects in the Project Control Center.

Before adding functionality to our code, you first need to finish adding the Task Drivers code to the Global.mpt file. To do this you need to copy all relevant Modules to the Global.mpt file. Containing the Modules we created so far, my Project Explorer looks like Figure 19-3.

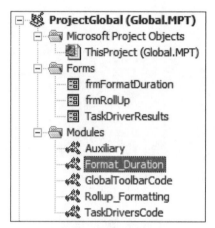

**Figure 19-3: Current Project
Explorer window**

The Global Toolbar code should now contain the following code:

```
Sub AddToolbar()
Dim MyBar As CommandBar
Dim MyButton As CommandBarButton
    On Error Resume Next
    Set MyBar = CommandBars("Global Macros")
    If MyBar Is Nothing Then
        Set MyBar = CommandBars.Add(Name:="Global Macros", _
        Position:=msoBarFloating, Temporary:=True)
        MyBar.Visible = True
    End If

    Set MyButton = Nothing
    Set MyButton = MyBar.Controls("Task Driver")
    If MyButton Is Nothing Then
        Set MyButton = MyBar.Controls.Add( _
            Type:=msoControlButton)
        With MyButton
            .Style = msoButtonCaption
            .Caption = "Task Driver"
            .OnAction = "TaskDrivers"
        End With
    End If
End Sub
```

I explained this code previously in Module 18. You need to copy to the Global.mpt file only those macros that you want available to any single project file. The Project Control Center (PCC) macros live in the Project Control Center.mpp file, as they need to work with the list of projects in that file. Therefore, you can keep PCC macros out of the Global.mpt file to help keep it simpler.

Designing the Get Resource Procedure

To read all resource data from each project you need to do the following:

1. Delete any existing resource data from the Project Control Center.
2. Call the procedure to get data after setting the Project Control Center task's Duration to the same overall Duration as the linked project.
3. Loop through all resources in the Linked Project.

For each resource, do the following:

1. Confirm that it is not a blank resource row and that it has work (it is assigned to at least one task).
2. Test to see if a resource with the same name already exists in the Project Control Center.

253

3. If the resource does not exist, add it to the Project Control Center project.

4. Assign the resource to the task in the Project Control Center.

5. Create a timescale collection for the assignment in the linked project for the entire Duration of the Linked Project.

6. For each time slice, add the value for the linked project's resource to the Project Control Center assignment.

The complex part of this macro is to understand that you need the timescale data for each resource in each linked project. You copy the weekly value for the total work for the resource into the same time slice for a new assignment in the Project Control Center project.

To understand this code you need to get it working and then look at the results. You can single step through the code to see what happens during each step. Remember that you are not copying every assignment from the linked project, but just the total work for each resource for each week.

The Comments for this macro could be as follows:

```
Sub GetResourceUsageData
'Loop through all resources in the Linked Project
'Only copy data if resource is not blank and has Work
'Point to the same resource in the PCC or if it doesn't exist,
    'add it
'Add an assignment for the resource to the task in the PCC
'Create a timescale collection for the assignment and the
    'Resource in the linked project for the whole duration of
    'the linked project
'For each time slice, add the value for the linked project
    'resource to the same time slice in the PCC assignment
End Sub
```

The code for the procedure is:

```
Sub GetResourceUsageData(prjPCC As Project, Tsk As Task, _
    prjLinked As Project)
'This procedure reads all Resource Usage data from the
'linked project to the PCC project.
Dim tsvsPCC As TimeScaleValues
Dim tsvsLinked As TimeScaleValues
Dim tsvLinked As TimeScaleValue
Dim Res As Resource
```

```
Dim ResPCC As Resource
Dim Assign As Assignment
   On Error Resume Next

'Loop through all resources in the Linked Project
   For Each Res In prjLinked.Resources
      'Point to the same Resource in the PCC or
         'if it doesn't exist, add it
      If Not Res Is Nothing Then
         If Res.Work > 0 Then
            'See if Resource exists in PCC already
            Set ResPCC = Nothing
            Set ResPCC = prjPCC.Resources(Res.Name)
            If ResPCC Is Nothing Then
               Set ResPCC = _
                  prjPCC.Resources.Add(Res.Name)
            End If

         'Add an Assignment for the Resource to the Task for
         'the Linked Project in the Project Control Center
            Set Assign = Tsk.Assignments.Add(Tsk.ID, _
                     ResPCC.ID, 1)

            'Create a timescale collection for the
            'Assignment and the Resource in the linked
            'project for the whole
            'duration of the Linked Project
               Set tsvsLinked = Res.TimeScaleData( _
                  prjLinked.ProjectStart, _
                  prjLinked.ProjectFinish, _
                  pjResourceTimescaledWork, _
                  pjTimescaleWeeks)
               Set tsvsPCC = Assign.TimeScaleData( _
                  Tsk.Start, Tsk.Finish, _
                  pjAssignmentTimescaledWork, _
                  pjTimescaleWeeks)
            'For each time slice, add the value for the
            'linked project Resource to the same
            'time slice in the Project Control Center
            'Assignment
```

```
         For Each tsvLinked In tsvsLinked
            'Add work for current time slot
            'to the same time slot in the PCC
            tsvsPCC(tsvLinked.Index).Value = _
            Val(tsvsPCC(tsvLinked.Index).Value) _
            + Val(tsvLinked.Value)
         Next tsvLinked
      End If
   End If
Next Res
End Sub
```

The good news is that explaining this code is about as complex as it gets! There are two collections of TimeScaleValues, one for each project. The Project Control Center collection is for the new assignment of the resource to the task with the linked project's Hyperlink. The other collection is for the linked project and will be for the total weekly work for each resource in turn. Both collections must be for the same date range and time units, which in this case is the Duration of the project in weeks.

You need to use On Error Resume Next because you want to trap attempts to point to a resource in the Project Control Center. If the attempt fails, then you know that the resource does not exist, so you can create it with the same name as in the linked project.

```
For Each Res In prjLinked.Resources
   If Not Res Is Nothing Then
      If Res.Work > 0 Then
         'See if Resource exists in PCC already
         Set ResPCC = Nothing
         Set ResPCC = prjPCC.Resources(Res.Name)
         If ResPCC Is Nothing Then
            Set ResPCC = prjPCC.Resources. _
               Add(Res.Name)
         End If
```

The preceding block of code is simple: loop through each resource, testing for blank rows in using the exactly the same steps you learned for tasks. You are only interested in copying data for resources that are assigned to a task (Work>0). To test if a resource with the same name already exists in the Project Control Center, first set the ResPCC Resource Object to Nothing. Now assign it to a resource with the same name as the linked project (Res.Name). If the resource already exists, you now have an Object variable (ResPCC) pointing to it. If the resource does not already exist, ResPCC will still be Nothing, so add the resource to the Project Control Center using Set ResPCC = prjPCC.Resources.Add(Res.Name). The Add method returns the Resource object of the newly added resource.

```
Set Assign = Tsk.Assignments.Add(Tsk.ID, ResPCC.ID, 1)
```

In the preceding code, Tsk points to the current task in the Project Control Center for the open linked project. This code adds an assignment of the current resource to it and is ready to add all the time slice values from the resource in the linked project. Assign is an assignment Object that points to the new assignment.

```
Set tsvsLinked = Res.TimeScaleData( _
   prjLinked.ProjectStart, _
   prjLinked.ProjectFinish, _
   pjResourceTimescaledWork, _
   pjTimescaleWeeks)
Set tsvsPCC = Assign.TimeScaleData( _
   Tsk.Start, Tsk.Finish, _
   pjAssignmentTimescaledWork, _
   pjTimescaleWeeks)
```

These two statements create the TimeScaleValues collections, one for the new assignment in the Project Control Center and one for the resource in the linked project. Both collections need to be for weekly work and cover the same time period. The Project Control Center task updates to the same duration as the linked project earlier in the update code.

```
For Each tsvLinked In tsvsLinked
   If tsvsPCC(tsvLinked.Index).Value <> "" Then
      tsvsPCC(tsvLinked.Index).Value = _
         Val(tsvLinked.Value)
   End If
Next tsvLinked
```

257

The previous code is the key to the entire procedure. I stripped the Comments out and outdented the code a little to help make the code easier to read. For every week, copy the week's value for the **resource** in the Linked Project in to the same week for the **assignment** in the Project Control Center.

The result is that all the Project Control Center tasks now have an assignment for each resource in the linked project for that task. The Resource Usage view in the Project Control Center now shows the total work for all resources across all the projects. This is truly a useful report!

Following is the code I added to the ReadAllProjectData procedure:

```
Dim Res As Resource
'Delete any current data such as resources
   For Each Res In ActiveProject.Resources
      Res.Delete
   Next Res
```

We need this code to delete all resources to make way for fresh data. I added the following code as well, just before the FileClose statement. The code calls the Get Data procedure and passes the current Project objects and the current task object (Tsk), so the ReadAllProjectData procedure knows the project and task with which to work.

```
'Get Resource Usage data
GetResourceUsageData prjPCC, Tsk, prj
```

Hands On Exercise

Exercise 19-3

Work with timescaled resource data.

1. Get the sample code to work. You will need to add several Hyperlinks to tasks so the macro has some projects (with resource assignments) to open.

2. Look at the results and single step through the code until you understand the function of the code.

Advanced Challenge: Add code to copy the Baseline Work for every week as well.

Module 20

Controlling Excel with Project VBA

Learning Objectives

After completing this module, you will be able to:

- Export data to Excel
- Open Excel templates from Microsoft Project and run a macro in the template
- Control Microsoft Excel from Microsoft Project
- Control Microsoft Project from Microsoft Excel

Using Excel for Project Reporting

Microsoft Excel is a fantastic reporting tool for project data. By creating reports in Excel, you provide a medium in which most people can happily edit, e-mail, or print your reports. Excel, like Microsoft Project, features a full implementation of VBA. However, most people are not aware of how easy it is to control everything in Excel from Project, and how easy it is to control everything in Project from Excel!

As stated previously in Module 06, VBA Automation is the process used to control one program from another. The first section in this module explains Automation. The rest of this module, as you should expect by now, creates a number of useful macros and code snippets that you can use in many of your Project and Excel macros.

Understanding VBA Automation

Automation is initiated by an Automation client (any of the Microsoft Office applications) by binding an Object to an Automation Server (most Office applications including Project and Excel). There are two techniques to bind to another application; **Early** binding and **Late** binding. Late binding occurs when you declare a variable with type Object. The Object variable is very flexible (a bit like the Variant variable); it can point to any object, including other applications. However, you must be careful to track what an Object variable is pointing to, otherwise errors occur. There is no IntelliSense when Late binding is used.

Early binding requires you to create a reference to the Object library used by the other application, and then use variable types relevant to the other application. For example, in Excel you could use Range objects, Workbooks, etc. For creating a reference, you get full IntelliSense and the compiler can detect when you try to assign objects like Workbooks to Excel Ranges. Early binding is the better option to use because it prevents a wide range of errors that the compiler catches for you, and makes creating code quicker and easier because of IntelliSense. I show you an example of Late binding, but otherwise, all code in this module uses Early binding only.

The only disadvantage with Early binding is that you need to reset references if you copy your macro to a PC with a different version of Excel or Project.

When searching Help for information on application Automation, use the search text "controlling one application from another".

Using Late Binding

Late binding refers to the idea that you bind your Object to the other application as late as possible with no compilation checks. For example, with the variable xlApp shown in the following code sample, there is nothing to stop you from assigning xlApp to an Excel Range, to a Word Range, or to any other object. While this might sound useful, it inevitably leads to confusing code and code problems that are difficult to fix.

The following code starts a new copy of Excel, displays a message in cell A1 and then leaves Excel open and active when the macro ends.

```
Sub StartExcelLateBinding()
Dim xlApp As Object
    Set xlApp = CreateObject("Excel.Application")
    xlApp.Visible = True
    xlApp.WorkBooks.Add
    xlApp.Range("A1") = "Hello World"
    Set xlApp = Nothing
End Sub
```

With Late binding, all variables are the Object type. CreateObject creates an object for the specified application. The Application object is the most useful object to bind to as it gives you access to everything (in this example) in Excel.

Applications that you launch with CreateObject always start hidden (their Visible property is set to False). To make the application visible to your user, set the Visible property to True. To add a new workbook and enter a text string into A1, the Excel VBA code would be as follows:

```
Workbooks.Add
Range("A1") = "Hello World"
```

If you try to run the same code in Project, the Project VBA compiler attempts to find a Workbooks collection in Project. Obviously, it does not exist so the compilation fails. To make the code work in Project, change it to the following:

```
xlApp.WorkBooks.Add
xlApp.Range("A1") = "Hello World"
```

This makes the compiler happy. When the code runs, it reads the xlApp variable and then communicates with the Excel Automation Server (part of Excel). It gets details of the WorkBooks collection so it can run the Add Method. You need to use the leading xlApp with Early binding as well.

Set xlApp = Nothing releases the xlApp Object and the connection between Project and Excel ends. The main advantage of Late binding is that it is Excel version independent.

Using Early Binding

Early binding requires you to create a reference to the other application's object library. To create a reference, complete the following steps:

1. In the VBE, click Tools ➤ References.

2. For a reference to Microsoft Excel, select the *Microsoft Excel Object Library XX.0* reference in the list of libraries. Figure 20-1 shows that I selected the Excel Library for Excel 2003 (version 11).

When you reopen the References dialog, all checked references appear at the top of the list.

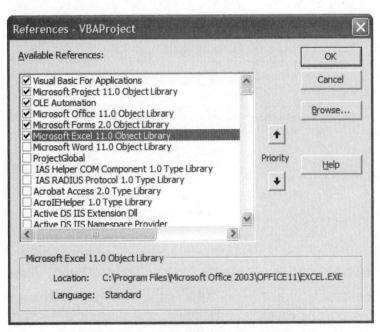

**Figure 20-1: References dialog with
Excel 2003 Library selected**

Following is the same example used for Late binding, but converted to Early binding:

```
Sub StartExcelEarlyBinding()
Dim xlApp As Excel.Application
    Set xlApp = CreateObject("Excel.Application")
    xlApp.Visible = True
    xlApp.WorkBooks.Add
    xlApp.Range("A1") = "Hello World"
    Set xlApp = Nothing
End Sub
```

There are three big differences between the Late binding and Early binding code samples:

1. By creating a reference, you have access to all of Excel's variable object types. The variable type Excel.Application is effectively the Excel application. With it, you can access all Excel's Objects, Methods, and Properties.

2. IntelliSense works, as shown in Figure 20-2.

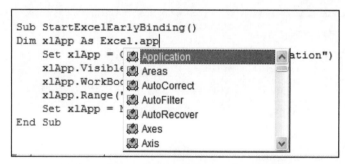

**Figure 20-2: IntelliSense works
with early binding**

3. You can click on any Excel Object, Method, or Property and then press F1 for Help, taking you directly to the relevant Excel VBA Help.

Having both IntelliSense and Excel VBA Help available makes it much easier for you to develop your macros, especially when you are learning. With Object variables there is no IntelliSense; you have to know in advance the correct Object, Method, or Property name and spelling. In addition, with Early binding, since xlApp is of type Excel.Application, you cannot use the xlApp variable for anything other than pointing to Excel Applications. If you do, the compiler flags a warning. This prevents many type-conversion errors when you run your code aiding faster development.

A disadvantage of Early binding is that the reference is dependant on a specific version of the referenced application. As explained in Module 6, references will automatically update when you upgrade to new versions, but if you send a macro to someone with an earlier version of the application than the one you referenced, the references will not update and compilation fails with an error.

If you do use Late binding because of version problems, it is often quicker to write your code with Early binding and then convert to Late binding with Object variables once the code is working.

 All of the following code samples assume you have a reference set to the Excel Object Library. Any version of Excel will work starting with Excel 95.

Connecting to an Already Open Copy of Excel

If the program supports it, your code runs more reliably if you start a new copy of the application to which you wish to bind. However, not all applications support multiple copies running at the same time. Excel happily runs multiple versions of itself, but Microsoft Project does not. If Excel is already open with information your macro needs opening a fresh copy of Excel is unnecessary. To connect to an already active copy of Excel use the following VBA code:

```
Sub ConnectToExistingExcelApplication()
Dim xlApp As Excel.Application
    On Error Resume Next
    Set xlApp = GetObject(, "Excel.Application")
    If xlApp Is Nothing Then
        MsgBox "Failed to connect to Excel, macro ended"
    Else
        MsgBox "Connected to existing Excel Application"
    End If
    xlApp.Visible = True

'Tidy up
    xlApp.UserControl = True
    Set xlApp = Nothing
End Sub
```

If you attempt to connect to Excel and a copy of Excel is not running, then a run time error occurs. That is why you need the On Error Resume Next statement, so you can test for a successful binding after attempting to connect using GetObject. Note also that GetObject has two parameters. Typically you do not need the first parameter, hence the leading comma.

If xlApp is Nothing returns True, then no copy of Excel is running. If you still need Excel, then go ahead and create one with CreateObject.

The other new code worth noting is xlApp.UserControl = True. Without it, if nothing was done with Excel, setting xlApp to Nothing also closes Excel. By using xlApp.UserControl = True Excel assumes it is under user control and does not close Excel when your Project macro sets xlApp to Nothing.

I use all the lines in the code above in all my macros controlling Excel and have had no problem using versions of Project 98 or later, and using Excel 95 or later. Call me lucky, but my experience is that each new version of Project and Excel has been backwards compatible. In fact, I still have a number of old Project 98 macros that currently run unchanged in Project 2003.

 If you try to use a feature in an older version of Project or Excel introduced in a later version, then it will not work. Any feature that exists in all versions almost always works unchanged in VBA for any version.

Exporting a List of Resources to Excel

The macro on which you are about to work exports a list of all resources in the active Project to Excel. This is a precursor to the WhoDoesWhatWhen macro, which exports to Excel all tasks and all resources in all projects in the Project Control Center.

The goal is simple: export a list of resources to Excel. Following is a set of Comments to describe the macro deliverables:

```
Sub ExportResourceNames()
'Start Excel and create a new Workbook
'Create Column Titles
'Export Resource Names and the Project Title
'Tidy up
Exit Sub
```

Below is the code to complete this macro. Much of it involves formatting Excel cells. Because this is not a book on Excel VBA, I recommend that you study the Excel VBA Help articles for information about Excel objects, methods, and properties. I also recommend that you single step through the code to see what happens with each statement. Developing Excel VBA code is easier when you know Excel well; just as developing Project VBA is easier when you know Project well.

```vba
Sub ExportResourceNames()
Dim xlApp As Excel.Application
Dim xlRange As Excel.Range
Dim Res As Resource

'Start Excel and create a new Workbook
   Set xlApp = CreateObject("Excel.Application")
   xlApp.Visible = True
   xlApp.WorkBooks.Add

'Create Column Titles
   Set xlRange = xlApp.Range("A1")
   With xlRange
      .Formula = "Who Does What When Report"
      .Font.Bold = True
      .Font.Size = 14
      .EntireColumn.ColumnWidth = 30
   End With
   With xlRange.Range("A2")
      .Formula = "As of: " & Format(Date, "mmm d yyyy")
      .Font.Bold = True
      .Font.Italic = True
      .Font.Size = 12
      .Select
   End With

   xlRange.Range("A4") = "Resource Name"
   xlRange.Range("B4") = "Project Title"
   With xlRange.Range("A4:B4")
      .Font.Bold = True
      .HorizontalAlignment = xlHAlignCenter
      .VerticalAlignment = xlVAlignCenter
   End With
```

```
'Export Resource Names and the Project Title
   Set xlRange = xlRange.Range("A5")
   For Each Res In ActiveProject.Resources
      If Not Res Is Nothing Then
         With xlRange
            .Range("A1") = Res.Name
            .Range("B1") = ActiveProject.Name
         End With
      End If
      Set xlRange = xlRange.Offset(1, 0)  'Point to next row
   Next Res

'Tidy up
   xlRange.Range("B1").EntireColumn.AutoFit
   Set xlApp = Nothing
End Sub
```

Although I call the preceding macro WhoDoesWhatWhen, this is only the first code writing iteration, so I export only resource information to Excel. The key to understanding Excel VBA is to learn how to use the Excel Range object. Search through Excel VBA Help for information about the Range Object and then experiment with using it in Excel VBA. Excel VBA code is easy to move to Project; you simply need an Excel Application object preceding the code or an Excel variable (like xlRange in the code above) that you specify using an Excel application object.

Running Excel VBA Code Using Project VBA

One way of organizing a larger macro is to use Project VBA to open an Excel template or a copy of an existing Excel Workbook, to export data to Excel, and then run a macro in the Excel file to do all the report formatting. One advantage of this method is that your worksheets can already include formatting and any needed formulas, reducing the amount of code you need to write in your macro.

To open a copy of an Excel template and run a macro in the template (assuming xlApp already points to an open copy of Excel), use the following code:

```
xlApp.Workbooks.Add "MyTemplate.xlt"
xlapp.Run "MacroNameInTemplate", OptionalArgument
```

The template name can include a full path and you can specify up to 30 arguments or parameters for the macro. The system returns control to your Project VBA macro after the Excel VBA macro completes.

Controlling Microsoft Project from Excel

Suppose you have VBA code in an Excel file with which you want to open a Microsoft Project file and then read and write some data. Although you can use Late binding in Excel to control Microsoft Project you should use Early binding instead. To set up a reference to Microsoft Project from Excel, use the following code:

1. In Excel's VBE, click Tools ➢ References

2. Select the *Microsoft Project Object Library* option from the list of libraries as shown in Figure 20-3.

3. Click the *OK* button.

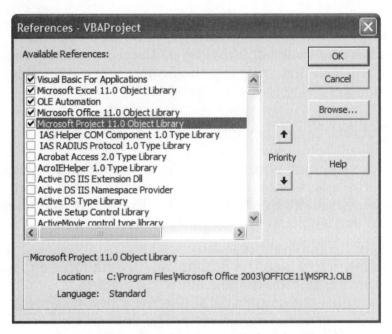

Figure 20-3: References dialog in Excel

Microsoft Project allows only a single running version of itself, so you must test for an already running version of the software with GetObject before launching a new copy. The code to do this follows:

```
Sub AutomateProjectFromExcel()
Dim projApp As MSProject.Application
   On Error Resume Next
   Set projApp = GetObject(, "MSProject.application")
   If projApp Is Nothing Then
      Set projApp = CreateObject("MSProject.Application")
   End If

   MsgBox "The name of the active project is: " _
      & projApp.ActiveProject.Name
   projApp.Visible = True

   'Tidy Up
   Set projApp = Nothing
End Sub
```

Do you recognize the similarities with the ConnectToExistingExcelApplication macro? MSProject is the key name to remember, as it appears in IntelliSense as well. Project is not a valid object type (in Excel), however, so remember to use MSProject. Now that you have the Project application object in Excel, you can control everything in Project using VBA from Excel.

Creating the S-Curves Macro in Excel

In Module 19. you learned how to export time phased data to csv files. I finish the S-Curve macro here, but I use Excel rather than csv files to export the data. Again, this is not the place to teach Excel VBA, so you need to read Excel VBA Help and single step through the code to understand Excel VBA code better.

The design of this macro is to use graphs, and a data table already existing in an Excel template, to receive the exported Project data, and then run an Excel macro to adjust the graph's data. Use the following code to create the S-Curve graph for the active project only. The deliverable Comments for this code are as follows:

```
Sub CreateSCurveGraph
'Setup Excel
'Open copy of Template
'Set up Range variable and delete any old data
'Export time phased data based on Project Summary Task
'Call Excel Template Macro
'Tidy up
End Sub
```

The Excel template should include formulas to create the cumulative totals. Although Microsoft Project calculates **cumulative work** automatically, it does not calculate **cumulative baseline work**. Because you need to create cumulative totals for both Work and Baseline Work, it is easy to use formulas to calculate both values. Following is the full code for the S-Curve macro:

```
Sub CreateSCurveGraph()
Dim xlApp As Excel.Application
Dim xlRange As Excel.Range
Dim tsvs As TimeScaleValues
Dim tsv As TimeScaleValue
   On Error Resume Next
   'Setup Excel
   Set xlApp = GetObject(, "Excel.Application")
   If xlApp Is Nothing Then
      Set xlApp = CreateObject("Excel.Application")
   End If
   xlApp.Visible = True

   'Open copy of Template
   xlApp.Workbooks.Add CurDir _
      & "\Module 20 Excel Code.xls"

   'Set up Range variable ready to export
   Set xlRange = xlApp.Range("Start")
   xlRange.CurrentRegion.Offset(3, 0).ClearContents
   xlRange.Range("A2:B3").ClearContents

'Export timed data based on Project Summary Task
   Set tsvs = ActiveProject.ProjectSummaryTask. _
       TimeScaleData( _
       ActiveProject.ProjectStart, _
       ActiveProject.ProjectFinish, _
       pjTaskTimescaledWork, pjTimescaleWeeks)
   For Each tsv In tsvs
      xlRange.Offset(tsv.Index, 0) = tsv.StartDate
      xlRange.Offset(tsv.Index, 1) = Val(tsv.Value) / 60
   Next tsv
   Set tsvs = Nothing
   Set tsvs = ActiveProject.ProjectSummaryTask. _
       TimeScaleData( _
       ActiveProject.ProjectStart, _
       ActiveProject.ProjectFinish, _
       pjTaskTimescaledBaselineWork, _
       pjTimescaleWeeks)
   For Each tsv In tsvs
      xlRange.Offset(tsv.Index, 2) = Val(tsv.Value) / 60
   Next tsv
```

273

```
    'Call Excel Template Macro
    xlApp.Run "SetupGraph"

    'Tidy up
    Set xlApp = Nothing
End Sub
```

There is nothing in this code that is new to you until you get to the following section:

```
    'Set up Range variable ready to export
    Set xlRange = xlApp.Range("Start")
    xlRange.CurrentRegion.Offset(3, 0).ClearContents
    xlRange.Range("A2:B3").ClearContents
```

Excel provides the ability to name cells (refer to Excel Help for complete instructions on how to name cells and ranges). In the sample template, I named cell A4 as Start, which provides a known starting cell. Even if I insert two extra rows as headers or titles, the named cell Start will move with the data titles row and the code continues to work, because it is all relative to the named cell Start. Set xlRange = xlApp.Range("Start") sets the variable xlRange to point to the named cell Start (cell address A4).

xlRange.CurrentRegion.Offset(3, 0).ClearContents deletes the contents of all cells as if you had pressed Ctrl+* in Excel. Offset(3,0) means that the selected (by CurrentRegion) area is moved down 3 rows so that the deletion does not touch the formulas in cells D5:E6. Therefore, delete Cell range A2:B3 separately. Single step through the code to see what happens during each step after you run the macro once to get data into Excel, and there is something for the macro to delete.

All remaining code (except for xlRange.Offset(tsv.Index, 2) = Val(tsv.Value) / 60) should be familiar to you by now. If xlRange points to cell A4, then for the first time slice (tsv.Index is 1) xlRange.Offset(tsv.Index,0) therefore points to A5. Offsets always go row, column so Offset(1,0) is one row down and zero columns to the right. Negative row numbers are rows up and negative columns are columns to the left.

This is a simple piece of code that allows the correct data to go into the correct cell using the For Each loop. The first For Each loop copies the start date of each week as well as the data. xlApp.Run "SetupGraph" is the code that runs the macro called SetupGraph in the Excel template.

What about the Excel VBA code? Since this is useful code, following are the SetupGraph macro Comments for the code.

```
Sub SetUpGraph()
'Get row number of last week and copy formulas down
'Delete all zeroes from bottom for accuracy
'Adjust source data ranges for chart
End Sub
```

In the above Comments, the reason we need to delete the zeroes is S-Curve lines normally stop on the last data point rather than continue in a flat line to the end of the time scale. This code starts from the last row and deletes all zeroes until the first non-zero entry. The effect on the graph is that it shows the date the project finishes and the baseline finish date. Following is the actual Excel VBA code:

```
Sub SetUpGraph()
Dim Row As Long
Dim rStart As Range
Dim R As Range
   Set rStart = Range("Start")

   'Get row of last week and copy formulas down
   Row = rStart.End(xlDown).Row
   rStart.Range("D3:E" & Row + 1 - rStart.Row).FillDown

   'Delete all zeroes from bottom for accuracy
   Set R = rStart.End(xlDown).Offset(0, 1)
   Do Until R <> 0 Or R.Row <= rStart.Row
      If R = 0 Then
         R.Range("A1,C1").ClearContents
      End If
      Set R = R.Offset(-1, 0)
   Loop
   Set R = rStart.End(xlDown).Offset(0, 2)
   Do Until R <> 0 Or R.Row <= rStart.Row
      If R = 0 Then
         R.Range("A1,C1").ClearContents
      End If
      Set R = R.Offset(-1, 0)
   Loop
```

```
    'Adjust source data ranges for chart
    ActiveSheet.ChartObjects(1).Activate
    ActiveChart.SetSourceData Source:=Sheets("SCurve") _
        .Range("A3:A" & Row & ",D3:E" & Row)
    rStart.Select
End Sub
```

All of this code is in the Module 20 Sample Code.xls file. The two macros combine to form the simplest and most efficient solution to creating an S-Curve graph in Excel. For these two macros to work correctly, you need an active project that contains tasks with resources assigned to them so there are Work values, and you must save a Baseline so there are Baseline Work values.

If Work and Cost values are the same as the Baseline Cost and Baseline Work values, then you will see only one line. After saving a Baseline, edit the schedule so that the current data is different from Baseline data. Then the two lines on the graph separate the next time you run the macro.

Hands On Exercise

Exercise 20-1

Automate using Microsoft Excel with Microsoft Project.

1. In a copy of one of your own project files insert a new Module

2. In Excel's VBE, click Tools ➢ References

3. Select the *Microsoft Excel Object Library* option from the list of libraries shown in Figure 20-3.

4. Click the *OK* button.

5. Edit the ExportResourceNames code described earlier to be an ExportTaskNames procedure.

6. In Excel add a reference to the Microsoft Project Object Library

7. Modify the AutomateProjectFromExcel procedure described earlier to read all task names with their Start and Finish dates.

8. Add to the code to format all summary task names in Excel with the Bold font style.

Completing the Who Does What When Macro

The goal of the Who Does What When macro is to produce a report in Excel to show the tasks assigned to every resource for all projects in the Project Control Center. Up to this point, our macro only exports a simple list of resources to Excel. The three remaining things we must accomplish are:

1. Add a timescale from today forward for 3 months. To keep the report simple, we will limit the timescale from the current week to 13 weeks.

2. Add task assignments for each resource.

3. Make sure our code works for every project in the Project Control Center.

The third item is something you already know how to do. The first two items are more difficult, but simple enough if we break the tasks into logical steps. The Comments for these steps are as follows:

```
Sub WhoDoesWhatWhen()
'Setup Excel
'Create Column Titles
'For every Project
'For every Resource
'For every Assignment
'Get weekly work for Assignment from this week for 13 weeks
'Point to top left of report
'Loop through all time slices entering the date
'  along the top of the report for each week
'Copy Resource Name, Project Name, Task ID, and Task Name
'For every time slice where Value<>"" copy hours
'End Assignment, Resource, Project
'Sort by Resource Name, Project, Task ID
'Create Pivot Table: Resource and Task by Project
End Sub
```

Merge these Comments with the existing ReadAllProjectData macro started earlier in this module. You can use some of the code from the ReadAllProjectData procedure, and the finished macro is as follows:

```
Option Explicit

Public Sub WhoDoesWhatWhen()
Dim StartOfWeek As Date
Dim EndOfPeriod As Date
Dim Tsk As Task
Dim prjPCC As Project
Dim prj As Project
Dim Path As String
Dim Res As Resource
Dim A As Assignment
Dim tsvs As TimeScaleValues
Dim tsv As TimeScaleValue
Dim xlApp As Excel.Application
Dim xlRange As Excel.Range
Dim Off As Long

'Calculate the date for the start of the week.
'    This macro assumes Monday is the start of each week
'    Calculate the date for this Monday
   StartOfWeek = Date - Weekday(Date) + vbMonday
   EndOfPeriod = StartOfWeek + (13 * 7)

'Start Excel
   On Error Resume Next
   'Setup Excel
   Set xlApp = GetObject(, "Excel.Application")
   If xlApp Is Nothing Then
      Set xlApp = CreateObject("Excel.Application")
   End If
   xlApp.Visible = True

'Create Column Titles
   Workbooks.Add
   Set xlRange = xlApp.Range("A1")
   CreateColumnTitles xlRange

'Point to top left of report
   Set xlRange = xlApp.Range("A4")

'Enter the date along the top of the report for each week
   For Off = 0 To 13
      xlRange.Offset(0, 4 + Off) = StartOfWeek + Off * 7
   Next Off
   Set xlRange = xlRange.Offset(1, 0)
```

```
'For Each task in the Project Control Center
   Set prjPCC = ActiveProject
   prjPCC.StartWeekOn = pjMonday
   For Each Tsk In prjPCC.Tasks
      If Not Tsk Is Nothing Then      'test for empty tasks

'Extract File path from the Hyperlink
         Path = Tsk.HyperlinkAddress
         Path = Replace(Path, "/", "\")
         Path = Replace(Path, "%20", " ")

'For every Project, open the project file read only with
'no updates from resource pools or external links.
         FileOpen Name:=Path, ReadOnly:=True, _
            noAuto:=True, openpool:=pjDoNotOpenPool
         Set prj = ActiveProject

'Make sure the project has its week starts on Monday
         prj.StartWeekOn = pjMonday

'For each Resource with work
         For Each Res In prj.Resources
            If Not Res Is Nothing Then

'For every Assignment, if it is in report date range
            For Each A In Res.Assignments
               If A.Start <= EndOfPeriod And _
                  A.Finish >= StartOfWeek Then
                  xlRange.Range("A1") = Res.Name
                  xlRange.Range("B1") = prj.Name
                  xlRange.Range("C1") = A.TaskID
                  xlRange.Range("D1") = _
                              A.TaskName

'Get weekly work for Assignment from this week for 13 weeks
                  Set tsvs = _
                  A.TimeScaleData( _
                  StartOfWeek, _
                  StartOfWeek + 13 * 7, _
                  pjAssignmentTimescaledWork, _
                  pjTimescaleWeeks)
```

```
'Copy Resource Name, Project Name, Task ID, Task Name
'For every time slice where Value<>"" copy hours
                For Each tsv In tsvs
                    If tsv.Value <> "" _ Then
                        xlRange.Offset( _
                        0, 3 + tsv.Index) = _
                        tsv.Value / 60
                    End If
                Next tsv
                Set xlRange = _
                    xlRange.Offset(1, 0)
            End If

'End Assignment, Resource, Project
            Next A
        End If
    Next Res

    'Close the project and don't save any changes
        prj.Activate  'Make sure project is active
        FileClose pjDoNotSave
    End If  'IF Not Tsk is Nothing

'End of Loop for all projects
    Next Tsk

'Format Report
'Sort by Resource Name, Project, Task ID
    FormatReport xlApp.Range("A4")

'Tidy up
    prjPCC.Activate    'Make sure its active
    Set prjPCC = Nothing
    Set prj = Nothing
    xlApp.Visible = True
End Sub
```

The preceding Comments evolved from the first set I described before I wrote the code. This is often what happens, so I left them as is. This code is not difficult to create when tackled in small blocks. If you break your macros into small blocks with a meaningful Comment describing what the block should do, then all you need to do is code each block in turn. Focus your testing and debugging on getting the individual blocks to work, then on getting the blocks to work together.

Let me describe what is happening with this code. You have already seen the first part, so the first new code is probably the following:

```
For Off = 0 To 13
    xlRange.Offset(0, 4 + Off) = StartOfWeek + Off * 7
Next Off
Set xlRange = xlRange.Offset(1, 0)
```

xlRange is an Excel range variable currently pointing to A4. Offset is a property that returns a range offset from the range to its left. So xlRange.Offset(0,4) is A4 plus zero rows down plus 4 columns to the right which is E4. Off is a Long variable. The For Off= 0 to 13 statement runs the xlRange.Offset statement 14 times, and writes 14 values into the 14 cells. The value written is the Date StartOfWeek plus 7 times the Off variable value. This enters weekly dates for the current week plus 13 more weeks. This is just what our deliverable describes! Alternatively, you could calculate the number of weeks to the end of the project and use that number instead of 13 weeks (three months)

Set xlRange = xlRange.Offset(1, 0) points the xlRange range to the cell one row down, same column. If A.Start <= EndOfPeriod And A.Finish >= StartOfWeek Then tests whether the current assignment is at least partly within the report period as defined by StartOfWeek and EndOfPeriod. This test means that the macro includes only tasks assigned to resources with Work in the report's date range. This makes the report more relevant and speeds up execution because it does not create rows with no data.

That is it! You should be familiar with the rest of the code. Note that because the procedure got too long, I broke out the code to create the Report Titles into the CreateColumnTitles and FormatReport procedures. I passed the range object for A4 to both procedures so they do not need to see or use xlApp. This avoids making a number of variables Global avoiding errors that are hard to find. The code and explanations for the CreateColumnTitles procedure is as follows:

```
Sub CreateColumnTitles(xlRange As Excel.Range)

'Create Column Titles
   With xlRange
      .Formula = "Who Does What When Report"
      .Font.Bold = True
      .Font.Size = 14
      .EntireColumn.ColumnWidth = 30
   End With
   With xlRange.Range("A2")
      .Formula = "As of: " & Format(Date, "mmm d yyyy")
      .Font.Bold = True
      .Font.Italic = True
      .Font.Size = 12
      .Select
   End With

   xlRange.Range("A4") = "Resource Name"
   xlRange.Range("B4") = "Project Title"
   xlRange.Range("C4") = "Task ID"
   xlRange.Range("D4") = "Task Name"
   With xlRange.Range("A4").EntireRow
      .Font.Bold = True
      .HorizontalAlignment = xlHAlignCenter
      .VerticalAlignment = xlVAlignCenter
      .NumberFormat = "mmm d yy"
      .WrapText = True
   End With
   xlRange.Columns("B").ColumnWidth = 20
   xlRange.Columns("D").ColumnWidth = 30
End Sub
```

When you know Excel VBA, none of the preceding code is difficult to write or understand. You could create most of it by recording a macro in Excel to do the necessary formatting, copying the code to Project, and then adding the xlRange or xlApp Objects in front of any Excel Object.

 Why did I export the resource and project names for every assignment? The answer is so that I can use Excel Pivot Tables on the data to create additional reports. One line for each week and task combination better supports the creation of Pivot tables, but the current format is more useful.

283

Following is the code and explanations for the FormatReport procedure:

```
Sub FormatReport(xlRange As Excel.Range)
'Does all report formatting including sorting
   xlRange.Columns("D").WrapText = True
   With Range(xlRange.Range("E1"), _
        xlRange.End(xlToRight).Address)
     .Orientation = 45
     .EntireRow.RowHeight = 48
     .EntireColumn.AutoFit
   End With
   xlRange.CurrentRegion.Offset(1, 4).NumberFormat = _
                              "#,##0\h"
   xlRange.Sort Key1:=xlRange, Order1:=xlAscending, _
      Key2:=xlRange.Range("B1"), Order2:=xlAscending, _
      Key3:=xlRange.Range("C1"), Order3:=xlAscending, _
      Header:=xlYes
End Sub
```

WrapText is a Method that wraps a long line of text into as many rows as needed within a single cell. With xlApp.Range(xlRange.Range("E1"), xlRange.End(xlToRight).Address) is more difficult to understand. This statement creates a range by specifying a start and end address using the address of xlRange for flexibility so it changes automatically in the future when needed, so that all Week Start dates are formatted at the same time.

The next few statements are self-explanatory, but the Sort method can be confusing. Think about how you sort in Excel using Tools ➢ Sort, in which you specify the columns, the sort order, and whether you want a header. That is exactly what the Sort code does. Note how the named parameters help you to understand the code.

Hands On Exercise

Exercise 20-2

Work with the Who Does What When Report.

1. Launch the WhoDoesWhatWhen Report. Provide a project in which each task has a Hyperlink to a project with current assignments.

2. Copy the code to your Global.mpt file and add a button on the Global Macros ToolBar.

3. Close Microsoft Project and then reopen it to confirm that the system adds a new button, and then test your code again. Module 20 Sample Code.mpp contains the complete code solution.

4. Add a fifth column before the time phased data for the total Work for the assignment.

5. Replace the number 13 (the number of weeks) with a constant that has a meaningful name.

6. Replace all other numbers with constants.

7. Edit the macro to export data for the next 6 months instead of 13 weeks.

Module 21

Create a Cost Margin Report

Learning Objectives

After completing this module, you will be able to:

- Create a macro to produce a Cost Margin report in Microsoft Project
- Create custom field formula with VBA
- Specify the Cost Rate Table used with each assignment

Understanding the Cost Margin Report

A Cost Margin Report calculates the difference between your customer billing rate and your internal cost for each project. Before you create this macro, you must do the following:

1. Reserve two custom task Cost fields (for example Cost1 and Cost2).

2. For each resource in each project, set your customer billing rate as the Standard Rate and set your internal cost as the Cost Rate Table B rate.

 To set the rate for Cost Rate Table B, double-click a resource, select the Costs tab, and then select the tab for Cost Rate Table B.

The Comments for this macro are as follows:

```
Sub CostMarginReport
'This procedure requires exclusive use of Cost1 and Cost2.
'All data in these fields will be over-written.
'Standard Rate is assumed to be Customer rate.
'Rate B for each Resource is assumed to be Internal Rate.

'Create Cost Margin Table for report
'Assign new Table
'Set Rate B for every Assignment
'Copy new Cost to Cost1
'Reset Rate A as rate for every Assignment
'Set Formula for Cost2 to calculate margin
End Sub
```

The code for this macro is as follows:

```
Sub CostMarginReport()
'This procedure requires exclusive use of Cost1 and Cost2.
'All data in these fields will be over-written.
'Standard Rate is Customer rate.
'Rate B for each Resource is Internal Rate.
Dim Tsk As Task
Dim Res As Resource
Dim Assign As Assignment
Const RateA = 0
Const RateB = 1
```

```
   On Error Resume Next

'Create and Apply copy of Task Sheet View
   ViewEditSingle Name:="Cost Margin Report", _
      Create:=True, Screen:=pjTaskSheet, _
      ShowInMenu:=False, HighlightFilter:=False, _
      Table:="Cost", Filter:="All Tasks", _
      Group:="No Group"
   ViewApply "Cost Margin Report"

'Create and Apply Cost Margin Table for report
   TableEdit Name:="Cost Margin Report", _
      TaskTable:=True, Create:=True, _
      OverwriteExisting:=True, FieldName:="ID", _
      Title:="", Width:=6, Align:=2, ShowInMenu:=True, _
      LockFirstColumn:=True, RowHeight:=1, AlignTitle:=1
   TableEdit Name:="Cost Margin Report", _
      TaskTable:=True, NewFieldName:="Indicators", _
      Title:="", Width:=6, Align:=2, _
      LockFirstColumn:=True, RowHeight:=1, AlignTitle:=1
   TableEdit Name:="Cost Margin Report", _
      TaskTable:=True, NewFieldName:="Name", _
      Title:="Task Name", Width:=40, Align:=pjLeft, _
      LockFirstColumn:=True, RowHeight:=1, AlignTitle:=1
   TableEdit Name:="Cost Margin Report", _
      TaskTable:=True, NewFieldName:="Cost", _
      Title:="Customer Cost", Width:=12, Align:=2, _
      LockFirstColumn:=True, RowHeight:=1, AlignTitle:=1
   TableEdit Name:="Cost Margin Report", _
      TaskTable:=True, NewFieldName:="Cost1", _
      Title:="Internal Cost", Width:=12, Align:=2, _
      LockFirstColumn:=True, RowHeight:=1, AlignTitle:=1
   TableEdit Name:="Cost Margin Report", _
      TaskTable:=True, NewFieldName:="Cost2", _
      Title:="Cost Margin", Width:=12, Align:=2, _
      LockFirstColumn:=True, RowHeight:=1, AlignTitle:=1
   TableApply Name:="Cost Margin Report"

'Set Rate B for every Assignment
   For Each Tsk In ActiveProject.Tasks
      If Not Tsk Is Nothing Then
         For Each Assign In Tsk.Assignments
            Assign.CostRateTable = RateB
         Next Assign
```

```
        'Copy new Cost to Cost1
           Tsk.Cost1 = Tsk.Cost
        End If
     Next Tsk

  'Reset Rate A as rate for every Assignment
     For Each Tsk In ActiveProject.Tasks
        If Not Tsk Is Nothing Then
           For Each A In Tsk.Assignments
              Assign.CostRateTable = RateA
           Next Assign
        End If
     Next Tsk

  'Set Formula for Cost2 to calculate margin
     CustomFieldSetFormula FieldID:=pjCustomTaskCost2, _
        Formula:="[Cost]-[Cost1]"
     CustomFieldProperties FieldID:=pjCustomTaskCost1, _
        Attribute:=pjFieldAttributeNone, _
        SummaryCalc:=pjCalcRollupSum, _
        GraphicalIndicators:=False, Required:=False
     CustomFieldProperties FieldID:=pjCustomTaskCost2, _
        Attribute:=pjFieldAttributeFormula, _
        SummaryCalc:=pjCalcRollupSum, _
        GraphicalIndicators:=False, Required:=False
  End Sub
```

After working with timephased data, this macro seems simple! The long first block of code is a recorded macro to create a new Table, complete with column titles and widths. To save space I removed the recorded Date Format because it is optional.

```
  'Set Rate B for every Assignment
     For Each Tsk In ActiveProject.Tasks
        If Not Tsk Is Nothing Then
           For Each A In Tsk.Assignments
              A.CostRateTable = RateB
           Next A

        'Copy new Cost to Cost1
           Tsk.Cost1 = Tsk.Cost
        End If
     Next Tsk
```

The preceding code loops through all tasks, and then loops through each task's assignments. If the task has any assignments, the code sets the Cost Rate Table to B. In Microsoft Project VBA, the number 1 represents Cost Rate Table B and RateB is a constant set equal to 1. After a task gets a new rate for all of its assignments, the code copies the newly calculated cost to the Cost1 field.

```
'Set Formula for Cost2 to calculate margin
   CustomFieldSetFormula FieldID:=pjCustomTaskCost2, _
      Formula:="[Cost]-[Cost1]"
   CustomFieldProperties FieldID:=pjCustomTaskCost2, _
      Attribute:=pjFieldAttributeFormula, _
      SummaryCalc:=pjCalcRollupSum, _
      GraphicalIndicators:=False, Required:=False
```

The preceding code adds the custom formula to calculate the margin and to force each summary task to sum the Total Margin for each of its subtasks. The code edits the Cost2 field to add a rollup sum to summary tasks so you see a summary of customer costs as well as margin costs. Figure 21-1 shows the result in Module 21 Sample Code.mpp.

	ⓘ	Task Name	Internal Cost	Customer Cost	Cost Margin	1 Jan '07 F S S M T W T F S	8 Jan '07 S M T W T F S	15 Jan S M T
0		⊟ Module 22 Sample Code	$6,000.00	$3,200.00	$2,800.00			
1		Task 1	$3,000.00	$1,600.00	$1,400.00	Res[50%]		
2		Task 2	$3,000.00	$1,600.00	$1,400.00		Res[50%]	

Figure 21-1: Cost Margin Report

Figure 21-2 shows the Global Toolbar after you copy the CostMarginCode Module to the Global.mpt file and add the following code to add the *CostMargin* button to the toolbar:

Figure 21-2: Global toolbar

```
   Set MyButton = Nothing
   Set MyButton = MyBar.Controls("CostMargin")
   If MyButton Is Nothing Then
      Set MyButton = MyBar.Controls.Add( _
            Type:=msoControlButton)
      With MyButton
         .Style = msoButtonCaption
         .Caption = "CostMargin"
         .OnAction = "CostMargin"
      End With
   End If
```

This code is the same as I used before, except for a different macro name for the Caption and OnAction properties.

Hands On Exercise

Exercise 21-1

Work with the Cost Margin Report.

1. Add code to handle an internal fixed cost. Use the task Cost3 field to hold the new cost and edit the Margin formula to include it.

2. Name the Module CostMarginCode then copy it to the Global.mpt file.

3. Add a button using the code supplied previously to the Global Macros button.

4. Test the code on different files.

5. Create a version that exports the report to Excel. You can do the Margin calculation with a formula in Excel.

Module 22

Consolidate Multiple Projects

Learning Objectives

After completing this module, you will be able to:

- Write a macro to create a snapshot report from multiple projects
- Understand options for consolidating projects

Creating Consolidated Project Reports

You create consolidated project reports by inserting any number of projects into a master project. To create a master project, open a new blank project in Microsoft Project and then click Insert ➤ Project. When you insert one project into another, you have two options:

1. The default option links each individual project into the master project. If you make changes to the master project, the subproject reflects the changes, and vice versa.

2. The other option allows you to insert individual projects into the master project **without** linking them. Using this option, the system **copies** each subproject into the master project. Changes in either the master project or a subproject are **not** reflected in the other.

To create a master project using the second option, deselect the *Link to project* option in the Insert Project dialog.

Table 22-1 details the advantages and disadvantages associated with using both linked and unlinked master projects.

ADVANTAGES	
Linked Version	**Unlinked Version**
1. The system reflects changes to either the master project or a subproject in the other immediately. 2. You do not need a macro. 3. The report is always current.	1. Because the master project is a copy of all files, this makes a great snapshot for audit purposes. 2. The master project consolidates all resource information across all inserted projects without using a shared resource pool file. 3. There are no links between files, so there is no risk of file corruption.
DISADVANTAGES	
Linked Version	**Unlinked Version**
1. Linked files are very prone to corruption if you move, overwrite, or rename any of them. 2. There is no snapshot or copy of schedules for an audit trail 3. You need to use a separate resource pool file to consolidate the resource data. This increases the risk of corruption by creating even more links.	1. The report does not stay current. 2. The report needs a macro to create a new master project reliably. Since projects are typically updated only once a week, having to run a macro is rarely a problem

Table 22-1: Advantages and Disadvantages of Consolidated project reports

I believe that the advantages of a consolidated resource report make consolidated projects without links the preferred solution. To easily create the consolidated project, you need a macro to use a list of projects and automatically create the consolidated project. The Project Control Center with its existing list of all current projects makes a great start for a consolidated report.

You do not want the consolidated report to mess up your Project Control Center, so the macro must create each report in a new file. Following are the Comments for this macro:

```
Sub ConsolidateProjects
'Set project variable to Project Control Center
'Create new project
'Set project variable to new project
'For each project in the Project Control Center
'Insert into the consolidated report
'Move timescale to today's date and Format in Weeks
'Open Save dialog for user to save the report
End Sub
```

The code to insert each project into a master project is the only code in this example that you have not seen before. The quickest and easiest way to do it is to record a macro while you insert one project into another. Make sure you deselect the *Link to project* option in the Insert Project dialog before you select the file name. The short but very useful macro code is as follows:

```
Sub ConsolidateProjectsReport()
Dim prjPCC As Project
Dim Tsk As Task
Dim Path As String

'Set project variable to Project Control Center
   Set prjPCC = ActiveProject

'Create new project
   FileNew

'For each project in the Project Control Center
'Insert into the consolidated report
   Application.DisplayAlerts = False
   For Each Tsk In prjPCC.Tasks
      If Not Tsk Is Nothing Then    'test for empty tasks
```

```
'Extract File path from the Hyperlink
        Path = Tsk.HyperlinkAddress
        If Left(Path, 1) = "." Then
            Path = prjPCC.Path & "\" & Path
        End If
        Path = Replace(Path, "/", "\")
        Path = Replace(Path, "%20", " ")
        Application.ConsolidateProjects _
            Filenames:=Path, AttachToSources:=False, _
            HideSubTasks:=True
    End If
  Next Tsk
  Application.DisplayAlerts = True

'Move timescale to today's date and format in weeks
  EditGoTo Date:=Date
  Application.TimescaleEdit _
    MajorUnits:=pjTimescaleMonths, _
    MajorLabel:=pjMonth_mmm_yyy, _
    MinorUnits:=pjTimescaleDays, _
    MinorLabel:=pjDayOfMonth_dd, MinorCount:=7

'Open Save dialog for user to save the report
  FileSaveAs
End Sub
```

As I previously mentioned, the only new code is the ConsolidateProjects Method. The first thing to note is that it belongs to the Application object, and therefore only works on the active project. The AttachToSources parameter matches the *Link to project* option in the Insert Project dialog. If you set HideSubTasks to True, the system collapses all subtasks automatically and displays only the project summary tasks for each subproject.

The preceding code provides a useful example for using a Project Object. In the For Each Tsk In prjPCC.Tasks statement, using ActiveProject does not work because the active project is the new consolidated project, and not the Project Control Center project. To access the tasks for each project in the Project Control Center, you need a project variable such as prjPCC.

Because this macro needs to work with the list of projects in the Project Control Center, it is not suitable for copying to the Global.mpt. This macro works better in the Project Control Center.mpp file.

Hands On Exercise

Exercise 22-1

Work with the Consolidated Report macro.

1. Test the code in the Consolidated Project Report macro and make sure it works.

2. Copy the code to your Project Control Center project.

3. Add a button for this macro to the My Macros toolbar in the Project Control Center project.

4. In the report project created by running the macro, apply the Resource Usage view to see the consolidated resource usage across all projects. You may want to rename the resources in some projects so that they all use exactly the same names.

Module 23

Changing Working Time

Learning Objectives

After completing this module, you will be able to:

- Write code to work with Calendars
- Use a tool to set non-working days to calendars in multiple projects

Working with Calendars

In Microsoft Project, calendars are useful tools, but are frequently ignored. I lost count long ago of the number of projects that do not even have a Christmas or New Year's Day break included! This means that most project administrators (anyone responsible for administrating and reporting across multiple projects) have the tedious job of updating many schedules to include all organizational days off plus any other days that are not going to have any project work done.

In Microsoft Project, click Tools ➤ Change Working Time to set any date or range of dates to use Default, Nonworking, or Nondefault working times. While calendars do not affect the calculation of task Durations, they do affect the calculation of Finish dates, so it is important to get them right. Know that there is a point of diminishing returns for the level of detail required in maintaining calendars. Generally, setting individual days to working or non-working is the threshold for diminishing returns and marking the calendar to exclude 2 hours when a resource visits the dentist goes beyond the call of duty.

Designing the Update Calendars Macro

To make updating the Standard calendar in multiple projects easy, you can write a VBA macro (UpdateCalendars macro) to do it for you. The UpdateCalendars macro needs to work with two sets of data: the list of projects in the Project Control Center and the list of calendar changes you want to make to all projects. As you already have macros in the Project Control Center, it makes sense for this macro to live there as well. Now you must find a home for the list of calendar changes. For this macro, we will reuse the text file Class to save the calendar changes in a text file. The text file can have a fixed name and live in the same folder as the Project Control Center for simplicity.

The goals of the calendar update macro are to:

- Update the Standard calendar of all projects in the Project Control Center.

- Allow user entry and retention of dates (minimum 1 day) for calendar edits.

- Allow Default, Nonworking, or Nondefault working settings.

- Delete dates in the past from the calendar changes list.

- Provide an easy to use data entry form for calendar exceptions (changes).

This is a complex macro so to make it simpler; it will be easier for you to build it in four iterations:

1. Create a UserForm to accept data entry for all calendar exceptions.

2. Add the class clsTextFile to save all calendar exceptions to a text file when the form closes. Load the exceptions into the UserForm from the text file when the UserForm opens.

3. Add a macro to loop through all projects in the Project Control Center and execute the changes to the Standard calendar.

4. Add the macro to the My Macros toolbar in the Project Control Center.

By creating four iterations, you break one complex macro into four simpler macros. The following subtopics divide your iterations into simpler goals.

Create the Calendar Exceptions UserForm

This is undoubtedly the most challenging iteration and the riskiest in terms of being able to complete the macro, so it is the best one to tackle first. The form should show a list of all calendar exceptions entered by the user. Each record needs a Start and Finish date plus the working/non-working/default setting, with all records sorted by Start Date for readability. In all likelihood, you won't have many rows to sort, so a simple **compare each record and swap if necessary** sort algorithm works well. Figure 23-1 shows the UserForm in design mode.

Figure 23-1: UpdateCalendars UserForm

The two controls in the lower left corner of the form are for entering a new Start and Finish date, and to edit any record the user selects. To help make data entry easier and more accurate the following features are included:

- There are only 3 valid entries for the Working column (Yes, No, and Default), so there is a *Toggle Working* button that cycles between the three values with No as the default value.

- When you enter a Start date into the Start field (bottom left control) and press the Enter key or click in the Finish Date control, the Start date is populated to the Finish Date box. This makes for quick entry of single day date ranges.

- Whenever the user clicks on an existing record, the selected record's Start and Finish dates populate the entry fields at the bottom of the UserForm. Clicking the *Update* button then updates the selected record with any new values.

Figure 23-2 shows the same form as in Figure 23-1 but active with a single calendar exception added.

Figure 23-2: UserForm in Action

Table 23-1 details all the controls, their type and the name given them in the sample code.

Control Type	Control Name	Use
ListBox	NonWorkingDays	Lists all calendar exceptions
TextBox	StartDate	Editing box to hold Start date for new or edited row
TextBox	FinishDate	Editing box to hold Finish date for new or edited row
CommandButton	Quit	Closes the Form
CommandButton	ToggleWorking	Toggles through all Working values
CommandButton	UpdateProjects	Calls the UpdatePCCCalendars routine to update all projects in the Project Control Center with all exceptions
CommandButton	DeleteException	Deletes the select row from the ListBox
CommandButton	AddException	Adds a row to the ListBox
CommandButton	Update	Updates values for selected row using values in the editing boxes

Table 23-1: Calendar Exceptions UserForm Controls

The most important control in this UserForm is the NonWorkingDays ListBox. You can add rows to ListBox controls using their AddItem method. When you want to add a number of rows with multiple column Lists, using the List property and an array is easier. Whenever I use NonWorkingDays in the following code, I am referring to the ListBox with that name.

Give all controls and buttons meaningful names as suggested by their captions or function. Table 23-1 provides the names used in the code that follows. There is a lot of code to make all these features work, but by taking the code one small block at a time there is nothing difficult. Following is the code:

```
Option Explicit

Private DataChanged As Boolean
Private ListCount As Long
Private Updating As Boolean

Private Sub UserForm_Initialize()
Dim DataArray(100, 3) As Variant
Dim Row As Long
   DataArray(0, 0) = "Dec 25 2007"
   DataArray(0, 1) = "Dec 26 2007"
   DataArray(0, 2) = "No"
   ListCount = 1
   NonWorkingDays.ColumnHeads = False
   NonWorkingDays.List() = DataArray
   NonWorkingDays.ColumnCount = 3
   SortList
End Sub

Private Sub NonWorkingDays_Click()
   If Not Updating Then
      StartDate = NonWorkingDays.List( _
            NonWorkingDays.ListIndex, 0)
      FinishDate = NonWorkingDays.List( _
            NonWorkingDays.ListIndex, 1)
   End If
End Sub

Private Sub Quit_Click()
   frmNonWorkingDays.Hide
End Sub

Private Sub StartDate_AfterUpdate()
   If IsDate(StartDate) Then
      FinishDate = StartDate
   End If
End Sub

Private Sub ToggleWorking_Click()
   If NonWorkingDays.ListIndex >= 0 Then
      Select Case NonWorkingDays.List( _
            NonWorkingDays.ListIndex, 2)
         Case "No"
            NonWorkingDays.List( _
               NonWorkingDays.ListIndex, 2) = "Yes"
```

```
            Case "Yes"
               NonWorkingDays.List( _
                  NonWorkingDays.ListIndex, 2) = "Default"
            Case "Default"
               NonWorkingDays.List( _
                  NonWorkingDays.ListIndex, 2) = "No"
         End Select
         DataChanged = True
      End If
End Sub

Private Sub Update_Click()
   Updating = True
   NonWorkingDays.List( _
      NonWorkingDays.ListIndex, 0) = _
      Format(CDate(StartDate), "mmm d yyyy")
   NonWorkingDays.List(NonWorkingDays.ListIndex, 1) = _
      Format(CDate(FinishDate), "mmm d yyyy")
   DataChanged = True
   SortList
   Updating = False
End Sub

Private Sub UpdateProjects_Click()
   'UpdatePCCCalendars
End Sub

Private Sub AddException_Click()
   Updating = True
   NonWorkingDays.List(ListCount, 0) = _
      Format(CDate(StartDate), "mmm d yyyy")
   NonWorkingDays.List(ListCount, 1) = _
      Format(CDate(FinishDate), "mmm d yyyy")
   NonWorkingDays.List(ListCount, 2) = "No"
   ListCount = ListCount + 1
   DataChanged = True
   SortList
   Updating = False
End Sub

Private Sub DeleteException_Click()
   NonWorkingDays.RemoveItem NonWorkingDays.ListIndex
   ListCount = ListCount - 1
   DataChanged = True
End Sub
```

```
Sub SortList()
'Sort List based on first column
Dim Ind1 As Long
Dim Ind2 As Long
Dim SwapMade As Boolean
Dim strDate1 As String, strDate2 As String
Dim StartDate As Date, FinishDate As Date, Reset As String
   If ListCount >= 2 Then
      Do
         SwapMade = False
         For Ind1 = 0 To ListCount - 2
            Ind2 = Ind1 + 1
            strDate1 = NonWorkingDays.List(Ind1, 0)
            strDate2 = NonWorkingDays.List(Ind2, 0)
            If IsDate((strDate1)) And _
                   (CDate(strDate2)) Then
               If CDate(strDate1) > _
                      CDate(strDate2) Then
                  'Copy first row
                  StartDate = _
                     NonWorkingDays.List(Ind1, 0)
                  FinishDate = NonWorkingDays. _
                           List(Ind1, 1)
                  Reset = NonWorkingDays.List( _
                              Ind1, 2)

                  'Move second row to 1st
                  NonWorkingDays.List(Ind1, 0) = _
                     NonWorkingDays.List(Ind2, 0)
                  NonWorkingDays.List(Ind1, 1) = _
                     NonWorkingDays.List(Ind2, 1)
                  NonWorkingDays.List(Ind1, 2) = _
                     NonWorkingDays.List(Ind2, 2)

                  'Re-save first row in second row
                  NonWorkingDays.List(Ind2, 0) = _
                     Format(StartDate, "mmm d yyyy")
                  NonWorkingDays.List(Ind2, 1) = _
                     Format(FinishDate, _
                            "mmm d yyyy")
                  NonWorkingDays.List(Ind2, 2) _
                     = Reset
                  SwapMade = True
               End If
            End If
```

```
        Next Ind1
    Loop Until SwapMade = False
  End If
End Sub


Private Sub UserForm_Terminate()
'Remove any dates that finish earlier than today
'Save data if any changes have been made
Dim Txt As New clsTextFile
Dim Line As Long
  For Line = 0 To ListCount - 1
    If IsDate(NonWorkingDays.List(Line, 1)) Then
      If CDate(NonWorkingDays.List(Line, 1)) _
                        < Date Then
        NonWorkingDays.RemoveItem Line
        ListCount = ListCount - 1
        DataChanged = True
      End If
    End If
  Next Line
End Sub
```

The above code is for frmNonWorkingDays1 in the Module 23 Sample Code Iteration1.mpp file. Code for iteration 2 is in UserForm frmNonWorkingDays Iteration2 and so on.

Note that the code is in 10 procedures and that each one on its own is not difficult. I will explain each procedure in turn.

```
Private Sub UserForm_Initialize()
Dim DataArray(100, 2) As String
Dim Row As Long
  DataArray(0, 0) = "Dec 25 2007"
  DataArray(0, 1) = "Dec 26 2007"
  DataArray(0, 2) = "No"
  ListCount=1
  NonWorkingDays.ColumnHeads = False
  NonWorkingDays.ColumnCount = 3
  NonWorkingDays.List() = DataArray
  SortList
End Sub
```

UserForm_Initialize runs when you first display the UserForm with the .show method. Use it to initialize controls. In Iteration 2 you add code to this procedure to read in existing calendar exceptions from a text file and display them in the List box.

DataArray is an array of strings with 3 columns and 101 rows. The index for each row and column starts at 0 so the declaration DataArray(100,2) does have 3 columns as the first column in the first row is accessed using DataArray(0,0). For initial testing purposes, the code adds only one row of data with entries for all three columns.

NonWorkingDays.List() = DataArray is the statement that sets the ListBox to have the same data displayed as entered into the Array. ListCount is a variable that keeps track of the number of rows of data. ListCount is especially important when you add code to save and read from text files.

```
Private Sub NonWorkingDays_Click()
   If Not Updating Then
      StartDate = NonWorkingDays.List( _
              NonWorkingDays.ListIndex, 0)
      FinishDate = NonWorkingDays.List( _
              NonWorkingDays.ListIndex, 1)
   End If
End Sub
```

Click on the ListBox to trigger this event. The code copies the data in the selected row into the two edit boxes at the bottom of the UserForm so the user can edit the dates. You cannot edit data directly in a ListBox.

```
Private Sub ExitForm_Click()
   frmNonWorkingDays.Hide
End Sub

Private Sub StartDate_AfterUpdate()
   If IsDate(StartDate) Then
      FinishDate = StartDate
   End If
End Sub
```

Click the *Exit* button to trigger the Quit_Click event and move your cursor away from the StartDate control by clicking somewhere else with the mouse or by pressing the Tab key to trigger the StartDate_AfterUpdate event. The Exit command button cannot be named Exit because Exit is a reserved word in VBA, hence the name ExitForm.

The StartDate_AfterUpdate event copies the Start date to the Finish date, but only if you enter a valid date. IsDate is a VBA function that tests the variant or string value passed to verify that it holds a valid date. If the date is valid, IsDate returns True and only then does the start date get copied to the Finish date. The idea is to make data entry a little quicker and easier. If the date range is for one day only, then no Finish date is required. If the date range is more than a day, the Finish date needs only editing. Either way you make the user's work a little bit easier.

```
Private Sub ToggleWorking_Click()
   If NonWorkingDays.ListIndex >= 0 Then
      Select Case NonWorkingDays.List( _
          NonWorkingDays.ListIndex, 2)
      Case "No"
         NonWorkingDays.List( _
            NonWorkingDays.ListIndex, 2) = "Yes"
      Case "Yes"
         NonWorkingDays.List( _
            NonWorkingDays.ListIndex, 2) = "Default"
      Case "Default"
         NonWorkingDays.List( _
            NonWorkingDays.ListIndex, 2) = "No"
      End Select
      DataChanged = True
   End If
End Sub
```

Click the *Toggle* command button to trigger the ToggleWorking_Click event. In the interest of data accuracy, this event cycles through the three possible values of No, Yes, and Default to make sure there are no typing errors or entry of a different value again.

NonWorkingDays.List(NonWorkingDays.ListIndex, 2) accesses the Working column of the ListBox for the currently selected row. List is a property that returns all data for the ListBox. NonWorkingDays.ListIndex returns the row number of the currently selected row (the top row is row zero). Number 2 is the third column of the row as the first column is column zero, and therefore the Working column. The code tests the current value then cycles through all three valid options in turn.

When the user edits the data, you must set the DataChanged flag to be sure that the edit is saved when the UserForm terminates.

```
Private Sub Update_Click()
   Updating = True
   NonWorkingDays.List(NonWorkingDays.ListIndex, 0) = _
      Format(CDate(StartDate), "mmm d yyyy")
   NonWorkingDays.List(NonWorkingDays.ListIndex, 1) = _
      Format(CDate(FinishDate), "mmm d yyyy")
   DataChanged = True
   SortList
   Updating = False
End Sub
```

Click the *Update* command button to trigger the Update_Click event. The statement most difficult to understand is Updating = True. In VBA UserForms, code in some events such as _Click or _Update can trigger other events in turn, such as other click or update events. Triggering more than one event can produce unexpected and undesirable results. For example, when you update the StartDate TextBox the Click event for the ListBox can also fire. By setting a flag (in this case Updating) to True and testing for it in other events and then only doing anything if the Updating Flag is False, you make sure that only one event's code is run at one time.

Again, the Format function formats the date into an international format that has a 3 character month name to avoid any chance of confusion between international d/m and m/d formats.

The DataChanged flag is set whenever a row of data is added or edited. That lets the _Terminate event know that it needs to re-save all data to the text file.

SortList is a call to the SortList procedure to sort the list of calendar exceptions by Start date. This makes the list easier to read and to check all relevant dates are included in the list.

```
Private Sub UpdateProjects_Click()
   'UpdatePCCCalendars
End Sub
```

Click the *UpdateProjects* command button to call the UpdateProjects_Click event. The code calls the UpdatePCCCalendars procedure to open all projects in the Project Control Center project to update their Standard calendar. Do not think about the UpdateProjects code for now, you will work on it in the third Iteration. In fact, notice that the call to UpdatePCCCalendars currently has a quote mark in front of it. This means it is a comment and UpdatePCCCalendars is therefore a placeholder waiting for you to develop the procedure.

```
Private Sub AddException_Click()
   Updating = True
   NonWorkingDays.List(ListCount, 0) = _
      Format(CDate(StartDate), "mmm d yyyy")
   NonWorkingDays.List(ListCount, 1) = _
      Format(CDate(FinishDate), "mmm d yyyy")
   NonWorkingDays.List(ListCount, 2) = "No"
   ListCount = ListCount + 1
   DataChanged = True
   SortList
   Updating = False
End Sub

Private Sub DeleteException_Click()
   NonWorkingDays.RemoveItem NonWorkingDays.ListIndex
   ListCount = ListCount - 1
   DataChanged = True
End Sub
```

AddException_Click and DeleteException_Click add or remove a row of data in the ListBox. AddException sets the Updating flag again to prevent any other event from interrupting it. Then it uses code very similar to the _Initialize event to add a row of data from the Edit boxes. For international date compatibility, use a three-character month for the Start and Finish dates.

In both events, the ListCount variable increments or decrements to reflect the new number of rows of data and the DataChanged flag is set to True to make sure the text file gets updated when the UserForm closes.

The next procedure is SortList. Rather than explain this code line by line, I explain what it has to accomplish instead. The code itself is nothing new. SortList has to perform the following steps:

1. Sort rows only if the number of rows is greater than or equal to two; there is no need to sort a list of one row!

2. Use a simple swap-two-list-rows-if-needed-until-the-list-is-sorted algorithm. Set the SwapMade flag to False before the loop starts. Set the SwapMade flag to True whenever two values are swapped. If after the loop has finished SwapMade is True, then the sort probably has not finished so loop again. If SwapMade is still False after looping through all rows, then the sort is complete and SortList can exit.

3. For each pair of StartDate values (for two consecutive rows) in the ListBox, if there are two valid Start dates compare their values and swap them if the second (lower) one is less than the first. If a swap is done, set the SwapMade flag to True to make sure looping continues until no swaps are made and the sort is therefore complete.

```
Private Sub UserForm_Terminate()
'Remove any dates that finish earlier than today
'Save data if any changes have been made
Dim Line As Long
    For Line = 0 To ListCount - 1
        If IsDate(NonWorkingDays.List(Line, 1)) Then
            If CDate(NonWorkingDays.List(Line, 1))<Date Then
                NonWorkingDays.RemoveItem Line
                ListCount = ListCount - 1
                DataChanged = True
            End If
        End If
    Next Line
End Sub
```

You have arrived at the last procedure. Well done! Close the UserForm by clicking the **X** button in the top right corner of the UserForm or close the Project with the UserForm in to trigger the UserForm_Terminate event. Clicking the *Exit* command button simply hides the UserForm and does not trigger the UserForm_Terminate event. Until you add the save to text file code, this event just deletes all old dates. The code used is simply a variation of previous code; there is nothing new in it. If you have problems understanding the code, single step through it and test each variable after each step. If all else fails, send me an email!

With all this working code you now have a working UserForm to enter and edit calendar exceptions. Iteration 2 adds the TextFile class so all calendar exceptions are read and saved to a text file.

Hands On Exercise

Exercise 23-1

Learn to use the Update Calendars macro.

1. Open the file Module 23 Sample Code Iteration1.mpp

2. Select Debug ➤ Compile. If no error messages appear your code has compiled correctly on your system. If errors do appear, see if you can resolve them, there should only be minor differences between systems.

3. Go to the first line of each procedure and press the F5 function key to add a breakpoint.

4. Display the UserForm by double-clicking it in Project Explorer.

5. Press the F5 function key to run the form. Use the different buttons and every time you hit a breakpoint, single step through your code making sure you understand what each line of code does.

6. Once you are happy you understand each procedure, remove the breakpoint for it by clicking on it then pressing the F9 function key again.

Add the Text Class to Store Calendar Exceptions

A text file is a useful place to save data such as calendar exceptions. Storing the data in the registry quickly becomes unwieldy and requires a lot of code specific to the data saved. Once written, a Text class is quickly reusable, and contains code that is easy to understand and maintain.

The Text class is the same one you created in Module 5 and updated in Module 19 to add write to text file functionality. To use it in another macro, use the Project Explorer in the Visual Basic Editor (VBE) to copy the clsTextFile Class Module from the Sample Module 20 file, to your file. To copy a Module, use your mouse to drag it while holding down the Ctrl key.

 TIP: Dragging data while holding the Ctrl key copies the selected file in Windows Explorer and selected text in all Office applications.

To add the text file as a data storage location, the steps you must perform are as follows:

1. Copy the Class clsTextFile to your project.

2. Add code in the UserForm_Initialize event to replace the setup of the DataArray with code to read the text file into the DataArray.

3. Add Code to the UserForm_Terminate event to save all data (after old exceptions have been deleted) to the text file, but only if the DataChanged flag is True.

For the Calendar Exceptions macro, you now need to replace the DataArray code used to test the UserForm with calls to the Text class and add calls to the text class to save all data in the Terminate event when needed. This only affects the UserForm_Initialize procedure and the UserForm_Terminate procedures that now look like the following code:

```
Private Sub UserForm_Initialize()
Dim DataArray(100, 3) As Variant
Dim Row As Long
Dim Txt As New clsTextFile
    Txt.FilePath = ActiveProject.Path _
            & "\NonWorking Dates.txt"
    Txt.FileOpenRead
    Do Until Txt.ISLastWord
        DataArray(ListCount, 0) = Txt.NextWord
        DataArray(ListCount, 1) = Txt.NextWord
        DataArray(ListCount, 2) = Txt.NextWord
        ListCount = ListCount + 1
    Loop
    Txt.FileClose
    NonWorkingDays.ColumnHeads = False
    NonWorkingDays.List() = DataArray
    NonWorkingDays.ColumnCount = 3
    SortList
End Sub
```

The use of the Text class is exactly as described in Module 5. As you are saving the data in a .txt file, any other program can easily update it if you wish. You do need to make sure, however, that each row in the text file has a valid Start date, Finish date and working status value of Yes or No.

Txt.FilePath = ActiveProject.Path & "\NonWorking Dates.txt" uses the path of the active project and the given file name to build a full path. When you first run the macro, the file name does not exist. The Text class handles this and simply sets the IsLastWord flag so the UserForm opens without fuss and displays an empty ListBox.

```
Private Sub UserForm_Terminate()
'Remove any dates that finish earlier than today
'Save data if any changes have been made
Dim Txt As New clsTextFile
Dim Ind As Long
    'Delete dates older than today
    For Ind = 0 To ListCount - 1
        If IsDate(NonWorkingDays.List(Ind, 1)) Then
            If CDate(NonWorkingDays.List(Ind, 1)) _
                            < Date Then
                NonWorkingDays.RemoveItem Ind
                ListCount = ListCount - 1
                DataChanged = True
            End If
        End If
    Next Ind

    'If any data has changed, save all data to the text file
again
    If DataChanged Then
        Txt.FilePath = ActiveProject.Path & _
                "\NonWorking Dates.txt"
        Txt.FileOpenWrite
        For Ind = 0 To ListCount - 1
            Txt.WriteLine NonWorkingDays.List(Ind, 0) _
                & "," & NonWorkingDays.List(Ind, 1) & "," _
                & NonWorkingDays.List(Ind, 2)
        Next Ind
        Txt.FileClose
    End If
End Sub
```

The first part of the _Terminate event is the same as previously written. The second block of code is new. Because the Txt class variable now exists for this procedure, its FilePath property needs to be set again. When the file is opened for write using the FileOpenWrite method, the file is created if it does not exist and over-written if it does.

The WriteLine method accepts a string created out of all three columns in the ListBox. The For Ind loop makes sure every row gets exported to the text file.

That is it! I hope you noticed that the code is once again made up of pieces of code you have already used. Increasingly, you will find that you develop macros from the same bits of code and simply bolt them together in different ways. When you get to this realization and achieve the ability to do it, you have crossed the watershed for learning Project VBA.

321

Hands On Exercise

Exercise 23-2

Learn more about the update calendars macro.

1. Open the file Module 23 Sample Code Iteration2.mpp.

2. Select Debug ➤ Compile.

3. Add a breakpoint to the different procedures in the text Class.

4. Run the UserForm again.

5. Single step through each procedure in the text class.

6. Once you understand what each procedure does, remove its breakpoint.

Apply Calendar Changes to All Projects

This iteration does the calendar editing to all projects in the Project Control Center. The code for the UpdatePCCCalendars procedure is:

```
Sub UpdatePCCCalendars()
Dim prjPCC As Project
Dim prj As Project
Dim Tsk As Task
Dim Path As String
Dim StartDate As Date, FinishDate As Date
Dim Working As String
Dim ListIndex As Long
'Set project variable to Project Control Center
   Set prjPCC = ActiveProject

   For Each Tsk In prjPCC.Tasks
      If Not Tsk Is Nothing Then
      'test for empty tasks

      'Extract File path from the Hyperlink and open it
         Path = Tsk.HyperlinkAddress
         If Left(Path, 1) = "." Then
            Path = prjPCC.Path & "\" & Path
         End If
         Path = Replace(Path, "/", "\")
         Path = Replace(Path, "%20", " ")

         FileOpen Name:=Path, ReadOnly:=False, _
            noAuto:=True, openpool:=pjDoNotOpenPool
         Set prj = ActiveProject

         'Loop through all rows in the ListBox
         'Set Calendar period to working status
         Do
            If frmNonWorkingDays1.NonWorkingDays. _
                 List(ListIndex, 0) = "" Then
               Exit Do
            End If
            StartDate = CDate(frmNonWorkingDays1 _
               .NonWorkingDays.List(ListIndex, 0))
            FinishDate = CDate(frmNonWorkingDays1 _
               .NonWorkingDays. List(ListIndex, 1))
            Working = frmNonWorkingDays1. _
               NonWorkingDays.List(ListIndex, 2)
```

```
            Select Case Working
               Case "No"
                  prj.BaseCalendars("Standard") _
                     .Period(StartDate, _
                     FinishDate).Working = False
               Case "Yes"
                  prj.BaseCalendars("Standard") _
                     .Period(StartDate, _
                      FinishDate).Working = True
               Case "Default"
                  prj.BaseCalendars("Standard") _
                     .Period(StartDate, _
                     FinishDate).Default
            End Select
            ListIndex = ListIndex + 1
         Loop
         FileClose pjSave
      End If
   Next Tsk
End Sub
```

Once again all this code is very similar to previous procedures on which we worked. What the UpdatePCCCalendars procedure has to do is:

1. Set a project variable to point to the Project Control Center project. This allows you to access its tasks while other projects are open.

2. Loop through all Project Control Center tasks.

3. Extract the file path from the Hyperlink and open the project that the Hyperlink points to.

4. For each row in the ListBox on the UserForm update the calendar of the active project. The calendar period can be set to Working, Nonworking, or Default.

5. Close and save the project.

I explained all the code in this procedure in earlier sections and modules. All that remains is for you to remove the single quote from the UpdateProjects_Click event so that UpdatePCCCalendars gets called. The event should now look like the following:

```
Private Sub UpdateProjects_Click()
   UpdatePCCCalendars
End Sub
```

Hands On Exercise

Exercise 23-3

Learn more about the Update Calendars macro.

1. Open the file Module 23 Sample Code Iteration3.mpp.

2. Select Debug ➤ Compile.

3. Add a breakpoint to the start of the UpdatePCCCalendars procedure.

4. Run the UserForm again.

5. Single step through the procedure until you are confident that you understand how it works.

Add the Macro to the Project Control Center Toolbar

The last Iteration is very simple, duplicate code to add a command button to the Project Control Center Toolbar to display the UserForm NonWorkingDays to complete the code. You can put the macro called to display the UserForm after Iteration 3 in the UpdateStandardCalendar Module. It should look like:

```
Public Sub ShowFrmNonWorkingDays()
    frmNonWorkingDays.Show
End Sub
```

The extra code in the GlobalToolbar module in the Global.mpt file should be as follows:

```
Set MyButton = Nothing
Set MyButton = MyBar.Controls("UpdateCalendars")
If MyButton Is Nothing Then
    Set MyButton = MyBar.Controls.Add( _
                   Type:=msoControlButton)
    With MyButton
        .Style = msoButtonCaption
        .Caption = "UpdateCalendars"
        .OnAction = "ShowFrmNonWorkingDays"
    End With
End If
```

Make sure you save all modules before testing your code.

Hands On Exercise

Exercise 23-4

Learn more about the Update Calendars macro.

1. Edit the code so that only selected projects in the Project Control Center get updated. To do this you need to use the Application.ActiveSelection.Tasks property to return all selected tasks so you can loop through them.

2. Design then build a macro to update resource calendars as well. You will need to add an extra column to the ListBox for the calendar name (resource or Base calendar) and then have a text file for each calendar or save the calendar name with each exception.

Module 24

Display Predecessor and Successor Tasks

Learning Objectives

After completing this module, you will be able to:

- Work with task links in Project VBA
- Use a macro to filter for all tasks preceding or succeeding a selected task
- Understand and develop recursive code

Working with Task Dependencies

Microsoft Project lets you create links between tasks so the software can calculate task Start and Finish dates based on these links. This is the preferred way to manage dependencies between tasks rather than the alternative, which is to enter dates for these tasks. Entering Constraints leads to large amounts of manual updating and, inevitably, inaccurate schedules when the manual updating gets left undone.

Schedulers often need to review all preceding and succeeding tasks for a particular task so they can review what is driving, or being driven by, a particular task. The macro in this Module works with the currently selected task and displays all its preceding and succeeding tasks based on existing Links. I call the macro LinkedTasks, which is useful for any schedule, and best suited to live in the Global.mpt file.

Designing the LinkedTasks Macro

The LinkedTasks macro performs all of the following:

- Requires the user to select the task on which to report. This task can be in any active project file, so it works using the ActiveCell.Task object.

- Expands all summary tasks to display all subtasks so link lines are visible in the Gantt Chart.

- Needs code to clear the Flag20 custom field then set Flag20 to Yes against every task that precedes or succeeds the originally selected task.

- If a linked-to task is a Summary Task, then it sets Flag20 to Yes for all subtasks as well

- Creates a Filter called Flag20 to display only tasks with Flag20 = Yes

- Applies the Filter Flag20 to show only preceding and succeeding tasks, which is the desired outcome

The difficulty in this macro is that you must work not only with immediate predecessors and successors of the selected task, but also with all of the predecessor's predecessors and all of the successor's successors, until your macro reaches the end of a chain of predecessor and successor tasks. To help make this problem clearer, I first walk through the logic needed to manually find all successors. These steps are as follows:

1. From the selected task, find the first successor.

2. Flag the successor and then find the first successor to the first successor.

3. Repeat the procedure to find the first successor to the first successor of the first successor and so on until reaching a task with no successors.

4. Find the second successor of the selected task.

5. Flag the successor and then find the first successor of the second successor.

6. Find the first successor of the first successor of the second successor and so on until reaching a task with no successors.

Besides ending up with a headache from trying to sort out what tasks have already been included and which have not, the solution rapidly becomes too complex. However, there is a surprisingly simple solution. If you select any one task, for all successors do the following:

1. Set its Flag20 field to Yes (provided you have not already tested this task).

2. Loop through all its successors and process them.

3. Set Flag20 for all its subtasks to Yes if the current task is a summary task.

So, the simplest solution is to repeat these three steps for every successor. Thankfully, VBA provides a feature called **recursive programming** that does exactly this. VBA allows you to call a routine and then let the routine call itself. The same code runs as many times as necessary using only a small amount of extra memory overhead for each procedure call. We can now state the solution as the following steps:

1. Set its Flag20 field to Yes (provided you have not already tested this task).

2. Call the successors procedure again using the task Id of the successor task if a successor for the current task exists.

3. Set Flag20 for all its subtasks to Yes if the current task is a Summary Task.

Your code now happily loops through all successors of all successors until there are no more successors to find. Add a similar procedure to work instead with predecessors and you have your solution. The solution therefore requires three procedures:

1. A main LinkedTasks procedure that does the following:

   - Shows the All Tasks filter and expands all Summary Tasks

   - Clears Flag20 for all tasks

   - Runs the first iteration of the DepPred and DepSucc procedures

   - Creates and then applies the Flag20 Filter

   - Reselects the original task

2. A DepPred procedure to process all predecessors for the original task. It must accept a Task Object parameter to process. It, in turn, passes a predecessor's Task Object when it next calls itself.

3. A DepSucc procedure to process all successors for the original task. It must accept a Task Object parameter to process. It, in turn, passes a successor's Task Object when it next calls itself.

The TaskDependency Object is critical to the LinkTasks macro.

 Note that the TaskDependency Object became available in Project 2000, so this macro does not work in Project 98.

Understanding the TaskDependency Object

In Microsoft Project, all tasks have a TaskDependencies collection. The TaskDependencies collection holds one TaskDependency Object for every link **To** the task and **From** the task. In other words, if you have three tasks (Task1, Task2 and Task3) linked together in a chain, the middle task, Task2, has two links, so two TaskDependency Objects. Task 1 and Task3 have one TaskDependency object each.

Each TaskDependency Object has two Methods: Add and Delete. With these Methods you can add and delete links between tasks. For our LinkedTasks macro, the TaskDependency Properties are more useful than the aforementioned methods. The key properties are:

- **From** Property that returns a Task Object of the preceding task

- **To** Property that returns a Task Object of the succeeding task

One thing you must keep in mind is that the TaskDependencies collection includes all predecessors and successors. To distinguish between the predecessor and successor, test the ID of the returned **From** and **To** Task Objects.

In Figure 24-1, examine the first TaskDependency for Task2. For the first TaskDependency the From task is Task1 and the To task is Task2. Therefore, when looking at the dependencies for Task2, if the **To** task ID is the same as the Task2 ID then the dependency is a predecessor. Similarly, if the **From** task ID is the same as the Task2 ID then we know that the dependency is a successor. With this understanding, you can quickly determine whether a TaskDependency is a predecessor or successor.

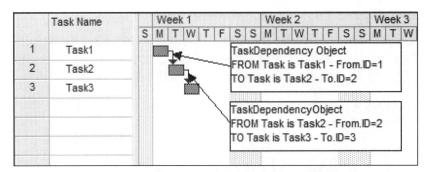

**Figure 24-1: TaskDependency Objects
with their From and To Properties**

Understanding the TaskLinks Macro Code

The Module 24 Sample Code.mpp file contains the necessary code ready for
you to copy to your Global.mpt file. The code is as follows:

```
Option Explicit
'This macro goes up all predecessors and down all successors
'to the active task and sets Flag20 for each one.
'The macro creates a filter for Flag20 to display only flagged
'tasks.

Sub LinkedTasks()
Dim TD As TaskDependency
Dim Tsk As Task
   On Error Resume Next
   Set Tsk = ActiveCell.Task
   If Tsk Is Nothing Then
      MsgBox "Cursor must be one a valid task", _
         vbCritical
      End
   ElseIf Tsk.TaskDependencies.Count = 0 Then
      MsgBox "There are no Dependencies to show", _
         vbInformation
      End
   End If
   FilterApply Name:="All Tasks"
   Application.OutlineShowAllTasks
   SelectAll
   SetTaskField Field:="Flag20", Value:="No", _
      AllSelectedTasks:=True
   EditGoTo Tsk.ID
```

```
      DepPred Tsk         'Detect all predecessors
      Tsk.Flag20 = False   'Force Successors to be tested
      DepSucc Tsk         'Detect all successors

     'Create then apply Filter. Reset Flag20 field to No
     FilterEdit Name:="Flag20", Create:=True, _
        OverwriteExisting:=True, TaskFilter:=True, _
        FieldName:="Flag20", Test:="Equals", _
        Value:="Yes", ShowSummaryTasks:=True
     FilterApply Name:="Flag20"
     EditGoTo Tsk.ID
     SelectRow
End Sub

Sub DepPred(Tsk As Task)
Dim Dep As TaskDependency
Dim SumT As Task
   If Tsk.Flag20 = False Then
      Tsk.Flag20 = True
      For Each Dep In Tsk.TaskDependencies
         If Dep.From.ID <> Tsk.ID Then
            DepPred Dep.From
         End If
      Next

      'Include any links to parent summary task
      If Tsk.OutlineLevel >= 2 Then
         Set SumT = Tsk.OutlineParent
         SumT.Flag20 = True
         For Each Dep In SumT.TaskDependencies
            If (Dep.From.ID <> SumT.ID) Then
               DepPred Dep.From
            End If
         Next
      End If
   End If
End Sub

Sub DepSucc(Tsk As Task)
Dim Dep As TaskDependency
Dim subT As Task
   If Tsk.Flag20 = False Then
      Tsk.Flag20 = True
      For Each Dep In Tsk.TaskDependencies
         If (Dep.To.ID <> Tsk.ID) Then
            DepSucc Dep.To
```

```
            End If
        Next

    'Include any links to sub tasks if this
    'task is a summary task
       If Tsk.Summary = True Then
          For Each subT In Tsk.OutlineChildren
             For Each Dep In subT.TaskDependencies
                If (Dep.To.ID <> subT.ID) Then
                   subT.Flag20 = True
                   DepSucc Dep.To
                End If
             Next
          Next
       End If

       'Test for successors to Summary Task of T
       If Tsk.OutlineLevel >= 2 Then
          DepSucc Tsk.OutlineParent
       End If
    End If
End Sub
```

Let's take a closer look at the code. Most of it is simple, but the recursive code needs careful thought.

```
Sub LinkedTasks()
Dim TD As TaskDependency
Dim Tsk As Task
   On Error Resume Next
   Set Tsk = ActiveCell.Task
   If Tsk Is Nothing Then
      MsgBox "Cursor must be on a valid task", vbCritical
      End
   ElseIf Tsk.TaskDependencies.Count = 0 Then
      MsgBox "There are no Dependencies to show", _
         vbInformation
      End
   End If
   FilterApply Name:="All Tasks"
   Application.OutlineShowAllTasks
   SelectAll
   SetTaskField Field:="Flag20", Value:="No", _
      AllSelectedTasks:=True
   EditGoTo Tsk.ID
```

First, the code confirms the validity of the active task and ends the macro if the task is blank or there are no Dependencies. Next, it shows all tasks and removes any filter by selecting the All Tasks filter. Finally, the start up block of code needs to reset all Flag20 values to No before once again selecting the original task.

```
DepPred Tsk            'Detect all predecessors
Tsk.Flag20 = False     'Force Successors to be tested
DepSucc Tsk            'Detect all successors
```

Tsk is a Task Object variable pointing to the original task. The procedure successively calls DepPred and then DepSucc to find all predecessors and successors of the passed Task Object Tsk. Between calling DepPred and calling DepSucc it resets the values for Flag20, otherwise DepSucc sees Task Tsk as previously tested because DepPred previously set Flag20 = True. Without resetting the values between the two calls, DepSucc won't look for all Successors.

```
'Create then apply Filter. Reset Flag20 field to No
FilterEdit Name:="Flag20", Create:=True, _
   OverwriteExisting:=True, TaskFilter:=True, _
   FieldName:="Flag20", Test:="Equals", _
   Value:="Yes", ShowSummaryTasks:=True
FilterApply Name:="Flag20"
EditGoTo Tsk.ID
SelectRow
```

To guarantee that the procedures do not crash on false assumptions that a Flag20 Filter exists and works correctly, the code creates or re-creates a Flag20 filter to only display tasks and summary tasks with Flag20 set to Yes.

The code applies the newly created Filter then selects the original task, by selecting the entire task row making the original task obvious to the user in the display.

 Tip: To show all tasks again, use the keyboard shortcut **F3** to apply the All Tasks filter. Applying the Flag20 Filter again shows all predecessors and Successors of the original task until you re-run the macro using another task or until the Flag20 field is changed by other means.

```
Sub DepPred(T As Task)
Dim Dep As TaskDependency
Static subT As Task
   If Tsk.Flag20 = False Then
      Tsk.Flag20 = True
      For Each Dep In Tsk.TaskDependencies
         If Dep.From.ID <> Tsk.ID Then
            DepPred Dep.From
         End If
      Next
```

Different tasks may be linked via numerous link paths, so to significantly speed the macro up for large schedules, test Flag20 and do nothing if the task has already been processed (Flag20=True).

Set Flag20 to True to include the current task in the result and then test for any additional predecessors and call DepPred again if it finds additional predecessors. This recursive feature calls DepPred once for every predecessor without requiring you to keep track of what is happening.

```
   'Include any links to parent summary task
   If Tsk.OutlineLevel >= 2 Then
      Set SumT = Tsk.OutlineParent
      SumT.Flag20 = True
      For Each Dep In SumT.TaskDependencies
         If (Dep.From.ID <> SumT.ID) Then
            DepPred Dep.From
         End If
      Next
   End If
```

If the current task is a subtask (OutlineLevel>=2) then check to see if the parent summary task has any predecessors as well.

```
Sub DepSucc(T As Task)
Dim Dep As TaskDependency
Dim subT As Task
   If Tsk.Flag20 = False Then
      Tsk.Flag20 = True
      For Each Dep In Tsk.TaskDependencies
         If (Dep.To.ID <> Tsk.ID) Then
            DepSucc Dep.To
         End If
      Next
```

The DepSucc procedure has a very similar structure to DepPred except that the first part looks for successors rather than predecessors. Like DepPred, DepSucc calls itself recursively, once for each new successor it finds. The **To** property always passes a Task Object of linked-**To** Task.

```
'Include any links to sub tasks if this task is a summary task
   If Tsk.Summary = True Then
      For Each subT In Tsk.OutlineChildren
         For Each Dep In subT.TaskDependencies
            If (Dep.To.ID <> subT.ID) Then
               subT.Flag20 = True
               DepSucc Dep.To
            End If
         Next
      Next
   End If
```

If the current task is a summary task, then check for successors to any of its child or subtasks, recursively calling DepSucc to handle each successor.

```
'Test for successors to Summary Task of T
If Tsk.OutlineLevel >= 2 Then
   DepSucc Tsk.OutlineParent
End If
```

DepSucc contains additional code to test whether the current task's summary Task has any successors.

Now we need a temporary toolbar to display when opening the Project with
the LinkedTasks code and a procedure to copy the Module to the Global.mpt
file. The code for both procedures follows as well as a procedure to delete the
Linked Tasks toolbar when your project closes:

```
Private Sub Project_Open(ByVal pj As Project)
Dim myBar As CommandBar
Dim myButton As CommandBarButton
   On Error Resume Next
   Set myBar = CommandBars("Linked Tasks ")
   If Not (myBar Is Nothing) Then
      Set myButton = myBar.Controls("Show Linked Tasks")
   End If

   'Only if macros not already copied to Global.mpt
   If myButton Is Nothing Then
      Set myBar = CommandBars.Add( _
            Name:=" Linked Tasks ", _
            Position:=msoBarFloating)
      myBar.Visible = True
      Set myButton = myBar.Controls.Add( _
                   Type:=msoControlButton)
      With myButton
         .OnAction = "CopyToGlobal"
         .Style = msoButtonCaption
         .Caption = "Copy to Global.mpt"
      End With
   End If
   EditGoTo Date:=Date
End Sub

Private Sub Project_BeforeClose(ByVal pj As Project)
'Closes the Toolbar
   On Error Resume Next
   Application.DisplayAlerts = False
   Application.OrganizerDeleteItem pjToolbars, _
      "Global.Mpt", "Linked Tasks "
   Application.DisplayAlerts = True
End Sub

Sub CopyToGlobal()
Dim myBar As CommandBar
Dim myButton As CommandBarButton
   On Error Resume Next
   Set myBar = CommandBars("Global Macros")
```

```
    If myBar Is Nothing Then
        Set myBar = CommandBars.Add( _
                Name:="Global Macros", _
                Position:=msoBarFloating)
    End If
    myBar.Visible = True
    Set myButton = myBar.Controls.Add( _
                Type:=msoControlButton)
    With myButton
        .OnAction = "LinkedTasks"
        .Style = msoButtonCaption
        .Caption = "Show Linked Tasks"
    End With
    Application.OrganizerMoveItem pjModules, _
        ActiveProject.Name, "Global.Mpt", "LinkedTasksCode"
End Sub
```

Project_Open runs automatically when you open your project. Project_Open creates a new toolbar called Linked Tasks and adds one button to copy the code to the Global.Mpt file and create a new button on the Global Macros toolbar. By now, your Global Macros toolbar should look like Figure 24-2.

**Figure 24-2: Global Macros
toolbar**

The CopyToGlobal procedure repeats previous code. It copies the module with your LinkedTasks code in it. You must rename the module to CopyToGlobal for the code to work. It then creates an extra button to run the LinkedTasks code. After running CopyToGlobal you can run the LinkedTasks macro from any active project.

Hands On Exercise

Exercise 24-1

Test the LinkedTasks macro code.

1. Get the code working and copied to the Global.Mpt file.

2. Test that LinkedTasks works for a small schedule and a large one with many tasks.

3. Edit the code so that applying the filter Flag20 highlights linked tasks rather than hiding unrelated tasks.

4. Click Format ➢ Bar Styles and create a new bar style for tasks with Flag20 set.

5. Create a new procedure and toolbar button to clear Flag20 so bar styles revert to normal.

Note: Steps #4-5 allow bars with Flag20 set to Yes to appear differently in the Gantt Chart.

6. Click Format ➢ Gridlines and add horizontal dotted lines to the Gantt Bars so your eye can follow the level a bar is on to its task Name.

Module 25

Miscellaneous Useful Code

Learning Objectives

After completing this module, you will be able to:

- Outline tasks using VBA
- Reorganize your tasks in different sequences
- Use formulas in custom fields
- Work with hyperlinks
- Work with subprojects in a master project
- Speed up your code execution
- Use the Windows API to open and save files

Indenting Tasks Using VBA

A frequently-asked question in the Microsoft Project programming newsgroup is, "How do I indent tasks based on an indent value in imported data?" For example, if you import data from Excel containing a column with the Outline Level in it, you can import the data with your tasks indented correctly using two different methods:

- If the data is in Excel or another supported data format, insert a heading row for the data. For the Task Name column, name it the Name column. Name the column containing the task Outline Level information Outline Level. Now open the Excel file using Microsoft Project and create a new map that maps Name column in Excel to the Name column in Project, and maps the Outline Level column in Excel to the Outline Level column in Project.

- If the data is not in a numeric format that easily moves to the Outline Level column, use VBA to interpret the data and indent tasks directly. For example if you have an Outline numbering system but no level number, then you can use VBA code to determine each task's Outline Level number and indent the task correctly.

Figure 25-1 shows some sample data you might need to import.

Task Name	Text1	Outline Number
Task1	1	1
Task2	2	2
Task3	2.1	3
Task4	2.2	4
Task5	2.2.1	5

**Figure 25-1: Data in Project
before Indenting**

Notice in Figure 25-1 that the Text1 field contains no periods for the two top level tasks (numbers 1 and 2). I designed the code to use a procedure to count the number of periods and another procedure to loop through all tasks, indenting them as required.

345

The code for these two procedures is as follows:

```
Sub IndentTasks()
Dim Tsk As Task
Dim Level As Long
    'Loop through all Tasks indenting as required
    For Each Tsk In ActiveProject.Tasks
        Level = NumberOfDecimals(Tsk.Text1)
        If Not Tsk Is Nothing Then
            Do Until Tsk.OutlineLevel = Level
                Tsk.OutlineIndent
            Loop
        End If
    Next Tsk
End Sub

Function NumberOfDecimals(OutlineNumber As String) As Long
'Return the number of periods in the OutlineNumber parameter
Dim instr1 As Long
Dim instr2 As Long
Dim Level As Long
    Level = 1
    instr1 = 1
    Do
        instr2 = InStr(instr1, OutlineNumber, ".")
        If instr2 = 0 Then
            Exit Do
        Else
            instr1 = instr2 + 1
            Level = Level + 1
        End If
    Loop
    NumberOfDecimals = Level
End Function
```

The IndentTask routine is a simple variation of previous loops shown in this workbook. You find the key feature in the following code:

```
Level = NumberOfDecimals(Tsk.Text1)
If Not Tsk Is Nothing Then
    Do Until Tsk.OutlineLevel = Level
        Tsk.OutlineIndent
    Loop
End If
```

In the NumberOfDecimals function, **Instr**, is a VBA function that searches for one string within another, and returns the start character position for the search string. It optionally accepts a start character position from which to start searching. You set this in the code using the instr1 variable. If you single step through the Instr code, you see that it very effectively counts the number of periods in the OutlineNumber string variable. Instr returns zero if it cannot find the search string in the main string after the start character number. When it returns a zero (instr2=0), then the system exits the loop and sets the Function's return value to the level count with the statement NumberOfDecimals = Level.

NumberOfDecimals is a function that returns the number of periods in the Text1 string that the macro passed to it. Level is a variable that counts the number of periods. Tsk.OutlineLevel provides the current outline level and Tsk.OutlineIndent is a method that indents the Tsk Task. The code continues to loop until the current task is indented to the value required by the number of periods in text1. Figure 25-2 shows the result.

Task Name	Text1	Outline Number
Task1	1	1
⊟ Task2	2	2
Task3	2.1	2.1
⊟ Task4	2.2	2.2
Task5	2.2.1	2.2.1

Figure 25-2: Code result

You must make sure the Outline value in Text1 is valid. For example, the code fails if 2.1 is followed by 2.1.1.1.

Later versions of Microsoft Project provide another way to indent tasks. You can set the OutlineLevel value directly and the task indents automatically. Strangely enough, Project VBA Help states that the OutlineLevel property is read-only; however, this is not true. This method should not work and yet it does in Project 2003. For both safety and compatibility issues, I recommend that you use the OutlineIndent method instead. To provide you with all the options, the alternative method is as follows:

```
Sub IndentTasksAlternative()
Dim Tsk As Task
    'Loop through all Tasks indenting as required
    For Each Tsk In ActiveProject.Tasks
        If Not Tsk Is Nothing Then
            Tsk.OutlineLevel = NumberOfDecimals(Tsk.Text1)
        End If
    Next Tsk
End Sub
```

Reorganizing Task Sequences

Reporting on projects sometimes requires you to report tasks in different sequence than their native order. You may have a requirement to re-number the tasks on your report. The problem, therefore, is to temporarily renumber tasks and then restore the original numbering. One solution is to sort the file and then to close the file without saving the sorting changes. If your VBA code is in the file, then this solution is messy and slow. Another solution is to take these steps in your code:

1. Copy the current task ID numbers to a custom task Number field, such as Number1.

2. Sort tasks as required such as by date, with the renumber option selected and produce the report.

3. Re-sort and renumber all tasks using the original ID numbers in the Number1 field.

Following is the code to perform these three steps:

```
Sub ReNumber()
Dim Tsk As Task
    'Loop through all Tasks copying the ID number
    For Each Tsk In ActiveProject.Tasks
        If Not Tsk Is Nothing Then
            Tsk.Number1 = Tsk.ID
        End If
    Next Tsk

    'Sort and print the project
    Sort key1:="Start", Ascending1:=True, _
        ReNumber:=True, Outline:=False
    Application.FilePrintPreview

    'Re-sort by the original ID number
    Sort key1:="Number1", Ascending1:=True, _
        ReNumber:=True, Outline:=False
End Sub
```

Creating Formulas in Custom Fields

It is not usually safe to assume that non-enterprise Views, Tables, Filters, or Formulas needed by your code actually exist in any project. Therefore, it is always a good idea to recreate them in your code. To add a Formula to a custom field use the following code:

```
Sub AddFormula()
    CustomFieldSetFormula FieldID:=pjCustomTaskText1, _
        Formula:="[Duration]/60/40 & ""w"""
    CustomFieldProperties FieldID:=pjCustomTaskText1, _
        Attribute:=pjFieldAttributeFormula, _
        SummaryCalc:=pjCalcFormula
End Sub
```

The resulting formula looks like this:

[Duration]/60/40 & "w"

The preceding formula calculates the Duration of each task as a number of 40 hour weeks. To get a double-quote to appear in the string for the formula ("w"), you need to type two sets of double-quotes as in ""w"". VBA interprets "" in your string as a single double-quote (") in the final string.

Working with Hyperlinks

You previously worked with VBA code that reads Hyperlinks in the Project Control Center code. In the Project Control Center, each task contains a Hyperlink to a .mpp file. The code reads the path to the file from the Hyperlink and then uses the path to open the file. In this section, I describe how the system stores Hyperlinks and how to add a Hyperlink to a task.

You can store Hyperlinks for tasks, resources, and assignments. In addition there is a Hyperlink Base field in the Properties dialog, accessed by clicking File ➤ Properties. The Hyperlink Base field provides a common location for all your Hyperlinks in the project. If you provide a value in the Hyperlink Base field, all Hyperlinks are relative to the Base address. For example, if a Hyperlink Base is G:\Projects then a Hyperlink to MyBusinessCase.Doc refers to the full path G:\Projects\MyBusinessCase.Doc. To read the Hyperlink Base field, use the code:

```
MyBase = ActiveProject _
    .BuiltinDocumentProperties("Hyperlink Base")
```

The following components make up a Hyperlink:

- A name that the system displays as the Hyperlink

- The address for the Hyperlink

- A sub address for a Hyperlink

- A ScreenTip displayed when you hover your mouse pointer over the Hyperlink

The sub address component that may not be familiar to you. A sub address lets you refer to a specific location in a file, such as a Bookmark in a Word document or a Named Range in an Excel workbook, as in the following examples:

- #My Excel File.xls#A20#

- #My Excel File.xls#NamedRange#

- #My Word Document.Doc#BookmarkName#

- #My project file.mpp#20#

Use the # (hash) character to separate an address from a sub address. Within Microsoft Project files, the sub address can be the ID number of any existing task. The limiting factor is that ID numbers change, so it would be better to use the Unique ID instead. Unfortunately, you cannot specify a Unique ID as a sub address in a Hyperlink!

A task's Unique ID can be very useful to Project VBA developers. If you need to use a unique value for any task, resource, or assignment, use the object's UniqueID. Unique ID's are unique for any individual project file and never change.

In Microsoft Project VBA, you can create, edit, and delete Hyperlinks for any task, resource, or assignment. Table 25-1 shows the key methods used with Hyperlinks.

Name	Method or Property	Description
EditClearHyperlink	Method	Remove a Hyperlink
EditHyperlink	Method	Edit a Hyperlink
FollowHyperlink	Method	Opens the file in the Address with the appropriate application and then jumps to the sub address if provided
HyperlinkAddress	Property – Read/Write	Address of Hyperlink (Required)
HyperlinkSubAddress	Property – Read/Write	Sub Address of Hyperlink (optional)
HyperlinkScreenTip	Property – Read/Write	Screen tip shown when mouse hovers over Hyperlink
InsertHyperlink	Method	Inserts a Hyperlink to the parent task, resource or assignment

Table 25-1: Hyperlink Methods and Properties

Working with Subprojects

Some macros need to work with data from consolidated projects that hold many subprojects. There is a simple loop to iterate through all tasks in all subprojects, which is as follows:

```
Sub Sub_Projects()
Dim Prj As Project
Dim Tsk As Task
    'Loop through all Tasks in all subprojects
    For Each Prj In ActiveProject.SubProjects
        For Each Tsk In Prj.Tasks
            If Not Tsk Is Nothing Then
                'Task Code
            End If
        Next Tsk
    Next Prj
End Sub
```

SubProjects is a property that returns a collection of all subprojects inserted in the active project. Remember that with subprojects, all data lives in the inserted file, not the consolidated file.

Making Your Code Run Faster

Microsoft Project VBA code runs surprisingly fast, but there are times, especially in larger schedules, where code takes a long time to run. The following tips help you make your VBA code run faster:

- Never work with tasks by selecting the tasks. Always use Task, Resource, or Assignment Objects instead.

- Do not move the cursor, because this slows down a macro while the screen updating catches up.

- If you are adding or editing many tasks or assignments, set the Calculation mode to Manual within your code, and then reset it to Automatic afterwards. Better still, read the calculation mode first, change it if necessary, and then return the application to the previous state which is likely the user's preference. With calculation set to Manual, Microsoft Project recalculates the schedule only once, saving processing time in the application.

- Updating the screen takes time. Use **Application.ScreenUpdating = False** to pause screen updating and **Application.ScreenUpdating = True** to restart screen updating.

If you want to display some form of progress indicator while you stop the screen from refreshing, or if your version of Project does not support the ScreenUpdating method, then display a blank project while your code works on your project in the background. Display progress messages for only those items that need refreshing. Once the code finishes, close the blank project to reveal your updated file.

- If you work with other applications such as Excel, use Excel templates as much as possible for the bare bones of the application. Keep macros that do formatting in the same Excel template and then call the Excel macros from your Project VBA code. This technique minimizes the amount of code working between application processes which is slow. Running code within the same application process is much faster.

- If you write code that loops through many tasks in your schedules, do not call functions or other procedures inside the loop's code. Calls to functions and procedures activate overhead processing that slows down code execution. While making a few calls in your code results in no perceptible execution slowdown, making a call for each one of 5,000 can noticeably slow your code execution. Instead, include all code in the same procedure within the loop. This may lead to an overly long procedure and code that is more difficult to maintain, but it runs faster!

With today's powerful computers, most macros run more than fast enough. The speed issues you are likely to encounter happen when you work with large schedules or with macros performing lots of work with other applications.

Timing Code Execution

If you want to speed up your code it helps if you can measure how long it is taking to run! The following code returns the time it takes to execute code:

```
Sub TimingCode()
Dim Tim As Single
Dim str As String
Dim L As Long
   Tim = Timer
   For L = 1 To 500000
      str = Format((L ^ 0.5) * (L ^ 0.5), "0.00") & " secs"
   Next L
   Debug.Print "The Loop took " & Timer - Tim
End Sub
```

Timer is a VBA function that returns the number of seconds as a single variable type. By saving the value of Timer at the beginning of the loop and then comparing it at the end of the loop, you get an accurate time measurement. I set the loop to a large number because the code runs very fast, even though it is doing square roots and multiplication. This large number of loop iterations makes the code execution take a few seconds. Converting the number to a string also adds more work, which takes more time for the code to execute.

Hands On Exercise

Exercise 25-1

Work with some of the useful code examples.

1. Experiment with the Outline Tasks code. Add a breakpoint to the code and single step through it to see how it works.

2. Review all the Methods and Properties starting with Outline. In the Immediate Window type ActiveCell.Task then press the O (capital o) key and look for Outline. Select any one of the Outline methods then press the F1 function key for Help on it.

3. Add timing code to some of your macros and run several tests to record the average time. See if you can speed up your code execution. Examine loops for opportunities to speed your code up.

Using the Windows API to Open and Save Files

Excel has two great methods for users to browse for file names, which are the **GetOpenFilename** and **GetSaveAsFilename** methods. Unfortunately, Microsoft Project does not have the same file methods as Excel. In fact, Project does not even have the FileDialog methods enabled in Microsoft Office, which is a shame! This leaves you, the Project VBA programmer, with two options:

- Add a reference to Excel and use Excel's File methods. This works, but there is no GetFolder option. When moving a macro to different computers with different versions of Excel, problems may occur.

- Use Windows API's to open the dialog boxes you see and use in all Microsoft Office applications.

In Module 20, you learned to use Excel File methods, so in this section I focus on using Windows API's only. Windows API's are pieces of code built into Windows that programmers can call in their programs to avoid re-coding basic file system functionality. There are three calls that interest us:

- Getting a file-open name

- Getting a file-save-as name

- Getting a folder name

When you write code that calls a Windows API, you must use care to get it to work. I've got good news and bad news for you on this topic:

- **Bad news** – The code required to call a Windows API is very low-level and very complex. Coding against Windows APIs is not something you can do in a hurry, and if your code works incorrectly, it can crash your program and even Windows itself.

- **Good news** – Programmers more knowledgeable than I have already written most of the code a typical Project VBA programmer ever needs. When you search the Web for the code you want you will find a number of sites with working code that you can copy and use. I based the code in the Module 25 Sample Code.mpp file on code I acquired from **http://www.msdn.microsoft.com**.

The code in Module 25 Sample Code.mpp in the clsBrowse module is very complex and there are several good reasons why it is not worth your time to try and understand it:

- It is working code on the Web that you can download and use for free.

- The next version of Visual Studio will integrate with and allow direct coding of Microsoft Project using Visual Studio languages such as VB. These languages have much simpler calls to File Open dialogs using the Dot Net Framework that do not use Windows API's. Coding calls to a Windows API is a skill set required by a continuously decreasing number of people.

Instead of explaining the Windows API code, I want to explain how to use the class clsBrowse provided in the Module 25 Sample Code.mpp file. Assuming you have copied the clsBrowse module into your project, the following topics provide examples of using basic clsBrowse features.

Using File Open

```
Sub BrowseFileOpen()
Dim Browse As New clsBrowse
    With Browse
        .DialogTitle = "My File Open Dialog"
        .Filter = "Project Files|*.mpp"
        .ShowOpen
        If .FileName = "" Then
            MsgBox "You clicked the Cancel Key"
        Else
            MsgBox "You selected file:" & vbCrLf _
                    & .FileName
        End If
    End With
End Sub
```

The name of the Class module is clsBrowse so Dim Browse As New clsBrowse assigns and then creates a fresh copy of clsBrowse. One of the great features of Classes is that the system displays all Properties and Methods in an Intellisense pick list when you type the name of your class variable followed by a period character. Figure 25-3 shows the Browse IntelliSense pick list when I am ready to select the DialogTitle item. DialogTitle is a property you use to set the title for the dialog.

```
Sub BrowseMultipleFileOpen()
Dim Browse As New clsBrowse
Dim Fil As Long
Dim str As String
    With Browse
        MsgBox "Hold the Ctrl Key down to select more than one file", vbInformation + vbOKOnly
        .DialogTitle = "My Multiple File Open Dialog"
    [DialogTitle]         t Files|*.mpp"
    [Directory]           = True
    [ExistFlags]
    [Extension]           = "" Then
    [FileName]            licked the Cancel button or pressed the Esc Key"
    [FileNames]
    [FileTitle]           lected files:" & vbCrLf
                       o .FileNames.Count
            str = str & .FileNames(Fil) & vbCrLf
        Next Fil
        MsgBox str
    End If
    End With
    Set Browse = Nothing
End Sub
```

Figure 25-3: IntelliSense pick list

ShowOpen is a method that uses the properties you set and shows a file open dialog. If you press the Escape key or click the *Cancel* button, the .Filename property returns "". Otherwise, the .FileName property returns the selected file displayed using MsgBox in the code above.

```
Sub BrowseMultipleFileOpen()
Dim Browse As New clsBrowse
Dim Fil As Long
Dim str As String
    With Browse
        MsgBox "Hold the Ctrl Key down to select more " _
            &"than one file", vbInformation + vbOKOnly
        .DialogTitle = "My Multiple File Open Dialog"
        .Filter = "Project Files|*.mpp"
        .AllowMultiSelect = True
        .ShowOpen
        If .FileTitles(1) = "" Then
            MsgBox "You clicked the Cancel button or " _
                & "pressed the Esc Key" + vbOKOnly
        Else
            str = "You selected files:" & vbCrLf
            For Fil = 1 To .FileNames.Count
                str = str & .FileNames(Fil) & vbCrLf
            Next Fil
            MsgBox str
        End If
    End With
    Set Browse = Nothing
End Sub
```

The only difference between the preceding code and the previous example is that I set the AllowMultiSelect property to True. This enables the user to press and hold either the Ctrl key or the Shift key to select multiple files. This returns a Filenames collection that holds all files selected and the following code loops through all selected file names:

```
For Fil = 1 To .FileNames.Count
   str = str & .FileNames(Fil) & vbCrLf
Next Fil
```

 All properties retain their values until the system terminates the class. This means that if you want to display the ShowOpen dialog a second time without AllowMultiSelect enabled, you need to reset it to False before calling ShowOpen again.

Using File Save as

```
Sub BrowseFileSaveAs()
Dim Browse As New clsBrowse
   With Browse
      .DialogTitle = "My File Save As Dialog"
      .Filter = "Project Files|*.mpp"
      .ShowSave
      If .FileName = "" Then
         MsgBox "You clicked the Cancel button or " _
            &"pressed the Esc Key"
      Else
         MsgBox "You selected file:" & vbCrLf _
               & .FileName
      End If
   End With
   Set Browse = Nothing
End Sub
```

BrowseFileSaveAs displays a browse dialog that lets the user browse to a folder and enter a file name as the Save As file name. What is different in this code example is that I use the ShowSave method instead of the ShowOpen method.

Using Get Folder

```
Sub BrowseGetFolder()
Dim Browse As New clsBrowse
   With Browse
       .DialogTitle = "My File Save As Dialog"
       .BrowseForFolder
       If .Directory = "" Then
          MsgBox "You clicked the Cancel button or " _
             & "pressed the Esc key", _
             vbInformation + vbOKOnly
       Else
          MsgBox "You selected folder:" & vbCrLf _
             & .Directory
       End If
   End With
   Set Browse = Nothing
End Sub
```

Sometimes you need a user to select a folder. For example, you might want to work with all files in a nominated folder. The BrowseGetFolder method shows a Select Folder dialog using the BrowseForFolder method. It returns the selected folder in the .Directory property.

Applying the clsBrowse Class to a New Project

Using the clsBrowse code is simple if you follow these steps:

1. Copy the clsBrowse module into your project file in Project Explorer in Project's VBE.

2. Copy one of the procedures above and edit the property settings to suit your needs.

 To set an initial folder for the file dialogs, set the .Directory property.

Hands On Exercise

Exercise 25-2

Use the clsBrowse Class.

1. Copy the clsBrowse class from Module 25 Sample Code.mpp into a project file.

2. Add the clsBrowse class to one of your own projects. Use a File Open or File Save as dialog. If you don't have a suitable project, create a new project to test the code.

3. Create a new Sub procedure in a new Module.

4. Add the Browse declaration code detailed above.

5. Create the code to request a filename to open, a file name to save to and a folder to use to save to with three separate calls to the Browse class object.

SECTION 3

WORKING WITH DATABASES

Learning Objectives

After completing the Modules in this Section, you will be able to:

- Read data from project databases to create multi-project reports
- Write data to a project database to create a new project
- Read data directly from .mpp files into other applications using OLEDB
- Read data from a Project Server database to create automated project reports

Developing Project Database Code

Many organizations choose to save their projects in databases to facilitate multi-project reporting. Often it can take a lot of time, effort, and money to create new reports or to change existing reports. This section focuses on creating VBA code, mostly in Excel, to read and write data to a project database. The goal is for you to learn how to use the sample code to easily create powerful, flexible reports with minimal effort using an excellent reporting tool, Microsoft Excel.

I include code samples for working with projects saved both in Access databases and SQL Server databases. Because the code for working with both database types is the same, except the code for connecting to them, all code is for Access after the first example for SQL Server.

Microsoft Project .mpd database files are the same as Access .mdb files. You can open .mpd files in Access by changing the file type to *All files (*.*)* then selecting your .mpd file.

Project Server stores all its projects in a SQL Server database. The last module of this section shows you how to read data from a Project Server database to create a powerful weekly report.

Warning: Project Server 2007 uses a very different data structure from Project Server 2003, so the code for Project Server 2003 will not work with Project Server 2007. Project Server 2007 has a separate reporting database. This reporting database and SQL Server's new reporting tools allow for easy custom reporting.

Because it is easier to read data directly from SQL Server using VBA code rather than using the Project Data Service (PDS), a partial API for Project Server, I do not cover the PDS in this book. If you want to develop code using PDS (remember that it is not supported in Project Server 2007) then download the Software Development Kit (SDK) from Microsoft.com. The download address is:

http://www.microsoft.com/downloads/details.aspx?FamilyID=4d 2abc8c-8bca-4db9-8753-178c0d3099c5&DisplayLang=en

365

Downloading the Sample Files

You can download the Microsoft Project sample files containing all of the sample code in this workbook at the following URL:

http://www.projectvbabook.com/dl

Microsoft Project 98 uses a different file format, so if you do have Project 98, make sure you download the Project 98 zip file. The Project 2000-2003 file format is suitable for use with any recent version of Microsoft Project, from 2000 to 2003.

Warning: Microsoft Project 2007 uses a different file format, so if you have Project 2007, you must open and re-save the files in Project 2007 format.

Module 26

Importing Data from Other Sources

Learning Objectives

After completing this module, you will be able to:

- Import data from Excel into Microsoft Project
- Import data from an Access database into Microsoft Project
- Import data from a SQL Server database into Microsoft Project

Importing Data from an Excel Workbook

The quickest way to import data from an Excel workbook into a Microsoft Project file is using Project's Import Wizard. To run the Import Wizard, complete the following steps:

1. In Microsoft Project, click File ➤ Open.

2. Click the *Files of type* pick list and select *Microsoft Excel Workbooks (*.xls)*.

3. Select your Excel file then follow the steps displayed by the Import Wizard.

4. To map the Excel fields to Project fields, create or edit an Import/Export Map.

The simplest way to import tasks, resources, and assignments from Excel is to use a Project Excel Template. To create a Project Excel Template:

1. In Microsoft Project, click File ➤ Save as.

2. Click the *Files of type* pick list and select *Microsoft Excel Workbooks (*.xls)*.

3. Type a name for your template and click the *Save as* button.

4. In the Export Wizard click the *Next* button.

5. Select the *Project Excel Template* option.

6. Click the *Finish* button to save the project as a Project Excel Template.

Microsoft Project creates the Project Excel Template file and recognizes it when you import the data from Excel. Sometimes, however, the format of the data you want to import is not suitable for the Import Wizard, and you need VBA code to interpret and import your Excel data. The following code imports tasks, resources, and assignments from a Project Excel Template:

```
Sub ImportFromExcel
'Open the file in Excel
'Use the Start date of Task1 for the Project's Start Date
'Import all Tasks
'   If a Task has a Predecessor ignore its dates
'   Indent Tasks as set by Outline Level
'Import all Resources
'Make Assignments of Resources on Tasks
'   If Work provided, ignore units
End Sub
```

Before the following code can work on your system, you must meet these pre-requisites:

- You must add a reference in the Project VBE to Microsoft Excel.

- You must modify the column constants at the top of the code to match the column numbers in your workbook. Note that the first column, column A, is column zero.

- Confirm that each task has only one predecessor and that the number in the Predecessors column is for an existing task with an ID number lower than the ID number for the current task.

- The first task must be the earliest task to start as its Start date is used as the project's Start date.

- You must format Duration in Days and format Work in Hours.

The VBA code for each of the Comments follows:

```vba
Sub ImportFromExcel()
Dim xlApp As Excel.Application
Dim xlR As Excel.Range
Dim ExcelPath as String
Dim Tsk As Task
Dim Res As Resource
Dim Assn As Assignment
Dim Units As Single
Dim Level As Long

'Constants for column numbers. First column is zero
Const colTskID = 0
Const colTskName = 1
Const colTskDuration = 2
Const colTskStart = 3
Const colTskFinish = 4
Const colTskPredecessors = 5
Const colTskOutlineLevel = 6
Const colTskNotes = 7

Const colResName = 1
Const colResMaxUnits = 8

Const colAssTaskName = 0
Const colAssResourceName = 1
Const colAssPctWorkComplete = 2
Const colAssWork = 3
Const colAssUnits = 4
```

```
Const TaskSheetName = "Task_Table"
Const ResourceSheetName = "Resource_Table"
Const AssignmentSheetName = "Assignment_Table"

'Open the file in Excel
   Set xlApp = CreateObject("Excel.Application")
   xlApp.Visible = True
   ExcelPath = xlApp.GetOpenFilename("*.xls,*.xls", _
            , "Find Excel Workbook")
   If Dir(ExcelPath) = "" Then
      MsgBox "File not found, macro ended", vbCritical
      End
   End If
   xlApp.Visible = False
   xlApp.Workbooks.Open ExcelFilePath
   'Use the Start date of Task1 for the
   'new Project's Start Date
   Set xlR = xlApp.Workbooks(1).Worksheets( _
         TaskSheetName).Range("A2")
   Application.FileNew
   ActiveProject.ProjectStart = xlR.Offset(0, colTskStart)

'Import all Tasks
'    If a Task has a Predecessor ignore its dates
   Do Until IsEmpty(xlR)
      Set Tsk = ActiveProject.Tasks.Add(CStr( _
            xlR.Offset(0, colTskName)))
      Tsk.Duration = xlR.Offset(0, colTskDuration) _
               * 8 * 60
      If xlR = 1 Then   'If first Task, do nothing
      ElseIf (IsEmpty(xlR.Offset( _
                  0,colTskPredecessors))) Then
         'Set Start date SNET constraint
         Tsk.ConstraintType = pjSNET
         Tsk.ConstraintDate = _
               CDate(xlR.Offset(0, colTskStart))
      Else
         'Set predecessor
         Tsk.TaskDependencies.Add _
            ActiveProject.Tasks(xlR.Offset( _
            0, colTskPredecessors))
      End If

'    Indent Tasks as set by Outline Level
      Level = xlR.Offset(0, colTskOutlineLevel)
```

371

```
        Do Until Tsk.OutlineLevel >= Level
           Tsk.OutlineIndent
        Loop

'       Add Notes
        Tsk.Notes = xlR.Offset(0, colTskNotes)
        Set xlR = xlR.Offset(1, 0)
      Loop

'Import all Resources
    Set xlR = xlApp.Workbooks(1).Worksheets( _
           ResourceSheetName).Range("A2")
    Do Until IsEmpty(xlR)
       Set Res = ActiveProject.Resources.Add( _
              CStr(xlR.Offset(0, colResName)))
       Res.MaxUnits = Val(xlR.Offset(0, colResMaxUnits))
       Set xlR = xlR.Offset(1, 0)
    Loop

'Make Assignments of Resources on Tasks
    Set xlR = xlApp.Workbooks(1).Worksheets( _
           AssignmentSheetName).Range("A2")
    Do Until IsEmpty(xlR)
       Set Tsk = ActiveProject.Tasks( _
              CStr(xlR.Offset(0, colAssTaskName)))
       Set Res = ActiveProject.Resources( _
              CStr(xlR.Offset(0, _
              colAssResourceName)))
       Units = Val(xlR.Offset(0, colAssUnits))
       Set Assn = Tsk.Assignments.Add( _
              ResourceID:=Res.ID, Units:=Units)

'    If Work provided, ignore units
       If Not IsEmpty(xlR.Offset(0, colAssWork)) Then
          Tsk.Type = pjFixedDuration
          Assn.Work = xlR.Offset(0, colAssWork) * 60
          Tsk.Type = pjFixedUnits
       End If
       Set xlR = xlR.Offset(1, 0)
    Loop

    'Tidy up
    xlApp.ActiveWorkbook.Close False
    xlApp.Quit
    Set xlApp = Nothing
End Sub
```

In Module 20, I showed you how to work with Excel. This code uses exactly the same techniques. xlApp.GetOpenFilename("*.xls,*.xls", , "Find Excel Workbook") gets Excel to prompt the user to find the Excel file to import. Before opening the file, use the Dir command to confirm the selected file exists and that the user has not clicked the Cancel button. Set xlApp to not visible again so that the focus is on Microsoft Project and the new project you are creating.

```
'Import all Tasks
'    If a Task has a Predecessor ignore its dates
  Do Until IsEmpty(xlR)
     Set Tsk = ActiveProject.Tasks.Add(CStr( _
                 xlR.Offset(0, colTskName)))
     Tsk.Duration = xlR.Offset(0, colTskDuration) _
                 * 8 * 60
     If xlR = 1 Then   'If first Task, do nothing
     ElseIf (IsEmpty(xlR.Offset( _
                 0,colTskPredecessors))) Then
        'Set Start date SNET constraint
        Tsk.ConstraintType = pjSNET
        Tsk.ConstraintDate = _
                 CDate(xlR.Offset(0, colTskStart))
     Else
        'Set predecessor
        Tsk.TaskDependencies.Add _
              ActiveProject.Tasks(xlR.Offset( _
              0, colTskPredecessors))
     End If

'    Indent Tasks as set by Outline Level
     Level = xlR.Offset(0, colTskOutlineLevel)
     Do Until Tsk.OutlineLevel >= Level
        Tsk.OutlineIndent
     Loop

'    Add Notes
     Tsk.Notes = xlR.Offset(0, colTskNotes)
     Set xlR = xlR.Offset(1, 0)
  Loop
```

The code is easy to understand once you understand the function of the xlR.Offset(0, colTskName) code. xlR is an Excel Range variable which is set to A2 in the Task_Table worksheet, the Resource_Table worksheet, and the Assignment_Table worksheet. Offset is a method that points to a number of rows and columns from the preceding range object. Offset(0,0) indicates no offset, but .Offset(0, colTskName) offsets zero rows down and colTskName columns to the right, where colTskName is a constant with the column number of the Task Name column. xlR.Offset(0, colTskName) that returns the task name for the current row.

Set xlR = xlR.Offset(1, 0) points the xlR Excel Range object to the cell below the current cell. This code, combined with the Do Until IsEmpty(xlR) code, loops through all rows of data. IsEmpty(xlR) returns False when xlR finally points to an empty cell.

```
'Import all Resources
   Set xlR = xlApp.Workbooks(1).Worksheets( _
         ResourceSheetName).Range("A2")
   Do Until IsEmpty(xlR)
      Set Res = ActiveProject.Resources.Add( _
            CStr(xlR.Offset(0, colResName)))
      Res.MaxUnits = Val(xlR.Offset(0, colResMaxUnits))
      Set xlR = xlR.Offset(1, 0)
   Loop
```

You can handle importing resources the same way you import tasks. In the preceding code sample, only the Resource Name and Maximum Units fields are imported.

```
'Make Assignments of Resources on Tasks
   Set xlR = xlApp.Workbooks(1).Worksheets( _
         AssignmentSheetName).Range("A2")
   Do Until IsEmpty(xlR)
      Set Tsk = ActiveProject.Tasks(CStr(xlR.Offset(0, _
            colAssTaskName)))
      Set Res = ActiveProject.Resources(CStr(xlR.Offset(0, _
            colAssResourceName)))
      Units = Val(xlR.Offset(0, colAssUnits))
      Set Assn = Tsk.Assignments.Add( _
            ResourceID:=Res.ID, Units:=Units)
```

```
'   If Work provided, ignore units
    If Not IsEmpty(xlR.Offset(0, colAssWork)) Then
       Tsk.Type = pjFixedDuration
       Assn.Work = xlR.Offset(0, colAssWork) * 60
       Tsk.Type = pjFixedUnits
    End If
    Set xlR = xlR.Offset(1, 0)
  Loop
```

Adding assignments is a little different from adding tasks and resources because you add an assignment to either a task or a resource. The preceding code sample adds assignments to a task since that more accurately reflects the manual steps you take when you assign a resource to a task. To make the code easier to understand and maintain, I added separate variables for the task, the resource, and the assignment. Although you can create assignments with one long statement, the resulting code is confusing and difficult to maintain and debug.

Tsk, Res, and Assn are objects that require the Set command. Units is a variable of type Single and uses the Val function to convert the data in the spreadsheet. Using Val handles a % sign without causing an error. The Assignment Add method treats Units of 0.5 and 50 as being the same (50%).

The Set Assn = Tsk.Assignments.Add(ResourceID:=Res.ID, Units:=Units) statement adds an assignment to the Tsk task with the Res resource at the units specified in the Units variable. Note that you need only the resource ID so you could save the ID number rather than the resource variable Res; however, the resource variable is more flexible as you can refer to all properties and methods when using it.

If there is work specified in the Work column, the next block of code sets the Task Type to Fixed Duration, edits the Work, and then restores the Task Type to Fixed Units. The result is an assignment with the original Duration and Work but with recalculated Units. Note that Work and Duration are always stored in minutes.

The code could import and save the original Task Type, and then restore it after editing the Work, but because both the project and the tasks are all new, Fixed Units is the standard default Task Type which is most flexible and useful. The Tidy Up code closes the workbook without saving changes, and then quits Excel and clears the xlApp variable.

Importing Data from an Access Database

People commonly use an Access database as an intermediate storage location when working with other databases. It is easy to import data from Access .mdb files or from any applications that uses the Access Jet Engine. The code for this topical section requires the following to work:

- Download the Module 26 sample code.mdb file from our web site and save it in a known location.

- Create a reference in the Project VBE to a Microsoft ActiveX Data Objects library, also known also as MDAC or ADODB library. Figure 26-1 shows the reference dialog with the latest version of the ADODB library checked. Any version is usable, but the newer the better.

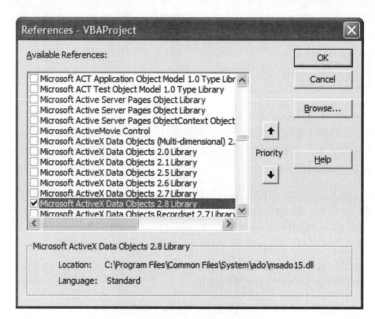

**Figure 26-1: Set a reference
to an ADODB library**

Assuming that you have exactly the same data used previously in the Excel file and stored the data in an .mdb file in three tables instead of three worksheets, then the code is as follows:

```
Sub ImportFromAccess()
Dim Conn As New ADODB.Connection
Dim rs As ADODB.Recordset
Dim MdbPath As String
Dim Tsk As Task
Dim Res As Resource
Dim Assn As Assignment
Dim Units As Single
Dim Level As Long
Dim FirstTask As Boolean
Dim Files As New clsBrowse

'Create Connection to the .mdb file
   With Files
      .DialogTitle = "Please Find .mdb file"
      .Filter = "Access Files|*.mdb"
      Files.ShowOpen
      Conn.ConnectionString = _
            "Provider=Microsoft.Jet.OLEDB.4.0;" _
            & "Data Source=" & Files.FileName _
            & ";Persist Security Info=False"
      Conn.Open
   End With

'Setup up new Project file
   Application.FileNew

'Import all Tasks
'   If a Task has a Predecessor ignore its dates
   Set rs = New ADODB.Recordset
   rs.Open "SELECT * FROM Task_Table ORDER BY ID", Conn
   ActiveProject.ProjectStart = rs![Start_Date]
   FirstTask = True
   Do Until rs.EOF
      Set Tsk = ActiveProject.Tasks.Add(CStr(rs![Name]))
      Tsk.Duration = rs!Duration * 8 * 60
      If FirstTask Then    'If first Task, do nothing
         FirstTask = False
      ElseIf (IsNull(rs!Predecessors)) Then
         'Set Start date SNET constraint
         Tsk.ConstraintType = pjSNET
         Tsk.ConstraintDate = CDate(rs!Start_Date)
      Else
         'Set predecessor
         Tsk.TaskDependencies.Add _
               ActiveProject.Tasks(rs!Predecessors)
      End If
```

377

```
'        Indent Tasks as set by Outline Level
        Level = rs!Outline_Level
        Do Until Tsk.OutlineLevel >= Level
           Tsk.OutlineIndent
        Loop

'        Add Notes
        If Not IsNull(rs!Notes) Then
           Tsk.Notes = rs!Notes
        End If
        rs.MoveNext
     Loop
     rs.Close

'Import all Resources
     rs.Open "SELECT * FROM Resource_Table " _
          & "ORDER BY [Name]", Conn
     Do Until rs.EOF
        Set Res = ActiveProject.Resources.Add(CStr(rs![Name]))
        Res.MaxUnits = rs!Max_Units / 100
        rs.MoveNext
     Loop
     rs.Close

'Make Assignments of Resources on Tasks
     rs.Open "SELECT * FROM Assignment_Table " _
          & "ORDER BY [Task_Name]", Conn
     Do Until rs.EOF
        Set Tsk = ActiveProject.Tasks(CStr(rs!Task_Name))
        Set Res = ActiveProject.Resources(CStr(rs!Resource_Name))
        Units = rs!Units
        Set Assn = Tsk.Assignments.Add( _
                   ResourceID:=Res.ID, Units:=Units)

'     If Work provided, ignore units
        If Not IsNull(rs!Scheduled_Work) Then
           Tsk.Type = pjFixedDuration
           Assn.Work = rs!Scheduled_Work * 60
           Tsk.Type = pjFixedUnits
        End If
        rs.MoveNext
     Loop
     rs.Close
```

```
    'Tidy up
    Set rs = Nothing
    Conn.Close
    Set Conn = Nothing
End Sub
```

To import data from a database using OLEDB, create and open a connection object and then set up and open a Recordset with the data you want. Importing data from a Recordset requires that you know the names of the source fields and how to navigate through the recordset. In the above code, navigation steps one record at a time using the MoveNext method to move from one record to the next. Look at the above code then copy and edit it to import data from your database.

Importing Data from a SQL Server Database

SQL Server is a common data source for projects. You may have workflow software that provides you with basic tasks or timesheet data that you want to import into Microsoft Project. Except for the code connecting to SQL Server, the code required to import data from SQL Server is very similar to that for Access. The code for this topical section requires you to do the following before it can work:

- You create a SQL Server database with the same tables, fields, and data as for the Access .mdb sample, or that you modify the code to work with your specific database.

- You create a reference in the VBE to a Microsoft ActiveX Data Objects library, known also as MDAC or ADODB library, as previously shown in Figure 26-1.

The following code imports data from a SQL Server database:

```
Sub ImportFromSQLServer()
Dim Conn As New ADODB.Connection
Dim rs As ADODB.Recordset
Dim MdbPath As String
Dim Tsk As Task
Dim Res As Resource
Dim Assn As Assignment
Dim Units As Single
Dim Level As Long
Dim FirstTask As Boolean
```

```
'Create Connection to the .mdb file
    Conn.ConnectionString = "Provider=sqloledb;" _
      & "Data Source=YourSqlServerName;" _
      & "Initial Catalog=Module 26 sample codeSQL;" _
      & "Integrated Security=SSPI;"
    Conn.Open

'Setup up new Project file
    Application.FileNew

'Import all Tasks
'    If a Task has a Predecessor ignore its dates
    Set rs = New ADODB.Recordset
    rs.Open "SELECT * FROM Task_Table ORDER BY ID", Conn
    ActiveProject.ProjectStart = rs![Start_Date]
    FirstTask = True
    Do Until rs.EOF
        Set Tsk = ActiveProject.Tasks.Add(CStr(rs![Name]))
        Tsk.Duration = rs!Duration * 8 * 60
        If FirstTask Then      'If first Task, do nothing
            FirstTask = False
        ElseIf (IsNull(rs!Predecessors)) Then
            'Set Start date SNET constraint
            Tsk.ConstraintType = pjSNET
            Tsk.ConstraintDate = CDate(rs!Start_Date)
        Else
            'Set predecessor
            Tsk.TaskDependencies.Add ActiveProject. _
          Tasks(rs!Predecessors)
        End If

'        Indent Tasks as set by Outline Level
        Level = rs!Outline_Level
        Do Until Tsk.OutlineLevel >= Level
            Tsk.OutlineIndent
        Loop

'        Add Notes
        If Not IsNull(rs!Notes) Then
            Tsk.Notes = rs!Notes
        End If
        rs.MoveNext
    Loop
    rs.Close
```

```
'Import all Resources
    rs.Open "SELECT * FROM Resource_Table " _
        &"ORDER BY [Name]", Conn
    Do Until rs.EOF
        Set Res = ActiveProject.Resources.Add(CStr(rs![Name]))
        Res.MaxUnits = rs!Max_Units / 100
        rs.MoveNext
    Loop
    rs.Close

'Make Assignments of Resources on Tasks
    rs.Open "SELECT * FROM Assignment_Table " _
        &"ORDER BY [Task_Name]", Conn
    Do Until rs.EOF
        Set Tsk = ActiveProject.Tasks(CStr(rs!Task_Name))
        Set Res = ActiveProject. _
            Resources(CStr(rs!Resource_Name))
        Units = rs!Units
        Set Assn = Tsk.Assignments.Add( _
            ResourceID:=Res.ID, Units:=Units)

'   If Work provided, ignore units
        If Not IsNull(rs!Scheduled_Work) Then
            Tsk.Type = pjFixedDuration
            Assn.Work = rs!Scheduled_Work * 60
            Tsk.Type = pjFixedUnits
        End If
        rs.MoveNext
    Loop
    rs.Close

'Tidy up
    Set rs = Nothing
    Conn.Close
    Set Conn = Nothing
End Sub
```

The only difference between this and the Access example is the code connecting to SQL Server. You do not need to browse for a .mdb file, but you must edit the connection string to match the name of your SQL Server database server and database name. To make this code work with your own SQL Server instance, you need the following:

- The computer name of your SQL Server.

- The name of the database you created to test your code.

- Tables and data setup as the code expects. For example, there must be a table called Task_Table.

- You must be a SQL Server user with at least read access to the tables.

You can download several files from our web site to help you create the SQL Server database as explained in table 26-1.

File Name	Use
Module 26.sql	SQL Server script that creates a database and all required Tables.
Test Sample Module 26 Tasks.csv	Test data for you to import into table Task_Table
Test Sample Module 26 Resources.csv	Test data for you to import into table Resource_Table
Test Sample Module 26 Assignments.csv	Test data for you to import into table Assignment_Table

**Table 26-1: Files you can use to
create a test database in SQL Server**

 You may need the help of your SQL Server database administrator (DBA) to set up a test SQL Server database if you do not know how to do this or do not have the correct rights on the system.

Hands On Exercise

Exercise 26-1

Import data from various sources.

1. Download and use the test data from our VBA download site, or use some data of your own and get the import routine most useful to you to work for you.

2. Single step through the code to make sure you understand what it does.

3. Make sure you are familiar with the clsBrowse class.

Module 27

Reading and Writing Data in a Database

Learning Objectives

After completing this module, you will be able to:

- Understand and use the PJDB.HTM file
- Loop through all projects in a database
- Read data from a database file for multi-project reports
- Create project schedules by writing data directly into a project database

Using the PJDB.HTM File

Use the PJDB.HTM file as your guide when reading and writing data from and to a project database, an .mdb file, a SQL Server database, or any other ODBC-compliant database. The PJDB.HTM file is located in one of Project's program folders and on the Project CD. Locate this file on your system before you dig into this module as I use information from the PJDB.HTM file to do some basic tasks. By default the English Language installation location for Project 2003 is:

C:\Program Files\Microsoft Office\OFFICE11\1033

 Before Microsoft Project 2003, the file name was **PR**JDB.HTM. In Project 2003, the name changed to PJDB.HTM. This module uses the later version of the name PJDB.HTM.

The PJDB.HTM file structure consists of two parts. Part 1 describes the project database and focuses on the "how to" side of working with a project database. It includes the following topics:

- About the Project Database

- Database Permissions and Configuration

- How Information is Stored in the Project Database

- Working with Projects in the Project Database

- Adding and Changing Rows in the Database

- Creating Project Schedule Data

- Customizing Project Data

- Managing Other Data in the Database

- Database Processing Order, Conventions, and Abbreviations

Part 2 describes every Field in every Table in the project database. The PJDB.HTM file topics provide vital information for correctly using a project database. In many cases, flags in different tables need to be set for edits to work. The PJDB.HTM file explains the required edits to flags and provides sample SQL code to make them happen. The PJDB.HTM file describes almost anything you can do to a project database; therefore, you do not need to rely on other information sources.

The PJDB.HTM explains that, for timephased data, the system stores this information in a Binary Large Object (BLOB) by default. To retrieve timescaled data stored in the database in a text readable format, complete these steps in Microsoft Project:

1. Click Tools ➤ Options.

2. Click the *Save* tab.

3. Select *Expand timephased data in the database* option.

4. Click the *OK* button.

5. Resave your project to your database.

Reading the timephased data accurately from the Project database is difficult because Project stores the data in one of the binary fields. I recommend that you do not read and write timephased data in the database. Instead, open the project and use the TimeScaleData method in Project VBA. Please note that storing time scaled data in text form adds considerable size to your project files and slows down file open and close.

Tip: Open your .mdb or .mpd files in Microsoft Access and click Tools ➤ Database Utilities ➤ Compact and Repair at least once a month. Continual editing of schedules is likely to bloat the database file size. This process also repairs any minor corruptions. Always remember to make a backup copy of your database before compacting it.

Warning: Failure to follow instructions to the letter in the PJDB.HTM file can cause corruption for the project and possibly corruption for the entire database! Do all testing of new code in a test database and maintain regular backups of production databases before you run code on them.

All of the following topical sections use an Access .mdb file. Except for the connection string, all remaining code works equally well on SQL Server. To change the connection string to work with SQL Server, copy the SQL Server connection code shown previously in Module 26.

While PJDB.HTM provides you with a data dictionary enhanced with sample code, you can also download an Entity Relationship Diagram (ERD) for the Project 2003 database from Microsoft at:

http://www.microsoft.com/downloads/details.aspx?FamilyID=b7 af9ec2-3ac1-4fc8-8e67-d908cdb9faf2&DisplayLang=en

Looping Through all Projects in a Database

The most common action programmers want to accomplish with a project database is to loop through all of the projects it contains. The following code outputs the titles of all projects you have stored in the database to the Immediate window:

```
Sub ReadProjectTitles()
Dim Conn As ADODB.Connection
Dim rs As ADODB.Recordset
Dim Files As New clsBrowse

'Create Connection to the database file
    Set Conn = New ADODB.Connection
    With Files
        .DialogTitle = "Please Find database file"
        .Filter = Array( _
            "Access Files|*.mdb", "Project Database|*.mpd")
        Files.ShowOpen
        If Files.FileName <> "" Then
            Conn.ConnectionString = _
                "Provider=Microsoft.Jet.OLEDB.4.0;" _
                & "Data Source=" & Files.FileName _
                & ";Persist Security Info=False"
            Conn.Open
        Else
            MsgBox "Macro halted by user, nothing done", _
                    vbInformation
        End
        End If
    End With

'Read all Project Titles
    Set rs = New ADODB.Recordset
    rs.Open "SELECT PROJ_NAME, PROJ_PROP_TITLE " & _
            "FROM MSP_Projects " & _
            "ORDER BY PROJ_NAME", Conn
```

```
    Do Until rs.EOF
       Debug.Print "Name used to save project: " _
              ;rs!PROJ_NAME, _
              "Name of Project Summary Task: " _
              ; rs!PROJ_PROP_TITLE
      rs.MoveNext
   Loop
   rs.Close

'Tidy up
   Set rs = Nothing
   Conn.Close
   Set Conn = Nothing
End Sub
```

In Module 26 I showed you how to browse for and then open an Access database file. In Microsoft Project, you can save projects either to a .mdb file or to a .mpd (Microsoft Project Database) file. The two file types are exactly the same; in fact, you can even open the .mpd file in Access. However, you need a way to let the user select whether to open .mdb files or .mpd files. The preceding code gives the user two file types to choose from in the File Type pick list. The two types need to be specified in an Array using the following code:

Filter = Array("Access Files|*.mdb", "Project Database|*.mpd").

Files.FileName <> "" confirms that the user has not clicked the *Cancel* button. rs.Open "SELECT PROJ_NAME, PROJ_PROP_TITLE FROM MSP_Projects ORDER BY PROJ_NAME", Conn reads the data from the database. The Pjdb.htm file tells you the name of the project table (MSP_PROJECTS) and the names of the fields (PROJ_NAME and PROJ_PROP_TITLE). PROJ_NAME is the name you enter for the project when you save the project file to the database. PROJ_PROP_TITLE is the name you enter in the Project Summary Task's name field, or the title you enter by clicking File ➢ Properties.

The PJDB.HTM file lists the field names in uppercase letters, but you do not need to observe that standard because field names are not case-sensitive. I covered the remaining code in previous modules.

Reading Data from a Database

In this example, I explain how to write Excel VBA code to read all assignment data for all projects in the database and to display this information as a Who Does What When report. The process for developing this code is as follows:

- Develop a View in Access/SQL Server to collect all required data.

- Create Excel VBA code to generate the report in a new Excel workbook and then read the data from the database.

Creating the Database View

This basic view pulls data from the Projects, Tasks, Resources, and Assignments tables. It sets the sort order by Resource, by Project, and then by Start date. The Excel code reads the column titles and inserts them into the Excel workbook in the same order as the View. What's nice about this is that editing the View to add or remove data automatically updates the report next time you run it.

The SQL code for the WhoDoesWhatWhen view is in the Module 27.mpd file, which you can download. This code is as follows:

```
SELECT MSP_PROJECTS.PROJ_ID,
    [ASSN_WORK]/60000 AS [Work (h)],
    MSP_RESOURCES.RES_NAME AS [Resource Name],
    MSP_TASKS.TASK_NAME AS [Task Name],
    MSP_PROJECTS.PROJ_PROP_TITLE AS [Project Title],
    MSP_TASKS.TASK_START_DATE AS Start,
    MSP_TASKS.TASK_FINISH_DATE AS Finish,
    [TASK_DUR]/600/8 AS [Dur (d)],
    MSP_TASKS.TASK_PCT_COMP AS [% Comp]
FROM MSP_TASKS INNER JOIN
    (MSP_RESOURCES INNER JOIN
    (MSP_PROJECTS INNER JOIN MSP_ASSIGNMENTS ON
    MSP_PROJECTS.PROJ_ID = MSP_ASSIGNMENTS.PROJ_ID)
    ON MSP_RESOURCES.RES_UID = MSP_ASSIGNMENTS.RES_UID) ON
    MSP_TASKS.TASK_UID = MSP_ASSIGNMENTS.TASK_UID
WHERE (((MSP_RESOURCES.RES_NAME) Is Not Null))
ORDER BY MSP_RESOURCES.RES_NAME,
    MSP_PROJECTS.PROJ_PROP_TITLE, MSP_TASKS.TASK_START_DATE
```

Note that the SQL code provides new names for the columns for easier reading.

Creating the Excel VBA Macro

Create a new workbook in Excel from which to run the following macro:

```
Sub WhoDoesWhatWhen()
Dim FileName As String
Dim Conn As ADODB.Connection
Dim rs As ADODB.Recordset
Dim fld As ADODB.Field
Dim R As Range
Dim Off As Long

'Create Connection to the database file
  Set Conn = New ADODB.Connection
  FileName = Application.GetOpenFilename( _
     "Access Files (*.mdb), *.mdb,Project Databases " _
     & "(*.mpd),*.mpd")
  If FileName <> "False" Then
     Conn.ConnectionString="Provider=" _
          & "Microsoft.Jet.OLEDB.4.0;" _
          & "Data Source=" & FileName
     Conn.Open
  Else
     MsgBox "Macro halted by user, nothing done", _
        vbInformation
     End
  End If

'Create Excel Report
  Workbooks.Add
  Set R = Range("A1")
  With R
     .Value = "Who Does What When"
     .Font.Bold = True
     .Font.Size = 14
  End With
  With R.Range("A2")
     .Value = "As of: " & Format(Date, "Long Date")
     .Font.Italic = True
     .Font.Size = 12
  End With
  Set R = Range("A4")
```

```
'Read Data
   Set rs = New ADODB.Recordset
   rs.Open "SELECT * FROM WhoDoesWhatWhen", Conn
   For Each fld In rs.Fields
       R.Offset(0, Off) = fld.Name
       Off = Off + 1
   Next fld
   R.CurrentRegion.Font.Bold = True

   R.Offset(1,0).CopyFromRecordset rs
   rs.Close

'Adjust column widths
   Range(R.Range("B1"), R.End(xlToRight)).EntireColumn.AutoFit

'Tidy up
   Set rs = Nothing
   Conn.Close
   Set Conn = Nothing
End Sub
```

One of the first things you discover about the preceding code is just how fast it runs! You could have 20 projects in a database and the code exports the data into a report in Excel within seconds. This code has all the makings of a true multi-project reporting tool.

 If you save multiple projects in a database, there is a risk of having all your schedule eggs in one basket. Make sure your backup process is thorough!

You might want to modify the Excel workbook report to do one of the following:

- Filter out completed assignments
- Limit the View to assignments starting in the next 3 months

Edit the code in the Read Data section as follows:

```
'Read Data
   Set rs = New ADODB.Recordset
   rs.Open "SELECT * FROM WhoDoesWhatWhen", Conn
   For Each fld In rs.Fields
       R.Offset(0, Off) = fld.Name
       Off = Off + 1
   Next fld
   R.CurrentRegion.Font.Bold = True

   R.Offset(1,0).CopyFromRecordset rs
   rs.Close
```

Set rs = New ADODB.Recordset creates a new object in memory to work with your data. A recordset is a set of records (rows) in your database. rs.Open "SELECT * FROM WhoDoesWhatWhen", Conn opens the new recordset. It includes the data in all columns, specified by the * asterisk notation, from the WhoDoesWhatWhen Query or View using the connection Conn. The connection provides the database path for Access, or the server name and database name for SQL Server.

A recordset object holds information about the data in it including the details of each field or column of data. Rs.Fields is a collection of all the fields in the recordset. For Each fld In rs.Fields sets the field variable fld to each field in turn. Off is a counter that the system uses to offset the range variable so each field ends up in its own column in the worksheet.

R.Offset(0, Off) = fld.Name copies the field's name into the relevant cell. To help you understand this code, single step through it and then hover your mouse over each bit to read its values. In the Immediate window, when this line is the next to be executed it is highlighted in yellow in the VBE. Type ? R.Offset(0, Off).Address and then press the Enter key. The VBE will print the address to which the code is referring at that time. By looking at the current value of the Off variable, you quickly understand how this code works. Remember that a little experimentation on your part is worth a thousand of my words.

R.CurrentRegion.Font.Bold = True applies Bold formatting to the row of titles. R.Range("A2").CopyFromRecordset rs is a very powerful statement. It automatically copies the data in the rs recordset object into Excel starting at the address pointed to by R.Offset(1,0). This address is the cell below R. Since R is still pointing to the first title cell, R.Offset(1,0) is the cell immediately below the first field title.

You can use the basics of this macro as a basis for other macros to create multi-project reports on projects in a database. I recommend that you get help from people experienced in using Access or SQL Server databases, so you can report on just the data you want. A big bonus from using this code is that you can edit the Query in Access or in the SQL Server View, and the code automatically adjusts to output on the information you now want without revising a line of code or updating macros on everyone's computers.

Writing Data to a Database

Project administrators often need to create new schedules based on information in a legacy system. If you have only a few tasks, using the code for importing data from Excel can work well. However, once the number of tasks gets above a certain number, which is dependent on the speed of your computer and network, using Excel can be slow. You may also want to create a new schedule in a database on your network from a computer that does not have Microsoft Project installed. In these cases, a useful technique is to create the schedule in a database and then open it in Microsoft Project.

Next I show you how to add tasks, resources, and assignments in the database. By working carefully with the PJDB.HTM file you can add anything else you want, but leave the creation of timephased data for VBA macros in Microsoft Project.

To add data to a project database, you can use any development system you want, from Visual Basic to ASP or to a variant of C. In this example, I use Excel VBA as it is the language most readers are likely to know and use. For the Excel VBA code to work, you must have the following:

- An Access database containing at least one project or one with the table structure already in place (the system creates table structures automatically when you save the first project in a new database).

- A copy of the PJDB.HTM file readily available.

- A reference in your code to the Microsoft ActiveX Data Objects library. Although any version will do, it is better to have the latest version. At the time of writing, 2.8 is the latest version number.

Following are the Comments for this code:

```
'Create Connection to the database file
'Get next highest project number
'Create a new Project and Project Summary task
'Create new Tasks
'Create a new Task Link
'Create a new Task Text1 field
'Create a new Resource
'Create a new Assignment
'Tidy Up
```

The code to add a simple project to the database using Excel VBA is as follows:

```
Sub CreateProject()
Dim FileName As String
Dim Conn As ADODB.Connection
Dim rs As ADODB.Recordset

Dim fld As ADODB.Field
Dim SQL As String
Dim ProjNum As Long

'Create Connection to the database file
   Set Conn = New ADODB.Connection
   FileName = Application.GetOpenFilename( _
      "Project Databases (*.mpd),*.mpd," _
         & "Access Files (*.mdb), *.mdb")
   If FileName <> "False" Then
      Conn.ConnectionString = _
            "Provider=Microsoft.Jet.OLEDB.4.0;" _
            & "Data Source=" & FileName
      Conn.Open
   Else
      MsgBox "Macro halted by user, nothing done", _
         vbInformation
      End
   End If
   Set rs = New ADODB.Recordset

'Get next highest project number
   SQL = "SELECT Max([PROJ_ID])+1 AS ProjNum FROM " _
            & "MSP_PROJECTS;"
   rs.Open SQL, Conn
   ProjNum = rs!ProjNum
   rs.Close
```

```
'Create a new Project and Project Summary task
   SQL = "INSERT INTO MSP_PROJECTS ( PROJ_ID, " _
        & "PROJ_NAME, PROJ_INFO_START_DATE, " _
        & "PROJ_EXT_EDITED ) " _
        & "VALUES (" & ProjNum & ", 'My Project', " _
        & "#1/1/2007#, '1');"
   Conn.Execute SQL
   SQL = "Insert into MSP_TASKS " _
        &"(PROJ_ID,TASK_UID,TASK_ID,TASK_NAME," _
        & "EXT_EDIT_REF_DATA ) " _
        & "values (" & ProjNum & ",0,0,'My Project','1' )"
   Conn.Execute SQL

'Create new Tasks
   SQL = "Insert into MSP_TASKS " _
        & "(PROJ_ID,TASK_UID,TASK_ID,TASK_NAME," _
        & "TASK_DUR,TASK_OUTLINE_LEVEL," _
        & "EXT_EDIT_REF_DATA ) " _
        & "values (" & ProjNum & ",1,1,'My Task 1', _
        & "4800,1,'1' )"

   Conn.Execute SQL
   SQL = "Insert into MSP_TASKS " _
        & "(PROJ_ID,TASK_UID,TASK_ID,TASK_NAME," _
        & "TASK_DUR,TASK_OUTLINE_LEVEL," _
        & "EXT_EDIT_REF_DATA ) " _
        & "values (" & ProjNum & ",2,2,'My Task 2', _
        & "9600,1,'1' )"
   Conn.Execute SQL

'Create a new Task Link
   SQL = "Insert into MSP_LINKS " _
        & "(PROJ_ID,LINK_UID,LINK_PRED_UID," _
        & "LINK_SUCC_UID,EXT_EDIT_REF_DATA ) " _
        & "values (" & ProjNum & ",1,1,2,'1' );"
   Conn.Execute SQL

'Create a new Task Text1 field
   SQL = "INSERT INTO MSP_TEXT_FIELDS " _
        & "(PROJ_ID,TEXT_CATEGORY,TEXT_REF_UID," _
        & "TEXT_FIELD_ID,TEXT_VALUE) " _
        & "values (" & ProjNum & ",0,1,188743731,'My Text1' )"
   Conn.Execute SQL
   SQL = "UPDATE MSP_PROJECTS " _
        & "Set PROJ_EXT_EDITED_TEXT='1' " _
        & "WHERE Proj_ID=" & ProjNum & ";"
   Conn.Execute SQL
```

```
'Create a new Resource
   SQL = "Insert into MSP_RESOURCES " _
         & "(PROJ_ID,RES_UID,RES_ID,RES_NAME," _
         & "RES_TYPE,EXT_EDIT_REF_DATA ) " _
         & "values (" & ProjNum & ",1,1,'My Resource',-1,'1' )"
   Conn.Execute SQL

'Create a new Assignment
   SQL = "Insert into MSP_ASSIGNMENTS " _
         & "(PROJ_ID,ASSN_UID,RES_UID,TASK_UID," _
         & "ASSN_UNITS,ASSN_WORK,EXT_EDIT_REF_DATA)" _
         & "values (" & ProjNum & ",1,1,1,0.5,240000,'1' )"
   Conn.Execute SQL

'Tidy Up
   Conn.Close
   Set Conn = Nothing
End Sub
```

Connecting to the Access database is nothing new for you. The first block of code to add data to the database is as follows:

```
'Get next highest project number
   SQL = "SELECT Max([PROJ_ID])+1 AS ProjNum FROM " _
         & "MSP_PROJECTS;"
   rs.Open SQL, Conn
   ProjNum = rs!ProjNum
   rs.Close
```

In all the tables, the **PROJ_ID** number is an essential piece of information. This number must be unique to your new project, so your first task is to read the maximum PROJ_ID number and increment it by 1 to create an ID for your new project. The SQL statement performs that step. The only field and row returned is the new project number. This technique guarantees a unique number. The code saves the new number in ProjNum for use whenever you need the PROJ_ID number.

```
'Create a new Project and Project Summary task
   SQL = "INSERT INTO MSP_PROJECTS ( PROJ_ID, " _
         & "PROJ_NAME, PROJ_INFO_START_DATE, " _
         & "PROJ_EXT_EDITED ) " _
         & "VALUES (" & ProjNum & ", 'My Project', " _
         & "#1/1/2007#, '1');"
   Conn.Execute SQL
   SQL = "Insert into MSP_TASKS " _
         &"(PROJ_ID,TASK_UID,TASK_ID,TASK_NAME," _
         & "EXT_EDIT_REF_DATA ) " _
         & "values (" & ProjNum & ",0,0,'My Project','1' )"
   Conn.Execute SQL
```

All sections essentially repeat the first section, so let's look at what is in the PJDB.HTM file and how that translates into VBA code. In PJDB.HTM, a section called *Creating a new, non-enterprise project* contains a list of all tables and fields that require values to add an item. A new project is unique because it requires a row of data in the MSP_PROJECTS table and in the MSP_Tasks table. The system requires a Project Summary task, Task 0 (zero) that holds data for the Project Summary Task.

Most of the instructions on adding a task, resource, or assignment provide the sample SQL code for you to edit and use. However, the new Project topic does not. The first SQL statement above carries the minimum information you must provide to create a new Project record in the MSP_PROJECTS table.

One interesting and vital field that must contain a value is the PROJ_EXT_EDITED field. Microsoft Project stores all its data in binary fields that are not available for editing and extracts these values to the database fields for you to read. If you add a new record or edit an existing record, then you must set the PROJ_EXT_EDITED flag in MSP_PROJECTS so that Project knows that you have changed the data deliberately. The next time you open the record, it knows to update the binary data based on the text data in the record. Each table has a field with EXT_EDITED and in some tables, like the MSP_TEXT_FIELDS table, it requires you to set an extra flag in the table as well. If you ignore these flag fields, the system will ignore your updates to the database, and at worst will corrupt the project.

#m/d/yyyy# is the date format for an Access database. For SQL Server a good international date format is 'yyyy-mm-dd'. Conn.Execute SQL executes the SQL statement using the Conn connection object. The next instruction adds a task to the MSP_TASKS table. Any task with a UID and ID of zero is a Project Summary Task (Task 0) and there can only be one for each project.

By carefully reviewing the PJDB.HTM file, and looking at data Microsoft already put into the database, it is not too difficult to determine the additional data you must add.

> When you add a new project to the MSP_PROJECTS table, all flags default to zero. For your project to have the options you expect, you need to set the PROJ_OPT fields to the desired settings. The easy way to determine the correct settings is to copy the settings from another project already saved into the database using Microsoft Project.

While creating this sample macro, I found that I needed to set the RES_TYPE field to -1 when adding a resource to force the resource to be a Work resource rather than a Material resource. Oddly, this is contrary to what the PJDB.HTM file says. Otherwise, I have not found any other discrepancies in the file. If you are even slightly in doubt, then copy the values from projects, tasks, resources, and assignments that you find in projects that you saved to the database using Microsoft Project.

Hands On Exercise

Exercise 27-1

Read and write data with a database.

1. Read the PJDB.HTM file to get familiar with the contents.

2. Create an .mpd file by saving an .mpp project in the .mpd file format.

3. Save two more projects to the same .mpd file but with different project titles.

4. Create queries in Access to read Queries from the .mpd database to show all milestones across all projects. Use the queries detailed above.

5. If it is useful for you, develop a macro to create a project in a database.

Note: If you wish, you can save the projects in a SQL Server database.

Module 28

Using the OLE DB

Learning Objectives

After completing this module, you will be able to:

- Understand how to use the OLE DB drivers
- Understand the limitations of OLE DB drivers
- Read data from a Project .mpp file using OLEDB

Understanding OLEDB

OLEDB is a Microsoft technology used for reading data from just about any source. Microsoft Project automatically installs an OLEDB driver you can use to read .mpp files directly from another application. Microsoft first provided OLEDB drivers when it released Microsoft Project 2000, but with limitations. Table 28-1 explains what features each version of Project provides.

Microsoft Project Version	Features Provided
98	No OLEDB driver available
2000	Read Only data for Tasks, Resources, Assignments (not time phased)
2002	Many more tables such as Calendars and custom fields, as well as time phased data. Unfortunately, the dates and times values it returns for daily time phased data are incorrect
2003	All data available with correct daily timephased data

**Table 28-1: OLEDB drivers
for Project versions**

Using the OLEDB Driver for Your Project Version

In one of Microsoft Project's program folders, look for the **PJOLEDB.HTM** file (called **PRJOLEDB.HTM** in Project 2002 and 2000). This file contains the OLEDB information you need including sample code. Once you connect to an .mpp file using OLEDB, reading its data is very similar to reading data from any other data source.

Pay close attention to the section in the pjoledb.htm file called *Limitations*. Read this section first as it will save you time and frustration! The key aspects of OLEDB are:

- It provides read access only, so you cannot write to .mpp files.

- It does not support multi-table queries; therefore, you can read from only one table at a time. It does support Shaped data sets as a way around this limitation. (See the example later in this module)

- You can read Recordsets in forward-only mode. OLEDB neither supports the MovePrevious, MoveFirst, and MoveLast methods, nor does it support the RecordCount property.

- The WHERE clause of your SQL statements does not support ANY, LIKE, and IS NOT.

- It does not support the Sum, Avg, Min, Max, Count, and StDev aggregate functions.

Using the OLEDB driver with Project 2007

At the time of this writing, Microsoft Project 2007 does not include an OLEDB driver. Microsoft tells us that there will be an OLEDB driver you can download, but only for use with Project 2000-2003 file formats. Your only options for reading data from Project 2007 are:

- Save your projects as .xml files and read the .xml file directly.

- Save your projects to a database and read from the database.

- Open the project in Microsoft Project and use automation to read data.

- Use Project Server 2007 and read data using the software's new PSI programming interface.

Connecting to an .MPP File Using OLEDB

Before OLEDB code can work, you must add a reference to a Microsoft ActiveX Data Object Library. At the time of writing, the 2.8 refresh is the latest version. The following code connects to an .mpp file you select and then closes the connection and returns a message indicating the successful connection. The following code runs in Excel VBA, but it works for VBA in any Office application. It can also run with little change in VB or VB.Net.

```
Sub OLEDBConnect()
Dim Conn As ADODB.Connection
Dim FileName As String
   On Error Resume next
   FileName = Application.GetOpenFilename(FileFilter:= _
        "Project Files (*.mpp),*.mpp", _
        Title:="Find Project file to report on")
   If Dir(FileName) <> "" Then
      Set Conn = New ADODB.Connection
'Connect to Project 2003
      Conn.ConnectionString = "Provider=" & _
      "Microsoft.Project" & ".OLEDB.11.0;" & _
      "PROJECT NAME=" & FileName
```

```
        Conn.Open
        If Err Then
           MsgBox "Could not connect to the Project file." & _
              vbCrLf & "Error: " & Err.Description, _
              vbCritical + vbOKOnly
        Else
           MsgBox "Successful Connection",
              vbInformation + vbOKOnly
              Conn.close
        End If
     End If
End Sub
```

GetOpenFilename is the same function used in earlier modules to let the user browse to a file. Dir() tests whether the user clicked the Cancel button or entered an invalid file. Conn.ConnectionString = "Provider=Microsoft.Project.OLEDB.11.0;PROJECT NAME=" & FileName is the connection string required for Project 2003. To connect when you have Project 2002 installed, edit the version number from 11 to 10. To connect when you have Project 2000 installed, edit the version number from 11 to 9. The remaining code displays a message depending on the success of the connection. If the connection open succeeds, the code closes the connection.

The next routine shows a more complete example, which reads tasks, resources, and time phased data for each Resource. Module 28 Sample Code.xls contains the sample code for this module:

```
Sub ReadData()
Dim rs As ADODB.Recordset
Dim cnnProject As ADODB.Connection
Dim strSelect As String
Dim R As Range
Dim Path As String
Dim strConn As String
   On Error Resume Next
   Path = Application.GetOpenFilename( _
        "Project Files (*.mpp), *.mpp", , _
        "Select file to report on")
   If Dir(Path) = "" Then
      MsgBox "File invalid or macro halted by user", _
         vbInformation
      Exit Sub
```

407

```
End If
strConn = "Provider=Microsoft.Project.OLEDB.11.0;" _
   & "Project Name=" & Path

Set rs = New ADODB.Recordset
Set cnnProject = New ADODB.Connection

cnnProject.Open strConn & ";"
If cnnProject Is Nothing Then
   MsgBox "Could not connect to the Project file." _
      & vbCrLf & "Error: " & Err.Description, _
      vbCritical + vbOKOnly
End If
'Copy Task details
strSelect = "Select TaskUniqueID, TaskName " _
         &"FROM Tasks Order by TaskID"
rs.Open strSelect, cnnProject
Set R = [A3]
R.CurrentRegion.Offset(2, 0).ClearContents
Do Until rs.EOF
   R.Range("A1") = rs!TaskName
   R.Range("B1") = rs!TaskUniqueID
   Set R = R.Offset(1, 0)
   rs.MoveNext
Loop
rs.Close

'Copy Resource details
strSelect = "Select ResourceUniqueID, ResourceName " _
         & "FROM Resources Order by ResourceName"
rs.Open strSelect, cnnProject
Set R = [D3]
R.CurrentRegion.Offset(2, 0).ClearContents
Do Until rs.EOF
   R.Range("A1") = rs!ResourceName
   R.Range("B1") = rs!ResourceUniqueID
   rs.MoveNext
   Set R = R.Offset(1, 0)
Loop
rs.Close

'Copy Daily details
'rsProjectResourcesTimephased.Open _
   "ResourceTimephasedByDay", cnnProject
```

```
On Error Resume Next
strSelect = "Select ResourceUniqueID, " _
        & "ResourceTimeStart, " _
        & "ResourceTimeFinish, ResourceTimeWork " _
        & "FROM ResourceTimephasedByDay " _
        & "ORDER BY ResourceTimeStart"
rs.Open strSelect, cnnProject
Set R = [G3]
R.CurrentRegion.Offset(2, 0).ClearContents
With rs
   Do Until .EOF
      If Val(rs!ResourceTimeWork) > 0 Then
         R = rs!ResourceUniqueID
         R.Offset(0, 1) = rs!ResourceTimeStart
         R.Offset(0, 2) = rs!ResourceTimeFinish
         R.Offset(0, 3) = _
                 rs!ResourceTimeWork / 60000
         Set R = R.Offset(1, 0)
      End If
      rs.MoveNext
   Loop
End With
rs.Close

'Copy Weekly details
strSelect = "SELECT ResourceUniqueID, " _
        & "ResourceTimeStart, " _
        & "ResourceTimeFinish, ResourceTimeWork " _
        & "FROM ResourceTimephasedByWeek " _
        & "ORDER BY ResourceTimeStart"
rs.Open strSelect, cnnProject
Set R = [L3]
R.CurrentRegion.Offset(2, 0).ClearContents
With rs
   Do Until .EOF
      If Val(rs!ResourceTimeWork) > 0 Then
         R = rs!ResourceUniqueID
         R.Offset(0, 1) = rs!ResourceTimeStart
         R.Offset(0, 2) = rs!ResourceTimeFinish
         R.Offset(0, 3) = _
                 rs!ResourceTimeWork / 60000
         Set R = R.Offset(1, 0)
      End If
      rs.MoveNext
   Loop
End With
rs.Close
```

```
    'Copy Monthly details
    strSelect = "SELECT ResourceUniqueID, " _
            & "ResourceTimeStart, " _
            & "ResourceTimeFinish, ResourceTimeWork " _
            & "FROM ResourceTimephasedByMonth " _
    rs.Open strSelect, cnnProject
    Set R = [Q3]
    R.CurrentRegion.Offset(2, 0).ClearContents
    With rs
        Do Until .EOF
            If Val(rs!ResourceTimeWork) > 0 Then
                R = rs!ResourceUniqueID
                R.Offset(0, 1) = rs!ResourceTimeStart
                R.Offset(0, 2) = rs!ResourceTimeFinish
                R.Offset(0, 3) = _
                        rs!ResourceTimeWork / 60000
                Set R = R.Offset(1, 0)
            End If
            rs.MoveNext
        Loop
    End With
    rs.Close
    cnnProject.Close
End Sub
```

The first code blocks should be familiar to you, so the first new code to discuss in this example reads Task data:

```
'Copy Task details
    strSelect = "Select TaskUniqueID, TaskName " _
        &"FROM Tasks Order by TaskID"
    rs.Open strSelect, cnnProject
    Set R = [A3]
    R.CurrentRegion.Offset(2, 0).ClearContents
    Do Until rs.EOF
        R.Range("A1") = rs!TaskName
        R.Range("B1") = rs!TaskUniqueID
        Set R = R.Offset(1, 0)
        rs.MoveNext
    Loop
    rs.Close
```

Using the strSelect variable is not required, but it makes for tighter code that is easier to understand. I took the field names directly from the pjoledb.htm file and its Tasks Table description. Use the rs.Open statement exactly as you would to open a recordset from a database. If you've worked through each module in this workbook, you have previously seen and used all the code shown here! This macro simply repurposes old snippets of code in order to accomplish new functionality.

Lastly, you must learn how to create Shaped recordsets. This is not simple, as it requires advanced SQL code. If you do not have access to anyone with good SQL skills, then the following example provides you with a good starting point:

```vba
Public Sub GetShapedData()
Dim strSQL As String
Dim cnnProject As ADODB.Connection
Dim rsPrj As ADODB.Recordset
Dim rsTsk As ADODB.Recordset
Dim rsAsn As ADODB.Recordset
Dim R As Range
Dim FileName As String
Dim strConn As String
    On Error Resume Next
    Worksheets("Shaped OLEDB").Select

    Set cnnProject = New ADODB.Connection
    Set rsPrj = New ADODB.Recordset
    Set rsTsk = New ADODB.Recordset
    Set rsAsn = New ADODB.Recordset
    Set R = [A1]
    R = "Projects"
    R.Range("B1") = "Tasks"
    R.Range("C1") = "Resources"
    R.Range("A1:C1").Font.Bold = True

    Set R = [A2]
    R.CurrentRegion.Offset(1, 0).ClearContents
    FileName = Application.GetOpenFilename( _
        "Project Files (*.mpp), *.mpp")
    If Dir(FileName) = "" Then
        MsgBox "File invalid or macro halted by user", _
        vbInformation
        Exit Sub
    End If
```

```
    strConn = "Provider=MSDataShape;Extended Properties= _
        & "'Project Name=" & FileName & "';" _
        & "Persist Security Info=False;Data " _
        & "Provider=MICROSOFT.PROJECT.OLEDB.11.0"

    cnnProject.Open strConn

    strSQL = "SHAPE {SELECT * FROM Project} " _
        & "APPEND ((SHAPE {SELECT * FROM Tasks} " _
            & "APPEND ({SELECT * FROM Assignments} " _
            & "as rsAsn " _
            & "RELATE 'TaskUniqueId' TO " _
                & "'TaskUniqueId')) as rsTasks " _
            & "RELATE 'Project' TO 'Project')"
    rsPrj.Open strSQL, cnnProject
    If Err Then
        MsgBox "Could not open Shaped Recordset." _
            & vbCrLf & "Error: " & Err.Description
        Exit Sub
    End If

    Do While Not rsPrj.EOF
        Set rsTsk = rsPrj!rsTasks.Value
        Do While Not rsTsk.EOF
            Set rsAsn = rsTsk!rsAsn.Value
            Do While Not rsAsn.EOF
                R.Range("A1") = rsPrj("ProjectTitle")
                R.Range("B1") = rsTsk("TaskName")
                R.Range("C1") = _
                    rsAsn("AssignmentResourceName")
                R.Range("D1") = _
                    rsAsn("AssignmentStart")
                R.Range("E1") = _
                    rsAsn("AssignmentFinish")
                R.Range("F1") = _
                    rsAsn("AssignmentWork") / 60000
                Set R = R.Offset(1, 0)
                rsAsn.MoveNext
            Loop
            rsTsk.MoveNext
        Loop
        rsPrj.MoveNext
    Loop
    rsAsn.Close
    rsTsk.Close
    rsPrj.Close
    cnnProject.Close
End Sub
```

The new code for you in the above example is the SQL Code and its SHAPE command which appends related recordsets together. You can then iterate through each recordset, and by keeping them in sync, you can simulate linked tables. The example above reads data from the Tasks, Resources, and Assignments tables.

Make sure you select a Project .mpp file which has Resource assignments when the macro prompts you for an .mpp file.

Hands On Exercise

Exercise 28-1

Work with the Microsoft Project OLEDB.

1. Test the sample code with one of your .mpp files.

2. Single step through the code to help understand what it does.

3. Edit the Resource data to return data for a specific Unique ID.

4. Edit the time phased data to create a report in Excel that looks like the week by week Resource Usage View in Project. You will need Project 2002 or 2003 to do this.

Module 29

Accessing Project Server Data from Excel

Learning Objectives

After completing this module, you will be able to:

- Understand and use the PJSVRDB.HTM file
- Develop a weekly report from Project Server data
- Loop through all projects in the Project Server database
- Read milestone data for all projects in the Project Server database
- Read all Issues and Risks for a project

Understanding the PJSVRDB.HTM File

Similar to the file called pjdb.htm that describes the Microsoft Project tables, Microsoft provides a file called **PJSVRDB.HTM** describing the tables in the Project Server Database. The pjsvrdb.htm file relates only to data in the Project Server tables, but does not address the separate Windows SharePoint Services database used for Risks, Issues, and Documents. Microsoft recommends that you do not work directly with SharePoint tables, choosing not to release a similar document to pjsvrdb.htm for the WSS database. When you work with Project Server, use both PJDB.HTM and PJSVRDB.HTM together as a reference set.

The Tables in the Project Server database fall into four main groups, as follows:

- **Project data** – The native data about any project is exposed in the Project Server database in a collection of tables labeled with the prefix "msp_." The system populates the project tables each time the project manager saves a project in the Project Server database.

- **Project Web Access data** – Once a project has been "published" to Project Web Access, the system stores the published data in a collection of tables labeled with the prefix "msp_web."

- **OLAP Cube data** – Each time the system processes the OLAP Cube, it stores the data in a collection of tables labeled with the prefix "msp_cube."

- **View data** – The system stores data used for the processing of business and presentation logic in Project Web Access in a collection of tables labeled with the prefix "msp_view."

It is very risky to update data in the Project Server tables. Microsoft provides a limited set of functionality through Project Server's PDS programming interface and you can also use Automation via Project Professional. The Microsoft product development team recommends using the new PSI interface introduced with Project Server 2007 to update projects.

The remaining topics in this module describe how to use Project Server data, culminating in a powerful Excel report. The macros read data via read-only Views.

Weekly Reporting on Project Server Data

Project Server holds lots of useful information for project stakeholders. Unfortunately, some project managers have a long list of excuses for not keeping their projects, Issues, and Risks up to date, making the Project Server Data less useful than it should be!

If you provide project managers with an Excel spreadsheet that, with a click, a button automatically filled out 80% of their weekly report, wouldn't this provide an incentive for project managers to update their projects, Issues, and Risks? I dedicate the rest of this module to creating such a spreadsheet to help you learn the basics of reading data from a Project Server database; including Issue and Risk data from the Windows SharePoint Services (WSS) database.

Looping through All Projects

Sooner than later, you will want to loop through all projects in the Project Server database. For example, you may want to republish them all after changing custom fields in the Enterprise Global file. The following code loops through all projects in Project Server and publishes each plan before closing them.

```
Sub LoopThroughAllProjects()
Dim Conn As New ADODB.Connection
Dim rs As ADODB.Recordset
'Create Connection to the .mdb file
   Set Conn = New ADODB.Connection
   Set rs = New ADODB.Recordset
   Conn.ConnectionString = "Provider=sqloledb;" _
       & "Data Source=YourSqlServerName;" _
       & "Initial Catalog=YourDatabaseName;" _
       & "Integrated Security=SSPI;"
   Conn.Open

'Open Recordset with all projects in
   Rs.Open "Select Proj_Name, Proj_ID FROM MSP_Projects" _
       & " WHERE (Proj_Version = 'Published')", Conn
```

```
'Open and Publish each project
   Do Until rs.EOF
      FileOpen "<>\" & rs!Proj_Name
      Application.PublishProjectPlan
      FileClose pjDoNotSave
      Rs.MoveNext
   Loop

'Tidy up
   rs.Close
   conn.Close
End Sub
```

To build the recordset open statement, you must look up the field names in pjsvrdb.htm. Because Project Server provides additional versions of projects, my code limits the recordset to the default Published versions only.

In the previous code example, the Open and Publish statements are the only ones we have not used before. To open a project from the Project Server database, you must first open Microsoft Project Professional and log into Project Server. Define the file name using the following structure:

```
FileOpen "<>\ProjectName.Version"
```

For example, to open the .Published version of any project, use the following code:

```
FileOpen "<>\ProjectName.Published"
```

Starting Project Professional and Logging into Project Server

In order for the previous example to work, you must already have Project Professional open and logged into Project Server. If you need to start Project Professional from another application and want to log into Project Server, the usual CreateObject statement does not work. With CreateObject, you cannot pass the Project Server address or login details, consequently the system starts Project Professional in Offline mode when you start it with the CreateObject command. The following code starts Project Professional in Online mode, reports the online status, and then exits the application.

```
Sub StartProject()
'Requires Reference to Microsoft Project
Dim projApp As MSProject.Application
   On Error Resume Next
   Shell "winproj.exe /s http://ServerName/ProjectServer/"
   Do Until Not (projApp Is Nothing)
      DoEvents
      Set projApp = GetObject(, "MSProject.Application")
   Loop
   Debug.Print projApp.Name
   Debug.Print projApp.Profiles. _
      ActiveProfile.ConnectionState
   projApp.Quit
   Set projApp = Nothing
End Sub
```

The Shell "winproj.exe /s http://ServerName/ProjectServer/" code opens Project Professional and logs into Project Server using Windows Authentication. Shell is a VBA command that lets you start an application and pass parameters as part of the command line. The /S parameter for winroj.exe allows you to pass the Project Server address. You can also pass a user name and a password using /U and /P parameters. Omitting /U and /P forces a login using Windows Authentication.

Shell runs the application command you pass, then returns control right back to the calling code. This means that your code tries to connect to Project Professional before it has started and logged in. The Do Until Not (projApp Is Nothing) statement keeps your code looping until the Set ProjApp statement succeeds, or until after Project Professional has successfully started and logged in.

DoEvents passes control to Windows so it can catch up with any actions it has queued, including getting Project Professional started and logged into Project Server. While you do not need this functionality for the weekly report, it is valuable for many applications that need to start Project Professional in online mode and to connect with Project Server.

Setting up the Excel Report

The basic Excel Report for Project Server projects includes the following features:

- The main worksheet, named Milestones, includes a pick list for all Project Titles. Selecting a project title or clicking an *Update* button reads all data for the report. The Project Title appears in cell A1 with the report date in cell A2. The report labels cell A1 ProjectTitle, labels cell A4 Milestones, and labels a cell hidden by the pick list (for example, K1) ProjIndex.

- The second worksheet, labeled Current Tasks, has its Title and Report date in cells A1 and A2. The contents are formulas linked to cells A1 and A2 in the Milestones Worksheet. Cell A4 is labeled CurrentTasks.

- The third worksheet, Issues, has the same layout as the Current Tasks Worksheet. The report labels cell A4 Issues.

- The fourth worksheet, Risks, features the same layout as the Issues Worksheet. The report labels cell A4 Risks.

- The fifth and final worksheet, Setup, is for temporary data. Initially it contains the list of Project Titles in Project Server to populate the pick list in the Milestones Worksheet. The report labels cell A1 Projects.

The macro read all column titles and data directly from the Project Server Database each time it runs. Download the file Module 29 Sample Code.xls from the Web site. The Workbook has the Worksheets already set up and contains all the VBA code. You must edit the Project Server computer and database names in the code to match your own names to get the code to work.

Reading a List of All Project Titles

The Milestones worksheet contains a pick list for all project titles, so the first step is to create a View in the ProjectServer database called ProjectTitles.

To make this code work, add the ProjectTitlesPublished View to your Project Server database. This requires your SQL Server administrator to add the View and make sure all Project Server users have read-only access to the View.

The ProjectTitlesPublished View has the following SQL Code:

```
CREATE VIEW dbo.ProjectTitlesPublished
AS
SELECT  TOP 100 PERCENT PROJ_ID, PROJ_PROP_TITLE AS Title
FROM    dbo.MSP_PROJECTS
WHERE (PROJ_VERSION = 'Published')
ORDER BY PROJ_NAME
```

The View returns the Proj_ID number and Title for each project. You must use the Proj_Id to refer to data in other Tables for the selected project. The system uses Proj_Id, not title, to define which task, resource, or assignment belongs to which project. A number is a more accurate and faster way of finding data for a project, especially as some Project Title fields include .Published at the end, while others do not.

After you have the ProjectTitlesPublished View in place and your Project Server user account has read access to it, with the GetProjectTitles code in place you are ready to add the pick list using the following steps:

1. Select or create a Milestones worksheet.

2. Click View ➤ Toolbars ➤ Forms.

3. Click the *Combo Box* button.

4. Draw the Combo Box from cell H1 to cell L1 and make it 1 row tall.

5. Right-click the Combo Box object and select *Format Control* from the shortcut menu.

6. Click the *Properties* tab and select the *Don't move or size with cells* option.

7. Click the *Control* tab and enter ProjLink in the *Cell link* field and then enter 20 in the *Drop down lines* field.

8. Click the *OK* button.

9. In the *Name* box in Excel (the white box at the left end of the *Formula bar*) enter the name *ProjectsDropDown* and press the Enter key.

The third step in creating the Milestones worksheet is writing the code to read the Project Titles from the Project Server database into the pick list, as follows:

```
Sub GetProjectTitles()
'This routine is called by the Open event in the ThisWorkbook
'Excel Object. It updates the drop down list with the latest
'Project Titles in Project Server.
Dim Conn As ADODB.Connection
Dim rs As ADODB.Recordset
Dim R As Range
    Set Conn = New ADODB.Connection
    Conn.ConnectionString = "Provider=sqloledb;" _
            & "Data Source=ServerName;" _
            & "Initial Catalog=" _
            & "ProjectServerDatabaseName;" _
            & "Integrated Security=SSPI;"
```

```
    Conn.Open
    Set rs = New ADODB.Recordset

    rs.Open "SELECT * FROM ProjectTitlesPublished", Conn

    'Create Report
    Set R = Range("Projects")
    R.CurrentRegion.ClearContents
    R.CopyFromRecordset rs

    'Reset Drop Down box
    Worksheets("Milestones").Shapes("ProjectsDropDown") _
        .Select
    With Selection
        .ListFillRange = "Setup!" & Range("Projects") _
            .Address & ":" & Range("Projects") _
            .End(xlDown).Offset(0, 1).Address
        .LinkedCell = "ProjIndex"
        .DropDownLines = 20
        .Display3DShading = False
    End With
    Range("A3").Select

    'Tidy up
    rs.Close
    Conn.Close
End Sub
```

As usual, I point out that you should be familiar with much of this code by now. rs.Open "SELECT * FROM ProjectTitlesPublished", Conn gets all data from the ProjectTitlesPublished View using the Connection Object created at the start of the routine. The system copies the data to the Setup worksheet to the cell labeled Projects.

Worksheets("Milestones").Shapes("ProjectsDropDown").Select selects the pick list combo box so you can work on it. Normally you do not need to select objects before working on them, but worksheet Form Objects are an exception.

.ListFillRange = "Setup!" " & Range("Projects").Address & ":" & Range("Projects").End(xlDown).Offset(0, 1).Address builds a text string that looks like "Setup!B2:B15". This code is an example where you must set a breakpoint and then hover your mouse over bits of the statement to see their values.

Run the GetProjectTitles macro and then click the pick list button to
determine if the project titles appear. If they do not appear on the pick list
look for the likely causes of this problem:

- The code cannot connect to the Project Server database because you
  have not changed the server and project server names for your
  environment.

- You have not created the ProjectTitlesPublished View in SQL Server or
  do not have read access to it.

- You have not set up the ProjIndex and Projects names on the required
  cells as described earlier.

- You have not named the Combo box ProjectsDropDown.

Figure 29-1 shows how pick list looks when built from the Project Server
sample database.

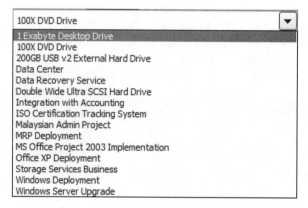

Figure 29-1: Project pick list

Your final step is to call the GetProjectTitles routine from the Workbook_Open
event. Create this event exactly the same way that you did for Microsoft
Project's Project_Open event. To create the Workbook_Open event:

1. Press Ctrl+R in the Excel VBE to display the Project Explorer.

2. Double-Click the *ThisWorkbook* object in the Microsoft Excel Objects
   folder.

3. Select *Workbook* in the *Object* pick list at the top left of code window.
   The default event added to the code window is Workbook_Open.

4. Enter the following code:

```
Private Sub Workbook_Open
   GetProjectTitles
End Sub
```

When your Workbook opens, the system calls GetProjectTitles to refresh the list of project Titles from the Project Server database. Your user now has a current list of all projects in Project Server.

Reading Milestone and Current Task Data

This macro reads milestones into Excel for all projects in the Project Server database. The macro reads data from a SQL Server View and writes the data to an Excel worksheet. Provided the layout of each worksheet is the same, there is no need for four separate routines to read data. Instead, let's write one routine with parameters for the name of a cell for the relevant worksheet, with a copy of the connection object and the SQL code needed to read the data for that worksheet. Now you have one routine to do all the work. To prepare for this common routine, we need the following:

- A View in SQL Server to read the correct data. Ask your database administrator to add the View you want and to set the column alias to the column titles you want to see in Excel. The macro copies the column titles automatically to the Excel workbook. Include the Proj_ID field in the View, but make it the last column shown. The code tests the last column and hides it if its title is Proj_ID.

- A named cell in the correct worksheet where the leftmost column title will appear, usually A4.

Create the following SQL Views in your Project Server database. The SQL code for the View Milestones is:

```
CREATE VIEW dbo.Milestones
AS
SELECT tsks.PROJ_ID, tsks.TASK_UID,
   tsks.TASK_IS_MILESTONE, tsks.TASK_NAME,
   tsks.TASK_START_DATE
FROM MSP_TASKS as tsks
WHERE (((tsks.TASK_IS_MILESTONE)<>0))
```

425

The SQL code for the CurrentTasks View is:

```
CREATE VIEW dbo.CurrentTasks
AS
SELECT tsks.PROJ_ID, tsks.TASK_UID,
   tsks.TASK_NAME, tsks.TASK_DUR,
   tsks.TASK_START_DATE, tsks.TASK_FINISH_DATE,
   tsks.TASK_PCT_COMP
FROM MSP_TASKS tsks
WHERE (((tsks.TASK_START_DATE)<Date()) AND
   ((tsks.TASK_PCT_COMP)<100))
```

The comments for the common routine are:

```
Sub GetData
   'Clear old data
   'Copy headings and data from Project Server
   'Format Data
   'Tidy up and Hide Proj_ID column
End Sub
```

The code for these comments is:

```
Sub GetData(RangeName As String, Conn As ADODB.Connection, _
         Sql As String)
Dim rs As ADODB.Recordset
Dim R As Range
Dim fld As ADODB.Field
Dim Off As Long
   Set rs = New ADODB.Recordset

   'Clear old data
   Set R = Range(RangeName)
   R.CurrentRegion.EntireColumn.Hidden = False

   'Copy headings and data from Project Server
   rs.Open Sql, Conn
   For Each fld In rs.Fields
      R.Offset(0, Off) = fld.Name
      Off = Off + 1
   Next fld
```

```
    With R.CurrentRegion
        .Font.Bold = True
        .VerticalAlignment = xlVAlignCenter
        .HorizontalAlignment = xlHAlignCenter
    End With
    R.Range("A2").CopyFromRecordset rs

    'Format Data
    With R.CurrentRegion.Offset(1, 0)
        .WrapText = True
        .VerticalAlignment = xlVAlignTop
    End With

    'Tidy up and Hide Proj_ID column
    Set R = Range(RangeName)
    With R.End(xlToRight)
        If .Text = "PROJ_ID" Then
            .EntireColumn.Hidden = True
        End If
    End With
    rs.Close
End Sub
```

The RangeName for getting all Milestones data is Milestones and it typically refers to A4 in the Milestones worksheet. The first block of code works on all cells in the current region. When you press Ctrl+Shift+8 (Ctrl+*) in Excel, the software selects all cells until it reaches either a blank row or column or the edge of the worksheet. The CurrentRegion method returns the same cell area. Clearing a report after a previous run includes showing any hidden columns and deleting all data.

The remaining code is once again a variation on previous code. Single-step through the code and look at the variables and properties to see their values as the code execution progresses through the routine.

Reading all Issues and Risks for a Project

The Issues and Risks features in Project Web Access are great for collaboration and make it easy for project personnel and managers to review and update them. However, when it comes to reporting, importing the Issues and Risks from the database and into your weekly report is an awkward process. If you have Microsoft Office 2003 installed, the easiest solution is to click the *Export to Excel* link under the list of Issues or Risks in Project Web Access. For our Excel report, however, you develop code to read Issues and Risks data directly into Excel from the Windows SharePoint Services (WSS) database.

The system stores Issues and Risks in the WSS database for Project Web Access. There is no Project Server documentation that describes how the system stores Issues and Risks data; however, I can tell you that the data is located in the UserData Table. Details about all users are in the *Users* Table. Table 29-1 describes the fields used for Issues, while Table 29-2 contains the fields used for Risks. To determine what fields hold other data, such as new fields you insert, add easily recognizable data into an Issue or Risk then look for it in the UserData table.

Field Name	Contains
datetime1	Date Due
int1	Issue ID
int3	Assigned to
int4	Owner
ntext3	Discussion
ntext4	Resolution
nvarchar1	Status
nvarchar2	Category
nvarchar3	Issue Title
nvarchar4	Priority
tp_Created	Date Created
tp_IsCurrent	1 if this version is current. 0 if this record is older version
tp_Listid	GUID for list (Issue or Risk)
tp_Modified	Date Modified
tp_SiteId	GUID for project site
tp_Version	Version number of record

Table 29-1: Field Names for basic Issue data

Field Name	Contains
datetime1	Date Due
float1	Probability
float2	Impact
float3	Cost
int1	Risk ID
int3	Assigned to
int4	Owner
ntext3	Description
ntext4	Mitigation
ntext5	Contingency Plan
ntext6	Trigger Description
nvarchar1	Status
nvarchar2	Category
nvarchar5	Trigger Type or own value
nvarchar6	Risk Title
tp_Created	Date Created
tp_IsCurrent	1 if this version is current. 0 if this record is older version
tp_Listid	GUID for list (Issue or Risk)
tp_Modified	Date Modified
tp_SiteId	GUID for project site
tp_Version	Version number of record

Table 29-2: Field Names for basic Risk data

The SQL code required to create the Issues View is as follows:

```
CREATE VIEW dbo.Issues
AS
SELECT TOP 100 PERCENT UD.ntext3 AS Discussion, User1.tp_Title
   AS Owner, UD.nvarchar3 AS [Issue Title], UD.ntext4 AS
   Resolution, UD.nvarchar1 AS Status, UD.nvarchar4 AS
   Priority, UD.datetime1 AS [Due Date], Prj.PROJ_ID
FROM YourWSSdatabase.dbo.UserData UD
   INNER JOIN YourWSSdatabase.dbo.UserInfo User1
   ON UD.tp_SiteId = User1.tp_SiteID AND UD.int4 =
   User1.tp_ID INNER JOIN dbo.MSP_WEB_PROJECTS Prj ON
UD.tp_ListId =
   Prj.WPROJ_ISSUE_LIST_NAME
WHERE      (UD.tp_IsCurrent = 1)
ORDER BY UD.nvarchar3
```

In the FROM clause of the SQL code, notice that the UserData table is in the YourWSSdatabase. You must edit that name to match your WSS database name. UD.tp_IsCurrent = 1 is important in this View. UD is an alias for the YourWSSdatabase.dbo.UserData Table. Tp_Current is always 1 for the current Issue or Risk. Because there is a record for every edit you make to an Issue or Risk, showing only the current record guarantees that you see the latest version and ignores all the older versions.

The Issues View sorts Issues by Issue Title. With the help of your DBA, it is easy to edit the fields and control the order of the data displayed. This in turn automatically changes the layout and content of the Excel report.

The SQL code to create the Risks View is as follows:

```
CREATE VIEW dbo.Risks
AS
SELECT TOP 100 PERCENT UD.nvarchar6 AS [Risk Title],
    User1.tp_Title AS Owner, UD.ntext3 AS Discussion,
    UD.ntext4 AS Resolution, UD.nvarchar1 AS Status,
    UD.datetime1 AS [Due Date], UD.nvarchar2 AS Category,
    UD.float1 AS Probability, UD.float2 AS Impact,
    UD.float3
    AS Cost, UD.ntext5 AS [Contingency Plan],
    UD.nvarchar5 AS [Trigger],
    UD.ntext6 AS [Trigger Description], Prj.PROJ_ID
FROM YourWSSdatabase.dbo.UserData UD INNER JOIN
    YourWSSdatabase.dbo.UserInfo User1 ON
    UD.tp_SiteId = User1.tp_SiteID AND
    UD.int4 = User1.tp_ID
    INNER JOIN dbo.MSP_WEB_PROJECTS Prj ON UD.tp_ListId =
    Prj.WPROJ_RISK_LIST_NAME
WHERE       (UD.tp_IsCurrent = 1)
ORDER BY UD.nvarchar6
```

In the FROM clause of the SQL code, notice that the UserData table is in the YourWSSdatabase. Again, you must edit that name to match your WSS database name. UD.tp_IsCurrent = 1 is important in this View. UD is an alias for the YourWSSdatabase.dbo.UserData Table. Tp_Current is always 1 for the current Issue or Risk. Because there is a record for every edit you make to an Issue or Risk, showing only the current record makes sure you see the latest version and ignore all the older versions.

The Risks View sorts Risks by Risk Title. With the help of your DBA, it is easy to edit the fields and control the data display order. This in turn automatically changes the layout and content of the Excel report. Because the Issues and Risks Views both refer to the WSS database by name, both Views can live in the Project Server database.

Writing the Final VBA Code for the Excel Report Macro

Before writing the final VBA code, let's review the pre-requisites for this macro. The items already in place are:

- All SQL Views to read the data. You can edit these Views which in turn changes the Excel report.

- The code to read all Project Titles in a pick list.

- Named cells in the Excel Workbook to mark where each set of data goes.

431

- A common routine (GetData) to read data for all worksheets.

There are two more routines required to complete the tool: UpdateReport and ClearReport. UpdateReport calls GetData once for each worksheet and provides the SQL code and the database connection Object. ClearReport is a utility function to clear all data from the report. The Comments for this code are:

```
Sub UpdateReport
   'Delete Old Data
   'Setup database connection
   'Get Proj_ID and update Project title from Project List
   'Fill Worksheets
   'Delete <div>, </div>,  
   'Tidy Up
End Sub
```

The contents of some Text fields are stored as HTML code, so the Delete <div>, </div>,   code removes the HTML tags to make the text more readable. Since the code only reads the text, removing the tags does not affect anything else. The code for UpdateReport is as follows:

```
Sub UpdateReport()
Dim Conn As ADODB.Connection
Dim rs As ADODB.Recordset
Dim ProjID As Long
Dim R As Range
Dim Sql As String
Const DaysAhead = 14
   'Delete Old Data
   ClearReport

   'Setup database connection
   Set Conn = New ADODB.Connection
   Conn.ConnectionString = "Provider=sqloledb;" _
           & "Data Source=(local);" _
           & "Initial Catalog=MPSSampleDatabase;" _
           & "Integrated Security=SSPI;"
   Conn.Open

   'Get Proj_ID and update Project title from Project List
   ProjID = Val(Range("Projects"). _
           Offset(Range("ProjIndex") - 1, 0))
   Range("ProjectTitle") = "Project Title: " & _
     Range("Projects").Offset(Range("ProjIndex") - 1, 1)
   Range("ProjectTitle").Range("A2") = "As of: " & _
     Format(Date, "Long Date")
```

```
'Fill Worksheets
Sql = "SELECT * FROM Milestones WHERE (PROJ_Id=" & _
      ProjID & ")"
GetData "Milestones", Conn, Sql

Sql = "SELECT * FROM CurrentTasks WHERE (PROJ_Id=" _
      & ProjID & ") AND ([Start Date]<'" _
      & Format(Date + DaysAhead, "yyyy-mm-dd") & "')"
GetData "CurrentTasks", Conn, Sql

Sql = "SELECT * FROM Issues WHERE (PROJ_Id=" & ProjID _
      & ")"
GetData "Issues", Conn, Sql

Sql = "SELECT * FROM Risks WHERE (PROJ_Id=" & ProjID _
      & ")"
GetData "Risks", Conn, Sql

'Delete <div>, </div>,  
With Range("Issues").CurrentRegion
    .Replace "<div>", ""
    .Replace "</div>", ""
    .Replace "< >", ""
End With
With Range("Risks").CurrentRegion
    .Replace "<div>", ""
    .Replace "</div>", ""
    .Replace " ", ""
End With

'Tidy Up
Conn.Close
End Sub
```

Most of the preceding code should be familiar to you by now except for ProjID = Val(Range("Projects").Offset(Range("ProjIndex") - 1, 0)). The pick list has a cell link property in which you designate a cell that the control uses to store the selected value. This value is a number for the selected project. For example, if you select the second project in the list, the linked cell contains the value 2. You now need code to translate the value 2 into the Proj_ID for the selected project.

In the Setup Worksheet your code stores a list of all Project ID's and their Project Titles. The system displays the titles in the list, but does not display the ID's. If your code reads down to the second project in the Setup list, then your code can read the Project_ID and the Project Title. That is the function of this code as it goes to the Projects named cell A1 in the Setup Worksheet and then goes down the number of cells in the linked cell named ProjIndex minus 1.

The returned value is in the Val function purely as a security measure. Your code expects a number in the ProjIndex cell, so just in case someone injects some malicious SQL code into a cell in the Project's range, forcing the value to be a number using the Val function adds a useful layer of protection. Good code security involves carefully forcing all data input by a user to a format that you expect. The likelihood of someone within your organization doing this is very remote; however good security is a habit and is the responsibility of everyone who can improve it.

Each call to GetData has three parameters: the name of the cell where GetData will write your data, the connection Object Conn, and the SQL code passed in the string variable Sql. Notice the simplicity of the SQL code to read Issues or Risks now that you have a SQL Server View in the background to do the difficult work. The SQL code is:

SELECT * FROM Risks WHERE (PROJ_Id=" & ProjID & ")"

This code also explains why you need to include the Proj_ID field in the Views. Your code must select only the Issues or Risks for the selected project. By placing the Proj_Id field last the GetData code can easily test for its presence and hide it because users do not need to see the Proj_ID data. If your Issues and Risks data includes more HTML tags than those for which we test here, simply add an extra Replace statement to delete them.

We now need a small routine to clear any existing data from the report before refreshing the data. Since you might edit the View to add new columns, change their order, or delete the column titles, GetData refreshes everything. The code to clear the report follows:

```
Sub ClearReport()
   With Range("Milestones").CurrentRegion
      .EntireColumn.Hidden = False
      .ClearContents
   End With
   With Range("CurrentTasks").CurrentRegion
      .EntireColumn.Hidden = False
      .ClearContents
   End With
   With Range("Issues").CurrentRegion
      .EntireColumn.Hidden = False
      .ClearContents
   End With
   With Range("Risks").CurrentRegion
      .EntireColumn.Hidden = False
      .ClearContents
   End With
End Sub
```

Note that the code shows any hidden columns as well so GetData starts with a completely clean Worksheet.

Creating a Project Program Report

You now have an effective reporting tool for individual reports in Excel. With this, it is not difficult to create a different Excel report for a program of projects. To create a program report you need to complete the following steps:

1. Add a custom enterprise Project field in the Enterprise Global file in Project Server to enter the program name. Use a value list in this field to avoid typing errors.

2. Create Views in SQL Server to select the data you want in the Program report.

3. Copy the Excel Project Report for a Program Report.

4. Edit the code to call the program Views instead of the project Views you used above.

Another version of the Report you can create is one for all projects for a particular Manager or Corporate Strategy. Add the necessary enterprise custom Project field in Project Server and the Views in SQL Server and another useful report is nearly finished!

Hands On Exercise

Exercise 29-1

Work with the Weekly report code.

1. Format the weekly report to make it more readable and attractive. Try adding a colored background and Red, Yellow, and Green flags for Milestones to show whether they are behind schedule, or for Issues and Risks on their Due Dates.

2. Add a worksheet for Comments needed in your weekly reports.

3. Add a macro button on the first worksheet to run the macro.

4. If you need to report by project program or all projects for different managers, create a new version of the Excel Report.

Module 30

Using Project 2007 VBA

Learning Objectives

After completing this module, you will be able to:

- Understand new features in Project 2007 VBA

- Write code using the new features in Project 2007 VBA

- Convert the SQL Statements in Module 29 to the Project Server 2007 Reporting Database

Introducing Project 2007 VBA

Microsoft Project 2007 introduces a number of very useful new features. These new features include:

- Multiple undo
- Task drivers (the Task Investigator)
- Calendars
- Visual Reporting
- Cell Formatting
- Deliverables (Project 2007 Professional only)

Project 2007 VBA provides full support for these key features. There are also a number of other, smaller improvements, all of which Project 2007 VBA supports. I will only discuss the main feature groups listed above.

 The information in this module is based on the Project 2007 SDK released for Beta 2. There may be some changes by the time Microsoft releases the full version, so we recommend you download the Project 2007 SDK from **www.microsoft.com** and search Project VBA Help for up-to-date information.

To find what is new for Project 2007 VBA:

1. Open the Visual Basic Editor (VBE) for Project 2007.
2. Press F1 for Help.
3. Search for the *What's New* topic.

In Project 2007 VBA, a number of Objects, Methods, and Properties used in Project 2003 VBA (such as the Global Object) now have alternatives where Project 2007 does things differently from Project 2003. These members no longer have descriptions in the Help files, but are still supported for compatibility. To see these hidden members in the Object Browser:

1. In the VBE press the F2 function key to open the Object Browser.
2. Right-click anywhere in the Object Browser window and then click *Show Hidden Members*.

To get full details of programming Project and Project Server 2007 download the Project Server 2007 SDK by searching for Project Server 2007 SDK at **www.microsoft.com**. The SDK includes full details of how to use the Project Server Interface (PSI) to control Project Server. PSI is a powerful development interface for programmers using Visual Studio.

Using Named Parameters

There are a number of new parameters and options for existing Methods and Objects in Project 2007 VBA. If a new parameter is optional, then Microsoft can safely add it to the end of the parameter list. However, if the new parameter is required, then it has to precede all optional parameters. This means that if you specify parameters by including a comma for each parameter, your code may fail in Project 2007 as you will have the wrong number or sequence of parameters.

The safest way to code all calls to objects and methods with parameters is to name the parameters. That way wherever new parameters are added, the naming ensures your code will continue to work with each new release of Microsoft Project. An example of a named parameter is:

```
Sort Key1:="ID", Ascending1:=True
```

The parameters are all separated from their values by := (colon then an equals).

Undoing a Macro

If you ever ran a macro without saving your project first and then regretted it once you saw the results, then this new feature is for you! Project 2007 has multiple levels of undo. The number of undo levels defaults to 20, but the following statement increases the levels to 30:

```
Application.UndoLevels = 30
```

Every time VBA code executes an undoable action, the system adds a new undo record onto the undo list. If your macro performs 50 undo actions, then with 30 undo levels 20 actions will be missed. Even if you increase the undo levels to 50, your user is likely to be very confused!

Project 2007 VBA allows you to group undoable actions together by giving them a single name (such as FormattingMacro, for example) and then that one name appears in the Undo list. The user can then undo all the actions of the macro in one easy undo.

To group many actions together, you need to create an Undo Transaction Set. To create an Undo Transaction Set copy and edit the following code:

```
Sub CreateUndoTransaction()
    Application.OpenUndoTransaction "Macro Changes"

    'Insert code that changes your project here

    Application.CloseUndoTransaction
End Sub
```

The following code is an edited example that simply adds 3 Tasks to a project.

```
Sub CreateUndoTransaction()
    Application.OpenUndoTransaction "Macro Changes"

    ActiveProject.Tasks.Add "Macro Inserted Task 1"
    ActiveProject.Tasks.Add "Macro Inserted Task 2"
    ActiveProject.Tasks.Add "Macro Inserted Task 3"

    Application.CloseUndoTransaction
End Sub
```

Figure 30-1 shows a project where a User entered Task 1 then ran a macro to add Tasks 2-4. The macro creates a transaction called **Macro Changes** to capture all Task additions. By clicking the *Undo* pick list button, you see Macro Changes at the top, as the most recent action. Click the *Macro Changes* item and the system removes all Tasks inserted by the macro.

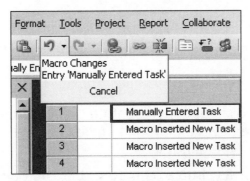

Figure 30-1: Undo list with the Macro Changes transaction

Rod Gill recommends that you capture the changes your macro makes to a project file in a VBA Undo Transaction which allows the user to easily undo the results of running the macro.

Managing Custom Fields

Project 2007 VBA handles custom Fields in a slightly different manner than previous versions. You still manage local Fields as with previous versions, but you must now manage all enterprise Fields for Project Server 2007 in Project Web Access (PWA). The basic changes are as follows:

- Enterprise custom field details are Read-Only in Project Professional.

- You can create as many Enterprise custom fields as you want (from PWA provided you have Admin rights).

- You can still customize local fields such as Text1 etc.

To read and write to the new Enterprise custom fields you need to use the GetField, SetField and FieldNameToFieldConstant methods. To read a project level Enterprise custom field called *Technical Reviewer* use the code:

```
Dim TechnicalReviewer as String
   TechnicalReviewer = ActiveProject.ProjectSummaryTask _
      .GetField(FieldNameToFieldConstant("Technical Reviewer"))
```

To write to the same field use:

```
ActiveProject.ProjectSummaryTask.SetField _
   FieldNameToFieldConstant("Technical Reviewer"), _
   "New Value"
```

GetField needs only a constant representing the field and SetField needs the same constant and the new value for the field. The Field Constant can be stored in a variable of type Long.

This new method is not as simple as before, but the gain is as many fields as you want using any name you want.

Controlling Visual Reports

Project 2007 VBA has a number of new objects and methods to support the new Visual Reports feature. The simplest way to learn about them is to record a macro as you create and view a Visual Report. The following recorded code creates a new report template and then displays it.

```
VisualReportsNewTemplate PjVisualReportsCubeType:=pjResourceTP
VisualReportsSaveCube _
    strNamePath:="C:\CubesPath\Resource Usage.cub", _
    PjVisualReportsCubeType:=pjResourceTP
VisualReportsView _
    strVisualReportTemplateFile:="C:\Templates\My Resource " _
    & "Usage.xlt"
```

Note that the new template method simply displays the New template view in Excel for the user to create the template.

Managing Calendars

Project 2007 offers new functionality to project schedulers. In previous versions, if shift times needed to be changed for all working days on a Calendar, then every day was an exception. In Project 2007 Exception Calendars allow you to define new base working hours so any edits (such as for vacations) can be seen as exceptions. There are two different types of Calendars: Exceptions and Work Week. You use Exception Calendars to create sub-calendars. For example, if a construction company has different winter and summer working hours, you can create a Winter and Summer Exception Calendar, each with different default working hours.

If a resource is taking a week of vacation, add a new working week that includes the vacation period. A Working week entry is called an EffectiveWeek in Project VBA. A resource can have an Exception and a Working Week that overrules the Exception calendar as well.

The following code creates a Calendar Exception for a Resource to show working extra hours before Christmas and then adds a Work Week for a vacation:

```
Sub AddException()
Dim cal As Calendar
   Set cal = ActiveProject.Resources("My Resource").Calendar

   ' Exception bitmask for Mon, Tue, Wed, Thu, Fri
   'is 00111110, or Hexadecimal 0x3E
   cal.Exceptions.Add Type:=pjWeekly, _
      Start:=#12/1/2007#, Finish:=#12/24/2007#, _
      Name:="BeforeXmas", DaysOfWeek:=&H3E&

   cal.Exceptions("BeforeXmas").Shift1.Start = #8:00:00 AM#
   cal.Exceptions("BeforeXmas").Shift1.Finish = #12:00:00 PM#
   cal.Exceptions("BeforeXmas").Shift2.Start = #1:00:00 PM#
   cal.Exceptions("BeforeXmas").Shift2.Finish = #7:00:00 PM#

   cal.EffectiveWeeks.Add Start:=#12/25/2007#, _
                Finish:=#1/3/2008#, Name:="Xmas vacation"

   For Each eWeekDay In _
               cal.EffectiveWeeks("Xmas vacation").WeekDays
      eWeekDay.Working = False
   Next
End Sub
```

All dates are specified in m/d/yyyy format. An error will occur if any EffectiveWeek conflicts or overlaps with another one.

Formatting Cell Background Colors

Another new feature in Project 2007 allows you to apply a background color to the cells in your project. There are two ways to set the background color of a cell as shown in the following code sample:

```
Font CellColor:=pjRed
ActiveCell.CellColor=pjBlue
```

Either way works, but the ActiveCell.CellColor method can be used to read the current cell background color as shown below:

```
Sub TestCellColor()
Dim ThisCellColor As String
Dim ColorIndex As Integer
   ColorIndex = ActiveCell.CellColor
   ThisCellColor = Choose(CSng(ColorIndex), "Black", "Red", _
      "Yellow", "Lime", "Aqua", "Blue", "Fuchsia", "White", _
      "Maroon", "Green", "Olive", "Navy", "Purple", "Teal", _
      "Grey", "Siver", "Automatic")
   MsgBox "The active cell's background color is: " _
      & ThisCellColor, vbInformation
End Sub
```

The CellColor Property returns a number from 0 to 16. If you look at the drop down list for colors in the Format ➢ Font dialog then 0 is Black, 1 is Red and so on down to the 17th item which is Automatic. The Choose function converts the number returned by the CellColor property to a string for the color.

Managing Deliverables

Deliverables are a new feature in Project Professional 2007 when used with Project Server 2007. The system allows you to create Tasks, flag them as Deliverables, and then use them to negotiate and track agreed dates when cross-project deliverables will occur. One project can create and update deliverables (called Commitment objects in Project VBA) and other projects can get and then accept changes to deliverables. Thus, using Deliverables is a better and more realistic way of managing cross-project relationships.

 At the time of writing, VBA sample code for tracking Deliverables was not available. Please visit our download site for current information about this feature at:

http://www.projectvbabook.com/dl.

Converting SQL Views from 2003 to 2007

Module 29 recommended that you create Views in SQL Server to read data for reports. In Project Server 2007, the main databases will not have a schema available as Microsoft wants to reserve the right to edit the schema in service packs and future releases. In fact, Microsoft warned that editing data in any database other than the Reporting Database is likely to cause problems. Changes to the Reporting Database are likely to be overwritten the next time you publish a project.

For all reporting needs in Project Server 2007, a separate Reporting Database is available. You must convert all previous Views you created against SQL Server with Project Server 2003 in order to use the Reporting Database for SQL Server 2007. Microsoft simplified this conversion for you because Issue and Risk data is available in the Reporting Database, so you no longer need to reference the Windows SharePoint Services database.

I created Project Server 2007 equivalents for all the Views used in Module 29. Please note that I created them using Beta release 2, so there may be some minor changes in the final version. In all samples, I include the original code as shown in Module 29 followed by Project Server 2007 equivalent code. The same code should work in SQL Server 2000 and 2005.

```
--Project Server 2003
CREATE VIEW dbo.ProjectTitlesPublished
AS
SELECT   TOP 100 PERCENT PROJ_ID, PROJ_PROP_TITLE AS Title
FROM     dbo.MSP_PROJECTS
WHERE (PROJ_VERSION = 'Published')
ORDER BY PROJ_NAME

--Project Server 2007
CREATE VIEW dbo.ProjectTitlesPublished
AS
Select ProjectUID as Proj_ID,
   Left(ProjectName,Len(ProjectName)-10) as Title
From dbo.MSP_EpmProject
Where Right(ProjectName,9)='Published'
```

There is no Version field available to test, but all project titles have the version name appended to them that you can test using the text *Right* function.

```
--Project Server 2003
CREATE VIEW dbo.Milestones
AS
SELECT tsks.PROJ_ID, tsks.TASK_UID,
   tsks.TASK_IS_MILESTONE, tsks.TASK_NAME,
   tsks.TASK_START_DATE
FROM MSP_TASKS as tsks
WHERE (((tsks.TASK_IS_MILESTONE)<>0))

--Project Server 2007
CREATE VIEW dbo.Milestones
AS
SELECT Tsks.ProjectUID, Tsks.TaskUID,
   Tsks.TaskName, Tsks.TaskStartDate
FROM dbo.MSP_EpmTask Tsks
WHERE (((Tsks.TaskIsMilestone)<>0))
```

Notice how using alias names for tables means that once the table name has been edited, most of the remaining SQL remains unchanged (give or take a few column name changes!)

```
--Project Server 2003
CREATE VIEW dbo.CurrentTasks
AS
SELECT tsks.PROJ_ID, tsks.TASK_UID,
   tsks.TASK_NAME, tsks.TASK_DUR,
   tsks.TASK_START_DATE, tsks.TASK_FINISH_DATE,
   tsks.TASK_PCT_COMP
FROM MSP_TASKS tsks
WHERE (((tsks.TASK_START_DATE)<GetDate()) AND
   ((tsks.TASK_PCT_COMP)<100))

--Project Server 2007
CREATE VIEW dbo.CurrentTasks
AS
SELECT tsks.ProjectUID, tsks.TaskUID,
   tsks.TaskName, tsks.TaskDuration/8 as Duration,
   tsks.TaskStartDate, tsks.TaskFinishDate,
   tsks.TaskPercentCompleted

FROM dbo.MSP_EpmTask as tsks
WHERE (((tsks.TaskStartDate)< GetDate()) AND
   ((tsks.TaskPercentCompleted)<100))
```

```
--Project Server 2003
CREATE VIEW dbo.Issues
AS
SELECT TOP 100 PERCENT UD.ntext3 AS Discussion, User1.tp_Title
   AS Owner, UD.nvarchar3 AS [Issue Title], UD.ntext4 AS
   Resolution, UD.nvarchar1 AS Status, UD.nvarchar4 AS
   Priority, UD.datetime1 AS [Due Date], Prj.PROJ_ID
FROM YourWSSdatabase.dbo.UserData UD
   INNER JOIN YourWSSdatabase.dbo.UserInfo User1
   ON UD.tp_SiteId = User1.tp_SiteID AND UD.int4 =
   User1.tp_ID INNER JOIN dbo.MSP_WEB_PROJECTS Prj
   ON UD.tp_ListId = Prj.WPROJ_ISSUE_LIST_NAME
WHERE (UD.tp_IsCurrent = 1)
ORDER BY UD.nvarchar3

--Project Server 2007
CREATE VIEW dbo.Issues
AS
SELECT Issues.Title, Issues.Discussion, Issues.Owner,
   Issues.Resolution, Issues.Status, Issues.Priority,
   Issues.DueDate, Issues.ProjectUID
FROM dbo.MSP_WssIssue as Issues
ORDER BY Issues.Title
```

As you can see, the Issues and following Risks Views are simpler than in Project Server 2003.

```
--Project Server 2003
CREATE VIEW dbo.Risks
AS
SELECT TOP 100 PERCENT UD.nvarchar6 AS [Risk Title],
   User1.tp_Title AS Owner, UD.ntext3 AS Discussion,
   UD.ntext4 AS Resolution, UD.nvarchar1 AS Status,
   UD.datetime1 AS [Due Date], UD.nvarchar2 AS Category,
   UD.float1 AS Probability, UD.float2 AS Impact,
   UD.float3
   AS Cost, UD.ntext5 AS [Contingency Plan],
   UD.nvarchar5 AS [Trigger],
   UD.ntext6 AS [Trigger Description], Prj.PROJ_ID
```

```
FROM YourWSSdatabase.dbo.UserData UD INNER JOIN
   YourWSSdatabase.dbo.UserInfo User1 ON
   UD.tp_SiteId = User1.tp_SiteID AND
   UD.int4 = User1.tp_ID
   INNER JOIN dbo.MSP_WEB_PROJECTS Prj ON UD.tp_ListId =
   Prj.WPROJ_RISK_LIST_NAME
WHERE  (UD.tp_IsCurrent = 1)
ORDER BY UD.nvarchar3


--Project Server 2003
CREATE VIEW dbo.Risks
AS
SELECT Risks.Title, Risks.Owner,
   Risks.Description as Discussion,
   Risks.Status, Risks.DueDate, Risks.Category,
   Risks.Probability, Risks.Impact, Risks.Cost,
   Risks.ContingencyPlan, Risks.TriggerDescription,
   Risks.ProjectUID
FROM dbo.MSP_WssRisk as Risks
ORDER BY Risks.Title
```

Another thing you want to do is rename the PROJ_ID field names in your VBA code to refer to ProjectUID instead. Project Server 2007 now uses full GUID's for each Project, Task Resource and Assignment. The idea is that each item will be unique within the Project Server databases and not just unique within each project.

If you want to change the name of a field in the final Excel Report, then simply rename the field in the SQL Server View using SqlName as ExcelName. For example *Risks.Description as Discussion* renames the Description field so it becomes Discussion in Excel.

Hands On Exercise

Exercise 30-1

Use new features in Project 2007 VBA code. **Note:** For this exercise, you need Project 2007 Standard or Professional.

1. Take any existing macro and a wrap a VBA Undo Transaction around it. Confirm that the Undo command can undo every action in your macro.

2. In the VBE, press the F2 function key display the Object Browser. Search the project library for the word "Report" (without the quotes). Read the Help topics on Report Objects and Methods that interest you.

3. Develop a macro to add an Exception calendar for the Standard calendar to be four 9-hour working days Monday to Thursday, with four hours on Friday. Make this effective from the beginning of next month for one year.

4. If you have Project Professional 2007 connected to Project Server 2007, click Project ➤ Project Information and note the names of any custom enterprise fields. In a new macro, read and write to a custom enterprise field using the code in the Managing Custom Fields topic.

Index

A

Automation ....*See* VBA Automation

B

Binary Large Object.. 388

Bloated files .... *See* Project files

BLOB .... *See* Binary Large Object

C

Calendars .... *See* Update Calendars macro

Class Modules 18, 65–69, 319–21, 360

   calling a Class..68

   creating a Class 65–69

   defined 18

   example of using a Class...319–21

   Property Get procedure 66

   Property Let procedure 66

   used with Windows API 360

   using a Class 68

Classes...*See* Class Modules

Code.................. 13, 15, 50, 55, 83–88, 90, 147–48, 197–98, 352–54, 365

   adding code to a UserForm 184–85

   compiling 50

   debugging 83–88

   developing Project database code 365

   entering and editing 13, 83–84

   estimating development time...84

   indenting 55

   maintenance for ease of debugging 90

   maintenance for ease of use.......................................88–90

   modifying recorded code 151

   recording a macro ....147–48 repairing corrupted .mpp files 155–56

running..83–88

selecting a module storage location 153–55

speeding up code execution.. 352–54

structuring 55, 197–98

timing code execution 354

using Events.. 189–93

using IntelliSense... 15

when to record 147

Code Window .... *See* Visual Basic Editor

Comments...23–24

Concatenate text strings .... *See* Data Types - Text data

Consolidated Project .... *See* Consolidated Project Report macro

Consolidated Project Report macro 297–300

master project defined.. 297

using a master project 297–98

writing the code 299–300

Constants...39–41

pj constants 41

vb constants.. 41

xl constants.. 41

Corrupted files .... *See* Project files

Corruption... *See* Project files

Cost Margin Report macro 289–93

Custom Fields.. 99–117, 124, 349

creating Formulas using VBA 349

defining 103–17

deleting 124

overview..99–101

testing for an NA date value 113

using a Value List..105–7

using Formulas 109–13

using formulas to support Project VBA... 102

using Graphical Indicators 113–17

Custom Outline Codes 119–23, 124

defined 119

defining the Code Mask 119–21

defining the Lookup Table 121–23
deleting 124

D

Data Types 43–50
converting data.. 49–50
Date data... 43–44
Number data 47–48
Text data 45–47
Variant data 49

Databases 365, 376–82, 387–400
creating a database View 391
developing Project database code.. 365
importing data from a SQL Server database................................... 379–82
importing data from an Access database 376–79
looping through all projects in a database.................................... 389–90
reading data from a database 391–95
using the pjdb.htm file... 387–89
writing data directly to a database... 395–400

DateAdd function .... *See* Data Types - Date data

DateDiff function... *See* Data Types - Date data

DatePart function .... *See* Data Types - Date data

DateSubtract function .... *See* Data Types - Date data

Digital Certificate .... *See* VBA Security

Do Loop.. *See* Loops - Do Loop

Downloading the sample Project files................................... 3, 95, 366

Driving Tasks macro.. 211–29
adding a UserForm 222–26
designing the main procedure 212–13
overview.. 211
running from a Toolbar 228–29
understanding task dependencies 213
understanding the Task Driver code.. 213–20

E

ElseIf statement.. *See* IF statement

Errors 173–77

   error handling options 173–74

   error types 173

   GoTo error handling 175–76

   Resume Next error handling 175

   selecting an error handling method 176

   using the Err Object 176–77

Events 189–93

   defined 189

   Project Events 189–90

   Task Events 190–93

Excel .... *See* VBA Automation

F

Fields .... *See* Custom Fields

File bloating .... *See* Project files

File Corruption .... *See* Project files

Files .... *See* Project files

Filters .... *See* Objects - Creating Views, Tables, and Filters

For Each Next Loop .... *See* Loops - For Each Next Loop

For Next Loop .... *See* Loops - For Next Loop

Format text strings .... *See* Data Types - Text data

Formulas .... *See* Custom Fields - using Formulas

Functions 18, 31

   defined 18

   differences with Procedures 31

G

Global.mpt file 234–40

   defined 234

   moving macros into 234–39

GoSub Subroutines 18

   defined 18

Graphical Indicators .... *See* Custom Fields - using Graphical Indicators

H

Help 33

Hyperlinks 199–206, 350–51

   used in the Project Control Center macro 199–206

   working with using VBA 350–51

I

IF statement 56–58

Immediate Window .... *See* Visual Basic Editor

Importing data 369–82

   from a SQL Server database 379–82

   from an Access database 376–79

   from Excel 369–75

InputBox function 30–31

InStr function .... *See* Data Types - Text data

IntelliSense .... *See* Entering and Editing Code

L

Left function .... *See* Data Types - Text data

Linked Tasks macro 331–41

   designing the code 331–33

   understanding the TaskDependency Object 333–34

   understanding the VBA code 334–41

Locals Window .... *See* Visual Basic Editor

Loops 58–60, 159–61, 389–90, 418–19, 421–27

   Do Loop 58–60

   For Each Next Loop 60

   For Next Loop 60

   looping through all projects in a database 389–90

   looping through all projects in the Project Server DB 418–19, 421–27

   looping through all tasks in a project 159–61

   Selected Tasks 160

   using a field to control looping 160–61

M

Master Project............................. *See* Consolidated Project Report macro

Menus ....*See* Objects - creating a new Menu

Methods 24–26

Microsoft Excel..*See* VBA Automation

Microsoft Project 2007 ....*See* Project 2007 new features

Microsoft Project Server 2007 ....*See* Project Server 2007 new features

Mid function ....*See* Data Types - Text data

Modules 17
   defined 17

MPP files ....*See* Project files

MsgBox function..29

O

Object Browser ....*See* Object Model - using the Object Browser

Object Browser Window ....*See* Visual Basic Editor

Object Model 129–42
   Application Methods..130–33
   Application Objects...130–33
   Application Properties 130–33
   Assignment Methods..138
   Assignment Objects...138
   Assignment Properties 138
   getting Help on 129
   overview..129
   Project Methods 134
   Project Objects 133–34
   Project Properties..134–35
   Resource Methods 137–38
   Resource Objects 137–38
   Resource Properties...137–38
   Task Methods 135–36
   Task Objects 135–36
   Task Properties..135–36
   using the Object Browser 138–42

Objects 24–26, 165–69

    creating a new Menu 167–69

    creating a new Toolbar.. 166

    creating Views, Tables, and Filters................................. 165

    understanding 24–26

OLE DB drivers 405–13

    availability in Project 2007 406

    availability in Project versions 405

    connecting to an .mpp file from another application 406–13

    features in each Project version......................................405–6

    locating the pjoledb.htm file 405

    OLEDB defined.. 405

    understanding 405

Outline Codes ....*See* Custom Outline Codes

P

Parameters 24–26

    named...25

PJDB.HTM ....*See* Databases - using the pjdb.htm file

PJSVRDB.HTM ....*See* Project Server database

Procedures..31, 233

    calling from another file 233

    differences with Functions 31

Project 2007 new features 439–45

    applying cell background formatting 444–45

    controlling Visual Reports 443

    managing Calendars 443–44

    managing custom fields 442

    undoing macro actions..440–42

    using named parameters... 440

Project Control Center macro 198–206, 252–58

    deliverables explained..199–200

    designing 198–99

    overview... 198

    understanding the code...200–206

    using timephased data..252–58

Project Explorer Window....................................*See* Visual Basic Editor

Project files..155–56

    controlling .mpp file size 155

Project Object Model .... *See* Object Model

Project Server 2007 ....*See* Project Server 2007 new features

Project Server 2007 new features 445–49

    converting SQL Views from Project Server 2003 445–49

    managing Deliverables..445

Project Server database 417–35

    developing a Weekly Report macro in Excel VBA..........................418–35

    launch Project and log into Project Server...................................419–20

    reading Risks and Issues..427–31

    understanding the pjsvrdb.htm file 417

Properties 24–26

Properties Window...*See* Visual Basic Editor

Q

Quickwatch dialog...*See* Code - debugging

R

References ....*See* VBA Automation

Registry 42–43

    DeleteSetting 43

    GetSetting 43

    SaveSetting 43

Right function ....*See* Data Types - Text data

S

S-Curves macro...*See* VBA Automation

Security ....*See* VBA Security

Set Non-Working Days in the Standard Calendar macro.................303

Splitting text strings ....*See* Data Types - Text data

Sub Procedures 17

    defined 17

Subprojects...352

T

Tables .... *See* Objects - Creating Views, Tables, and Filters

TaskDependency Object .... *See* Linked Tasks macro

Tasks 345–49

   indenting tasks 345–48

   reorganizing task sequence 348–49

Timephased data 243–58

   exporting to a .csv file 246–48

   overview 243

   reading 244–46

   used with the Project Control Center 252–58

   writing 250–51

Toolbars .... *See* Objects - creating a new Toolbar

Toolbox .... *See* Visual Basic Editor

U

Update Calendars macro 305–26

   calendars overview 305

   designing Iteration 1 326

   designing Iteration 2 319–21

   designing Iteration 3 323–24

   designing Iteration 4 326

UserForm Window .... *See* Visual Basic Editor

UserForms 19, 181, 182, 184–85

   adding code 184–85

   creating 182

   defined 19

   overview 181

   use in the Driving Tasks macro 222–26

V

Value List .... *See* Custom Fields - using a Value List

Variables 37–39, 41, 42

   controlling variable Scope 41–42

   Declaring 37

forcing Declared variables 41

naming convention 38–39

Private...38

protecting variables 42

Public 38

sharing with another file...42

Static 38

VBA...3

defined 3

Project VBA defined..95

skills needed to write code 4

support for VBA macros 5

VBA Automation 73–75, 263–84

add references to other applications 73–75

connecting to Excel 267–68

controlling Project from Excel..271–72

creating the S-Curves macro 272–76

creating the Who Does What When macro 278–84

defined 73, 263

early binding defined 263

exporting to Excel 268–70

late binding defined.. 263

opening an Excel template...270–71

running existing Excel code 270–71

using early binding..265–67

using Excel for project reporting... 263

using late binding..264–65

VBA Security 75–79

create a Digital Certificate 76–79

Views............................... *See* Objects - Creating Views, Tables, and Filters

Visual Basic Editor.. 9, 12

Code Window 9

Immediate Window 9

Locals Window 9

Object Browser Window 9

Project Explorer Window 9, 12

Properties Window 9, 12

Toolbox 9

UserForm Window 9
Watch Window 9

Visual Reports ....*See* Project 2007 new features

W

Watch Window ....*See* Visual Basic Editor

Who Does What When macro ....*See* VBA Automation

Windows API 356–60

    using 356–60

    using File Open 357–59

    using File Save As 359

    using Get Folder 360

    using with a Class Module 360

With statement 27